THE
ENORMOUS
ROOM

THE ENORMOUS ROOM

E. E. CUMMINGS

A typescript edition with drawings by the author

Introduction by Susan Cheever

Edited by George James Firmage

Afterword by Richard S. Kennedy

LIVERIGHT
A DIVISION OF W. W. NORTON & COMPANY
NEW YORK | LONDON

For information about permission to reproduce selections from this book,
write to Permissions, Liveright Publishing Corporation, a division of
W. W. Norton & Company, Inc., 500 Fifth Avenue, New York, NY 10110

For information about special discounts for bulk purchases, please contact
W. W. Norton Special Sales at specialsales@wwnorton.com or 800-233-4830

Manufacturing by Courier Westford
Book design by Fearn Cutler de Vicq
Production manager: Louise Parasmo

Library of Congress Cataloging-in-Publication Data

Cummings, E. E. (Edward Estlin), 1894–1962, author.
The enormous room / E.E. Cummings ; a typescript edition with drawings by
the author ; introduction by Susan Cheever ; edited, with a note on The Enor-
mous Room, by George James Firmage ; afterword by Richard S. Kennedy.
pages cm
ISBN 978-0-87140-928-7 (pbk.)
1. World War, 1914–1918—France—Fiction. 2. Concentration camp inmates—
Fiction. 3. Concentration camps—Fiction. 4. Americans—France—Fiction.
5. Ambulance drivers—Fiction. 6. La Ferté-Macé (France)—Fiction. 7. Autobio-
graphical fiction. 8. War stories. I. Firmage, George James, editor. II. Title.
PS3505.U334E56 2014   813'.52—dc23   2014019907

Liveright Publishing Corporation
500 Fifth Avenue, New York, N.Y. 10110
www.wwnorton.com

W. W. Norton & Company Ltd.
Castle House, 75/76 Wells Street, London W1T 3QT

1 2 3 4 5 6 7 8 9 0

CONTENTS

Introduction

SUSAN CHEEVER

On April 7, 1917—the day after the United States entered the First World War—E. E. Cummings did what was expected of a young man in his prime. A twenty-three-year-old Harvard graduate who knew how to drive a car, he joined the Norton-Harjes Ambulance Corps and headed for the battle-fields of France. Everything that happened after that was entirely unexpected.

On board the *La Touraine* to Europe, the seasick Edward Estlin Cummings made friends with a fellow Ivy Leaguer named William Slater Brown, a wealthy Columbia School of Journalism student who shared Cummings' rebellious sense of mischief. Brown and Cummings were marooned in Paris for five weeks—the end of April and May in Paris—before they were fitted for uniforms and sent to the Western Front to serve under the command of Harry Anderson, a former garage mechanic from the Bronx who disliked the French.

Cummings and Brown adored the French, had already learned to speak good French, and had had a glorious time in Paris. They liked the French soldiers near their encampment between Ham and St. Quentin and made friends with them. The Norton-Harjes Ambulance Corps, established by wealthy Harvard man Richard Norton primarily for other Harvard men, consisted of about fifty men and twenty vehicles—mostly Fords and Fiats.

Although Cummings was now on the Western Front a few miles from the Somme, which at the time was one of the most dangerous places on earth for poets—Rupert Brooke had already been killed there the year before and Wilfred Owen would follow shortly before the Armistice—there was a lull in the fighting in the summer of 1917. Cummings and Brown, both copious letter writers, carelessly wrote home, describing demoralization among the French troops and incompetence among the American officers. Brown especially made no secret of his scorn for the Allies. Both men were challenging and annoying to their superior officers. Before long, French and American officials began to scrutinize their letters looking for evidence of treason.

Cummings always reacted to authority with rebellion and so he and Anderson—his commanding officer—quickly became enemies. It did not take long for Cummings and Brown to be reassigned from ambulance drivers to ambulance washers and polishers. When Anderson refused Cummings and Brown a pass to visit Paris, Cummings was furious. "I took a mouthful of cigarette smoke and blew it flat in his face," he wrote his mother.

Eventually one day when the Corps was encamped at Ollezy, Cummings and Brown were arrested and questioned. Cummings was asked to say that he hated the Germans. "I love the French very much," was all he would say. He was asked to agree that Brown was disloyal to the Allies; he refused. He stayed in custody, was transported by car and then by train further west to a holding camp in Normandy—Le Depôt de Triage de La Ferté-Macé.

He arrived at the Depôt, a grim former seminary, at night and was led into a room so dark he could see nothing at all. Yet in that darkness he heard the sounds of many men, a strained cough here, the rustle of straw as someone rolled over on a pallet there, the sound of water sloshing in a bucket—this was actually an enormous room, about eighty by forty feet, where he and Brown would spend the next three months with forty or so men as the most literary, gallant, and lighthearted of prisoners.

Although being moved west away from the Somme made Cummings and Brown much safer from the dreadful battlefields of the Western Front, conditions at La Ferté-Macé were grim. A holding center for dozens of different kinds of men—defectors, pacifists, troublemakers, or men who had been in the wrong place at the wrong time—it had scant provisions for its inmates, who slept in the same room on bug-infested straw pallets with buckets serving as latrines. The floors were cold, the walls wet from condensation in the old chapel. The daily routine began at 6:30 and included some exercise in a courtyard and two meals of watery soup. Cummings and Brown, who had miraculously ended up in the same place, were gallant as always and pretended to be delighted by the turn of events that landed them in prison.

All his life, Cummings acted as if the world was a lighthearted place, which would reward his gallant faith with resources and benevolence. More than just an aristocratic noblesse oblige, his attitude was that delight and generosity would be repaid with safety. He leaned into the universe with a trust that sometimes seemed risky but always rewarded him.

As a result, Cummings as a prisoner had a better time than his worried parents back in cushy Cambridge. "You can't imagine, Mother mine, how interesting a time I am having," he wrote Rebecca Cummings. After describing the snoring in the room at night and the smells that, if knives had been permitted, could have been cut with a knife, he joked, "Not for anything in the world would I change it . . . I know you will believe me when I reiterate that I am having the time of my life!" At last, Cummings decided, he and Brown were free of the brutal stupidity of Harry Anderson and the military caste system and free to enjoy the variety of the world—free that is in a manner of speaking.

In letters home, Cummings cheerfully described the bucket toilets as well as the panoply of characters he came across in the holding camp. Cummings met a man named Count Charles Bragard who had known the painter Paul Cézanne; Fritz, a Norwegian ship's stoker; a handsome bearded gypsy whom Cummings dubbed "The Wanderer"; and "The Bear," a handsome Pole. Another prisoner had been a brilliant equine portraitist—he asked if Cummings knew his friend Cornelius Vanderbilt. "I was confronted by a perfect type," Cummings cheerfully wrote in his memoir, "the apotheosis of injured nobility,the humiliated victim of perfectly unfortunate circumstances,the utterly respectable gentleman who has seen better days."

While Cummings was drinking watery coffee, scratching an increasingly itchy skin, and hobnobbing with exotic strangers, his father was in the kind of towering, fearful rage a Harvard professor and Unitarian minister could muster. After getting a telegram from Richard Norton, founder of the ambulance corps, saying that their son was in a concentration camp, Edward Cummings went into action. First he wrote to the American Embassy in Paris, then to the United States State Department, who gave him a bureaucratic runaround. No one knew where Cummings' son was; it was wartime in France.

On October 26, the State Department made an error that compounded Edward Cummings' fury—he got a telegram saying that his son, one H. H. Cummings, had gone down on the ship *Antilles*, torpedoed by the Germans. In the two days it took for this mistake to be corrected, Edward Cummings' anger doubled. Finally, he wrote a letter to President Wilson, a plea from one father to another, asking for information on his son's where-abouts. Whether his letter did the trick, or whether La Ferté-Macé was designed for three-month stays, Cummings was finally released and sent home in January.

For all his gallantry, for all his ballyhoo over the delights of prison, Cummings arrived home skinny and sick, exhausted and depressed, and plagued by malnutrition and a variety of skin problems. His friend Hildegarde Watson, who gave a fancy lunch in New York to celebrate his return, noted that her friend Estlin Cummings had lost his smile.

Edward Cummings, in the meantime, had not lost his rage. He planned to bring an international lawsuit against the Red Cross, the French government, and perhaps the United States State Department. Luckily for us, E. E. Cummings was not too sick to realize the futility of his father's anger. Instead of a lawsuit, he suggested to his father that he would write a book that would be an indictment of the powers that be and a furious account of the dreadful way the Cummings family had been treated. Edward agreed and even offered to pay his son for writing it.

The Enormous Room is a vivid, detailed memoir of three months, but in some ways it is also the key to all of Cummings' voluminous work in prose and poetry. Here are the physical details described so graphically that the reader feels hungry and exhilarated and faint. Here is the delight in all the things that others see as adversity. Here is the collision of an aristocratic Yan-kee gentleman's code with physical hardship. Here is the strength of character, the furious elegance, and the assumption that the world is good that drove everything E. E. Cummings would write in the forty years ahead of him.

Introduction
to the First Edition (1922)

"FOR THIS MY SON WAS DEAD, AND IS ALIVE AGAIN; HE WAS LOST AND IS FOUND."

He was lost by the Norton-Harjes Ambulance Corps.
He was officially dead as a result of official misinformation.
He was entombed by the French Government.
It took the better part of three months to find him and bring him back to life,—with the help of powerful and willing friends on both sides of the Atlantic. The following documents tell the story.

104 Irving Street,
Cambridge, December 8, 1917.

President Woodrow Wilson,
    White House,
        Washington, D.C.

Mr. President:
It seems criminal to ask for a single moment of your time.

But I am strongly advised that it would be more criminal to delay any longer calling to your attention a crime against American citizenship in which the French Government has persisted for many weeks,—in spite of constant appeals made to the American Minister at Paris; and in spite of subsequent action taken by the State Department in Washington, on the initiative of my friend Hon.——.

The victims are two American ambulance drivers,—Edward Estlin Cummings of Cambridge, Mass., and W—— S—— B——....

More than two months ago these young men were arrested, subjected to many indignities, dragged across France like criminals, and closely confined in a Concentration Camp at La Ferté-Macé; where according to latest advices they still remain,—awaiting the final action of the Minister of the Interior upon the findings of a Commission which passed upon their cases as long ago as October 17.

Against Cummings both private and official advices from Paris state that there is no charge whatever. He has been subjected to this outrageous treatment solely because of his intimate friendship with young B——, whose sole crime is,—so far as can be learned,—that certain letters to friends in America were misinterpreted by an over-zealous French censor.

It only adds to the indignity and irony of the situation, to say that young Cummings is an enthusiastic lover of France, and so loyal to the friends he has made among the French soldiers, that even while suffering in health from his unjust confinement, he excuses the ingratitude of the country he has risked his life to serve, by calling attention to the atmosphere of intense suspicion and distrust that has naturally resulted from the painful experience which France has had with foreign emissaries.

Be assured, Mr. President, that I have waited long—it seems

like ages—and have exhausted all other available help before venturing to trouble you.

1. After many weeks of vain effort to secure effective action by the American Ambassador at Paris, Richard Norton of the Norton-Harjes Ambulance Corps to which the boys belonged, was completely discouraged, and advised me to seek help here.

2. The efforts of the State Department at Washington resulted as follows:

i. A cable from Paris saying there was no charge against Cummings and intimating that he would speedily be released.

ii. A little later a second cable advising that Edward Estlin Cummings had sailed on the Antilles and was reported lost.

iii. A week later a third cable correcting this cruel error, and saying the Embassy was renewing efforts to locate Cummings,— apparently still ignorant even of the place of his confinement.

After such painful and baffling experiences, I turn to you,— burdened though I know you to be, in this world crisis, with the weightiest task ever laid upon any man.

But I have another reason for asking this favor. I do not speak for my son alone; or for him and his friend alone. My son has a mother,—as brave and patriotic as any mother who ever dedicated an only son to a great cause. The mothers of our boys in France have rights as well as the boys themselves. My boy's mother had a right to be protected from the weeks of horrible anxiety and suspense caused by the inexplicable arrest and imprisonment of her son. My boy's mother had a right to be spared the supreme agony caused by a blundering cable from Paris saying that he had been drowned by a submarine. (An error which Mr. Norton subsequently cabled that he had discovered six weeks before.) My boy's mother and all American mothers have a right to be protected against all needless anxiety and sorrow.

Pardon me, Mr. President, but if I were president and your son were suffering such prolonged injustice at the hands of France; and your son's mother had been needlessly kept in Hell as many weeks as my boy's mother has,—I would do something to make American citizenship as sacred in the eyes of Frenchmen as Roman citizenship was in the eyes of the ancient world. Then it was enough to ask the question, "Is it lawful to scourge a man that is a Roman, and uncondemned?" Now, in France, it seems lawful to treat like a condemned criminal a man that is an American, uncondemned and admittedly innocent!

Very respectfully,

Edward Cummings

This letter was received at the White House. Whether it was received with sympathy or with silent disapproval, is still a mystery. A Washington official, a friend in need and a friend indeed in these trying experiences, took the precaution to have it delivered by messenger. Otherwise, fear that it had been "lost in the mail" would have added another twinge of uncertainty to the prolonged and exquisite tortures inflicted upon parents by alternations of misinformation and official silence. Doubtless the official stethoscope was on the heart of the world just then; and perhaps it was too much to expect that even a post-card would be wasted on private heart-aches.

In any event this letter told where to look for the missing boys,—something the French Government either could not or would not disclose, in spite of constant pressure by the American Embassy at Paris and constant efforts by my friend Richard Norton, who was head of the Norton-Harjes Ambulance organization from which they had been abducted.

Release soon followed, as narrated in the following letter to Major—— of the Staff of the Judge Advocate General in Paris.

February 20, 1918

My dear Mr. ——

Your letter of January 30th, which I have been waiting for with great interest ever since I received your cable, arrived this morning. My son arrived in New York on January 1st. He was in bad shape physically as a result of his imprisonment: very much under weight, suffering from a bad skin infection which he had acquired at the concentration camp. However, in view of the extraordinary facilities which the detention camp offered for acquiring dangerous diseases, he is certainly to be congratulated on having escaped with one of the least harmful. The medical treatment at the camp was quite in keeping with the general standards of sanitation there; with the result that it was not until he began to receive competent surgical treatment after his release and on board ship that there was much chance of improvement. A month of competent medical treatment here seems to have got rid of this painful reminder of official hospitality. He is, at present, visiting friends in New York. If he were here, I am sure he would join with me and with his mother in thanking for the interest you have taken and the efforts you have made.

W—— S—— B—— is, I am happy to say, expected in New York this week by the S. S. Niagara. News of his release and subsequently of his departure came by cable. What you say about the nervous strain under which he was living, as an explanation of the letters to which the authorities objected, is entirely borne out by first-hand information. The kind of badgering which the youth received was enough to upset a less sensitive temperament. It speaks volumes for the character of his environment that such treatment aroused the resentment of only one of his companions, and that even this manifestation of normal human sympathy was regarded as "suspicious." If you are right in characterizing

B——'s condition as more or less hysterical, what shall we say of the conditions which made possible the treatment which he and his friend received? I am glad B—— wrote the very sensible and manly letter to the Embassy, which you mention. After I have had an opportunity to converse with him, I shall be in better position to reach a conclusion in regard to certain matters about which I will not now express an opinion.

I would only add that I do not in the least share your complacency in regard to the treatment which my son received. The very fact that, as you say, no charges were made and that he was detained on suspicion for many weeks after the Commission passed on his case and reported to the Minister of the Interior that he ought to be released, leads me to a conclusion exactly opposite to that which you express. It seems to me impossible that any well-ordered Government would fail to acknowledge such action to have been unreasonable. Moreover, "detention on suspicion" was a small part of what actually took place. To take a single illustration, you will recall that after many weeks' persistent effort to secure information, the Embassy was still kept so much in the dark about the facts that it cabled the report that my son had embarked on The Antilles and was reported lost. And when convinced of that error, the Embassy cabled that it was renewing efforts to locate my son. Up to that moment, it would appear that the authorities had not even condescended to tell the United States Embassy where this innocent American citizen was confined; so that a mistaken report of his death was regarded as an adequate explanation of his disappearance. If I had accepted this report and taken no further action, it is by no means certain that he would not be dead by this time.

I am free to say, that in my opinion no self-respecting Government could allow one of its own citizens, against whom there had been no accusation brought, to be subjected to such prolonged indignities and injuries by a friendly Government without vigorous remonstrance. I regard it as a patriotic duty, as well as a matter of personal self-respect, to do what I can to see that such remonstrance is made. I still think too highly both of my own Government and the Government of France to believe that such an untoward incident will fail to receive the serious attention it deserves. If I am wrong, and American citizens must expect to suffer such indignities and injuries at the hands of other Governments without any effort at remonstrance and redress by their own Government, I believe the public ought to know the humiliating truth. It will make interesting reading. It remains for my son to determine what action he will take.

I am glad to know your son is returning. I am looking forward with great pleasure to conversing with him.

I cannot adequately express my gratitude to you and to other friends for the sympathy and assistance I have received. If any expenses have been incurred on my behalf or on behalf of my son, I beg you to give me the pleasure of reimbursing you. At best, I must always remain your debtor.

With best wishes,

Sincerely yours,
Edward Cummings

I yield to no one in enthusiasm for the cause of France. Her cause was our cause and the cause of civilization; and the tragedy is that it took us so long to find it out. I would gladly have risked my life for her, as my son risked his, and would have risked it again had not the departure of his regiment overseas been stopped by the armistice.

France was beset with enemies within as well as without. Some of the "suspects" were members of her official household. Her Minister of Interior was thrown into prison. She was distracted with fear. Her existence was at stake. Under such circumstances excesses were sure to be committed. But it is precisely at such times that American citizens most need and are most entitled to the protection of their own government.

Edward Cummings

THE
ENORMOUS
ROOM

I Begin a Pilgrimage

We had succeeded, my friend B and I, in dispensing with almost three of our six months' engagement as Conducteurs Volontaires, Section Sanitaire Vingt-et-Un, Ambulance Norton-Harjes, Croix-Rouge Américaine, and at the Moment which subsequent experience served to capitalize had just finished the unlovely job of cleaning and greasing (nettoyer is the proper word) the own private flivver of the chef de section, a gentleman by the convenient name of Mr. A. To borrow a characteristic cadence from Our Great President: the lively satisfaction which we might be suspected of having derived from the accomplishment of a task so important in the saving of civilization from the clutches of Prussian tyranny was in some degree inhibited, unhappily, by a complete absence of cordial relations between the man whom fate had placed over us and ourselves. Or, to use the vulgar American idiom, B and I and Mr. A. didn't get on well. We were in fundamental disagreement as to the attitude which we, Americans, should uphold toward the poilus in whose behalf we had volunteered assistance, Mr. A. maintaining "You boys want to keep away from those dirty Frenchmen" and "We're here to show those bastards how they do things in America",to which we answered by seizing every opportunity for fraternization. Inasmuch as eight dirty Frenchmen were attached to the section in various capacities(cook,provisioner,chauffeur,mechanician,etc.)and the section itself was affiliated with a branch of the French army,fraternization was easy. Now when he saw that we had not the slightest intention of adopting his ideals,Mr. A.(together with the sous-lieutenant who acted as his translator—for the chef's knowledge of the French language,obtained during several years' heroic service,consisted for the most part in "Sar var","Sar marche",and "Deet donk moan vieux")confined his efforts to denying us the privilege of acting as conducteurs,on the ground that our personal appearance was a disgrace to the section. In this,I am bound to say,Mr. A. was but sustaining the tradition conceived originally by his predecessor,a Mr. P.,a Harvard man,who until his departure from Vingt-et-Un succeeded in making life absolutely miserable for B and myself. Before leaving this painful subject I beg to state that,at least as far as I was concerned,the tradition had a firm foundation in my own pre-

disposition for uncouthness plus what Le Matin(if we remember correctly)cleverly nicknamed La Boue Héroïque.

Having accomplished the nettoyage(at which we were by this time adepts,thanks to Mr. A.'s habit of detailing us to wash any car which its driver and aide might consider too dirty a task for their own hands)we proceeded in search of a little water for personal use. B speedily finished his ablutions. I was strolling carelessly and solo from the cook-wagon toward one of the two tents—which protestingly housed some forty huddling Americans by night—holding in my hand an historic morceau de chocolat,when a spic not to say span gentleman in a suspiciously quiet French uniform allowed himself to be driven up to the bureau by two neat soldiers with tin derbies,in a Renault whose painful cleanliness shamed my recent efforts. This must be a general at least,I thought,regretting the extremely undress character of my uniform,which uniform consisted of overalls and a cigarette.

Having furtively watched the gentleman alight and receive a ceremonious welcome from the chef and the aforesaid French lieutenant who accompanied the section for translatory reasons,I hastily betook myself to one of the tents,where I found B engaged in dragging all his belongings into a central pile of frightening proportions. He was surrounded by a group of fellow-heroes who hailed my coming with considerable enthusiasm. "Your bunky's leaving" said somebody. "Going to Paris" volunteered a man who had been trying for three months to get there. "Prison you mean" remarked a confirmed optimist whose disposition had felt the effects of French climate.

Albeit confused by the eloquence of B's unalterable silence,I immediately associated his present predicament with the advent of the mysterious stranger,and forthwith dashed forth bent on demanding from one of the tin-derbies the high identity and sacred mission of this personage. I knew that with the exception of ourselves everyone in the section had been given his permission de sept jours—even two men who had arrived later than we and whose turn should consequently have come after ours. I also knew that at the headquarters of the Ambulance,7 rue François premier,se trouvait Monsieur Norton,the supreme head of the Norton-Harjes fraternity,who had known my father in other days. Putting two together I decided that this potentate had sent an emissary to Mr. A. to demand an explanation of the various and sundry insults and indignities to which I and my friend had been subjected,and more particularly to secure our long-delayed permission. Accordingly I was in high spirits as I rushed toward the bureau.

I didn't have to go far. The mysterious one,in conversation with monsieur le sous-lieutenant,met me half-way. I caught the words:"And Cummings(the first and last time that my name was correctly pronounced by a Frenchman),where is he?"

"Present" I said,giving a salute to which neither of them paid the slightest attention.

"Ah yes" impenetrably remarked the mysterious one in positively sanitary English. "You shall put all your baggage in the car,at once"—then,to tin-derby-the-first,who appeared in an occult manner at his master's elbow—"Allez avec lui,chercher ses affaires,de suite."

My affaires were mostly in the vicinity of the cuisine,where lodged the cuisinier,mécanicien,menuisier,etc. who had made room for me(some ten days since)on their own initiative,thus saving me the humiliation of sleeping with nineteen Americans in a tent which was always two-thirds full of mud. Thither I led the tin-derby,who scrutinized everything with surprising interest. I threw mes affaires hastily together(including some minor accessories which I was going to leave behind,but which the t-d bade me include)and emerged with a duffle-bag under one arm and a bed-roll under the other,to encounter my excellent friends the dirty Frenchmen aforesaid. They all popped out together from one door,looking rather astonished. Something by way of explanation as well as farewell was most certainly required,so I made a speech in my best French:

"Gentlemen,friends,comrades—I am going away immediately and shall be guillotined tomorrow."

—"Oh hardly guillotined I should say" remarked t-d,in a voice which froze my marrow despite my high spirits;while the cook and carpenter gaped audibly and the mechanician clutched a hopelessly smashed carburetor for support.

One of the section's voitures,a F.I.A.T.,was standing ready. General Nemo sternly forbade me to approach the Renault(in which B's baggage was already deposited)and waved me into the F.I.A.T.,bed,bed-roll and all;whereupon t-d leaped in and seated himself opposite me in a position of perfect unrelaxation which,despite my aforesaid exultation at quitting the section in general and Mr. A. in particular,impressed me as being almost menacing. Through the front window I saw my friend drive away with t-d number 2 and Nemo;then,having waved hasty farewell to all les américains that I knew—3 in number—and having exchanged affectionate greetings with Mr. A.(who admitted he was very sorry indeed to lose us),I experienced the jolt of the clutch—and we were off in pursuit.

Whatever may have been the forebodings inspired by t-d number 1's attitude,they were completely annihilated by the thrilling joy which I experienced on losing sight of the accursed section and its asinine inhabitants—by the indisputable and authentic thrill of going somewhere and nowhere under the miraculous auspices of someone and noone—of being yanked from the putrescent banalities of an official non-existence into a high and clear adventure,by a deus ex machina in a grey-blue uniform and a couple of tin derbies. I whistled and sang and cried to my vis-à-vis: "By the way, who is yonder distinguished gentleman who has been so good as to take my friend and me on this little promenade?"—to which, between lurches of the groaning F.I.A.T., t-d replied awesomely, clutching at the window for the benefit of his equilibrium: "Monsieur le Ministre de Sûreté de Noyon."

Not in the least realizing what this might mean, I grinned. A responsive grin, visiting informally the tired cheeks of my confrere, ended by frankly connecting his worthy and enormous ears which were squeezed into oblivion by the oversize casque. My eyes, jumping from those ears, lit on that helmet and noticed for the first time an emblem, a sort of flowering little explosion, or hair-switch rampant. It seemed to me very jovial and a little absurd.

"We're on our way to Noyon, then?"

T-d shrugged his shoulders.

Here the driver's hat blew off. I heard him swear, and saw the hat sailing in our wake. I jumped to my feet as the F.I.A.T. came to a sudden stop, and started for the ground—then checked my flight in mid-air and landed on the seat, completely astonished. T-d's revolver, which had hopped from its holster at my first move, slid back into its nest. The owner of the revolver was muttering something rather disagreeable. The driver(being an American of Vingt-et-Un)was backing up instead of retrieving his cap in person. My mind felt as if it had been thrown suddenly from fourth into reverse. I pondered and said nothing.

On again—faster, to make up for lost time. On the correct assumption that t-d does not understand English the driver passes the time of day through the minute window:

"For Christ's sake, Cummings, what's up?"

"You got me" I said, laughing at the delicate naïveté of the question.

"Did y' do something to get pinched?"

"Probably" I answered importantly and vaguely, feeling a new dignity.

"Well, if you didn't, maybe B—— did."

"Maybe" I countered, trying not to appear enthusiastic. As a matter of fact I was never so excited and proud. I was, to be sure, a criminal! Well, well, thank God that settled one question for good and all—no more section sanitaire for me! No more Mr. A. and his daily lectures on cleanliness, deportment, etc. In spite of myself I started to sing. The driver interrupted:

"I heard you asking the tin lid something in French. Whadhesay?"

"Said that gink in the Renault is the head cop of Noyon" I answered at random.

"GOODNIGHT. Maybe we'd better ring off, or you'll get in wrong with"—he indicated t-d with a wave of his head that communicated itself to the car in a magnificent skid; and t-d's derby rang out as the skid pitched t-d the length of the F.I.A.T.

"You rang the bell then" I commended—then to t-d: "Nice

car for the wounded to ride in" I politely observed. T-d answered nothing....

Noyon.

We drive straight up to something which looks unpleasantly like a feudal dungeon. The driver is now told to be somewhere at a certain time,and meanwhile to eat with the Head Cop,who may be found just around the corner—(I am doing the translating for t-d)—and,oh yes,it seems that the Head Cop has particularly requested the pleasure of this distinguished American's company at déjeuner.

"Does he mean me?" the driver asked innocently.

"Sure" I told him.

Nothing is said of B or me.

Now,cautiously,t-d first and I a slow next,we descend. The F.I.A.T. rumbles off,with the distinguished one's backward-glaring head poked out a yard more or less and that distinguished face so completely surrendered to mystification as to cause a large laugh on my part.

"Vous avez faim?"

It was the erstwhile-ferocious speaking. A criminal,I remembered,is somebody against whom everything he says and does is very cleverly made use of. After weighing the matter in my mind for some moments I decided at all costs to tell the truth,and replied:

"I could eat an elephant."

Hereupon t-d led me to the Kitchen Itself,set me to eat upon a stool,and admonished the cook in a fierce voice:

"Give this great criminal something to eat in the name of the French Republic!"

And for the first time in three months I tasted Food.

T-d seated himself beside me,opened a huge jack-knife,and fell to,after first removing his tin derby and loosening his belt.

One of the pleasantest memories connected with that irrevocable meal is of a large gentle strong woman who entered in a hurry,and seeing me cried out:

"What is it?"

"It's an American,my mother" t-d answered through fried potatoes.

"Pourquoi qu'il est ici?" the woman touched me on the shoulder,and satisfied herself that I was real.

"The good God is doubtless acquainted with the explanation" said t-d pleasantly. "Not myself being the—"

"Ah,mon pauvre" said this very beautiful sort of woman. "You are going to be a prisoner here. Every one of the prisoners has a marraine,do you understand? I am their marraine. I love them and look after them. Well,listen: I will be your marraine,too."

I bowed,and looked around for something to pledge her in. T-d was watching. My eyes fell on a huge glass of red pinard. "Yes,drink" said my captor,with a smile. I raised my huge glass.

"A la santé de ma marraine charmante."

—This deed of gallantry quite won the cook(a smallish,agile Frenchman)who shovelled several helps of potatoes on my already empty plate. The tin-derby approved also: "That's right,eat,drink,you'll need it later perhaps." And his knife guillotined another delicious hunk of white bread.

At last,sated with luxuries,I bade adieu to my marraine and allowed t-d to conduct me(I going first,as always)upstairs and into a little den whose interior boasted two mattresses,a man sitting at the table,and a newspaper in the hands of the man.

"C'est un américain" t-d said by way of introduction. The newspaper detached itself from the man who said: "He's welcome indeed: make yourself at home Mr. American"—and bowed himself out. My captor immediately collapsed on one mattress.

I asked permission to do the same on the other,which

favor was sleepily granted. With half-shut eyes my Ego lay and pondered: the delicious meal it had just enjoyed; what was to come; the joys of being a great criminal...then, being not at all inclined to sleep, I read Le Petit Parisien quite through, even to Les Voies Urinaires.

Which reminded me—and I woke up t-d and asked: "May I visit the vespasienne?"

"Downstairs" he replied fuzzily, and readjusted his slumbers.

There was no one moving about in the little court. I lingered somewhat on the way upstairs. The stairs were abnormally dirty. When I reentered, t-d was roaring to himself. I read the journal through again. It must be about three o'clock.

Suddenly t-d woke up, straightened and buckled his personality, and murmured: "It's time, come on."

Le bureau de Monsieur le Ministre was just around the corner, as it proved. Before the door stood the patient F.I.A.T. It was ceremoniously informed by t-d that we would wait on the steps.

Well! Did I know any more?—the American driver wanted to know.

Having proved to my own satisfaction that my fingers could still roll a pretty good cigarette, I answered: "No", between puffs.

The American drew nearer and whispered spectacularly: "Your friend is upstairs. I think they're examining him." T-d got this; and though his rehabilitated dignity had accepted the makin's from its prisoner, it became immediately incensed:

"That's enough" he said sternly.

And dragged me tout-à-coup upstairs, where I met B and his t-d coming out of the bureau door. B looked peculiarly cheerful. "I think we're going to prison all right" he assured me.

Braced by this news, poked from behind by my t-d, and waved on from before by M. le Ministre himself, I floated vaguely into a very washed neat businesslike and altogether American room of modest proportions, whose door was immediately shut and guarded on the inside by my escort.

Monsieur le Ministre said:

"Lift your arms."

Then he went through my pockets. He found cigarettes, pencils, a jack-knife, and several francs. He laid his treasures on a clean table and said: "You are not allowed to keep these. I shall be responsible." Then he looked me coldly in the eye and asked if I had anything else?

I told him that I believed I had a handkerchief.

He asked me: "Have you anything in your shoes?"

"My feet" I said, gently.

"Come this way" he said frigidly, opening a door which I had not remarked. I bowed in acknowledgement of this courtesy, and entered room number 2.

I looked into six eyes which sat at a desk.

Two belonged to a lawyerish person in civilian clothes, with a bored expression, plus a mustache of dreamy proportions with which the owner constantly imitated a gentleman ringing for a drink. Two appertained to a splendid old dotard (a face all skee-jumps and toboggan-slides) on whose protruding chest the rosette of the Legion pompously squatted. Numbers five and six had reference to Monsieur, who had seated himself before I had time to focus my slightly bewildered eyes.

Monsieur spoke sanitary English, as I have said.

"What is your name?"—"Edward E. Cummings."—"Your second name?"—"E-s-t-l-i-n" I spelled it for him.—"How do you say that?"—I didn't understand.—"How do you say your name?"—"Oh" I said; and pronounced it. He explained in French to the mustache that my first name was Edouard, my second "A-s-tay-l-ee-n", and my third "Say-u-deux m-ee-n-zhay-s"—and the mustache wrote it all down. Monsieur then turned to me once more:

"You are Irish?"—"No" I said, "American."—"You are Irish by family?"—"No, Scotch."—"You are sure that there was never an Irishman in your parents?"—"So far as I know" I said, "there never was an Irishman there."—"Perhaps a hundred years back?" he insisted.—"Not a chance" I said decisively. But Monsieur was not to be denied: "Your name it is Irish?"—"Cummings is a very old Scotch name" I told him fluently, "it used to be Comyn. A Scotchman named The Red Comyn was killed by Robert Bruce in a church. He was my ancestor and a very well-known man."—"But your second name, where have you got that?"—"From an Englishman, a friend of my father." This statement seemed to produce a very favorable impression in the case of the rosette, who murmured: "Un ami de son père, un anglais, bon!" several times. Monsieur, quite evidently disappointed, told the mustache in French to write down that I denied my Irish parentage; which the mustache did.

"What does your father in America?"—"He is a minister of the gospel" I answered.—"Which church?"—"Unitarian." This puzzled him. After a moment he had an inspiration: "That is the same as a Free Thinker?"—I explained in French that it wasn't and that mon père was a holy man. At last Monsieur told the mustache to write: Protestant; and the mustache obediently did so.

From this point our conversation was carried on in French, somewhat to the chagrin of Monsieur, but to the joy of the rosette and with the approval of the mustache. In answer to questions, I informed them that I was a student for five years at Harvard (expressing great surprise that they had never heard of Harvard), that I had come to New York and studied painting, that I had enlisted in New York as conducteur volontaire, embarking for France shortly after, about the middle of April.

Monsieur asked: "You met B—— on the paquebot?" I said I did.

Monsieur glanced significantly around. The rosette nodded a number of times. The mustache rang.

I understood that these kind people were planning to make me out the innocent victim of a wily villain, and could not forbear a smile. C'est rigolo, I said to myself; they'll have a great time doing it.

"You and your friend were together in Paris?" I said "Yes." "How long?" "A month, while we were waiting for our uniforms."

A significant look by Monsieur, which is echoed by his confreres.

Leaning forward Monsieur asked coldly and carefully: "What did you do in Paris?" to which I responded briefly and warmly "We had a good time."

This reply pleased the rosette hugely. He wagged his head till I thought it would have tumbled off. Even the mustache seemed amused. Monsieur le Ministre de Sûreté de Noyon bit his lip. "Never mind writing that down" he directed the lawyer. Then, returning to the charge:

"You had a great deal of trouble with Lieutenant A.?"

I laughed outright at this complimentary nomenclature. "Yes, we certainly did."

He asked:"Why?"—so I sketched "Lieutenant" A. in vivid terms,making use of certain choice expressions with which one of the "dirty Frenchmen" attached to the section,a Parisien,master of argot,had furnished me. My phraseology surprised my examiners,one of whom(I think the mustache)observed sarcastically that I had made good use of my time in Paris.

Monsieur le Ministre asked:Was it true(a)that B and I were always together and(b)preferred the company of the attached Frenchmen to that of our fellow-Americans?—to which I answered in the affirmative. Why? he wanted to know. So I explained that we felt that the more French we knew and the better we knew the French,the better for us;expatiating a bit on the necessity for a complete mutual understanding of the Latin and Anglo-Saxon races if victory was to be won.

Again the rosette nodded with approbation.

Monsieur le Ministre may have felt that he was losing his case,for he played his trump card immediately:"You are aware that your friend has written to friends in America and to his family very bad letters." "I am not" I said.

In a flash I understood the motivation of Monsieur's visit to Vingt-et-Un:the French censor had intercepted some of B's letters,and had notified Mr. A. and Mr. A.'s translator,both of whom had thankfully testified to the bad character of B and(wishing very naturally to get rid of both of us at once)had further averred that we were always together and that consequently I might properly be regarded as a suspicious character. Whereupon they had received instructions to hold us at the section until Noyon could arrive and take charge—hence our failure to obtain our long overdue permission.

"Your friend" said Monsieur in English,"is here a short while ago. I ask him if he is up in the aeroplane flying over Germans will he drop the bombs on Germans and he say no,he will not drop any bombs on Germans."

By this falsehood(such it happened to be)I confess that I was nonplussed. In the first place,I was at the time innocent of third-degree methods. Secondly:I remembered that,a week or so since,B myself and another American in the section had written a letter—which,on the advice of the sous-lieutenant who accompanied Vingt-et-Un as translator,we had addressed to the Under-Secretary of State in French Aviation—asking that inasmuch as the American government was about to take over the Red Cross(which meant that all the sections sanitaires would be affiliated with the American,and no longer with the French army)we three at any rate might be allowed to continue our association with the French by enlisting in l'Escadrille Lafayette. One of the "dirty Frenchmen" had written the letter for us in the finest language imaginable,from data supplied by ourselves.

"You write a letter,your friend and you,for French aviation?"

Here I corrected him:there were three of us;and why didn't he have the third culprit arrested,might I ask? But he ignored this little digression,and wanted to know:Why not American aviation?—to which I answered:Ah,but as my friend has so often said to me,the French are after all the finest people in the world.

This double-blow stopped Noyon dead,but only for a second.

"Did your friend write this letter?"—"No" I answered truthfully.—"Who did write it?"—"One of the Frenchmen attached to the section."—"What is his name?"—"I'm sure I don't know" I answered;mentally swearing that,whatever might happen to me,the scribe should not suffer. "At my urgent request" I added.

Relapsing into French,Monsieur asked me if I would have any hesitation in dropping bombs on Germans? I said no,I wouldn't. And why did I suppose I was fitted to become aviator? Because,I told him,I weighed 135 pounds and could drive any kind of auto or motorcycle.(I hoped he would make me prove this assertion,in which case I promised myself that I wouldn't stop till I got to Munich;but no.)

"Do you mean to say that my friend was not only trying to avoid serving in the American army but was contemplating treason as well?" I asked.

"Well, that would be it, would it not?" he answered coolly. Then, leaning forward once more, he fired at me: "Why did you write to an official so high?"

At this I laughed outright. "Because the excellent sous-lieutenant who translated when Mr. Lieutenant A. couldn't understand advised us to do so."

Following up this sortie, I addressed the mustache: "Write this down in the testimony—that I, here present, refuse utterly to believe that my friend is not as sincere a lover of France and the French people as any man living!—Tell him to write it" I commanded Noyon stonily. But Noyon shook his head, saying: "We have the very best reason for supposing your friend to be no friend of France." I answered: "That is not my affair. I want my opinion of my friend written in; do you see?" "That's reasonable" the rosette murmured; and the mustache wrote it down.

"Why do you think we volunteered?" I asked sarcastically, when the testimony was complete.

Monsieur le Ministre was evidently rather uncomfortable. He writhed a little in his chair, and tweaked his chin three or four times. The rosette and the mustache were exchanging animated phrases. At last Noyon, motioning for silence and speaking in an almost desperate tone, demanded:

"Est-ce que vous détestez les boches?"

I had won my own case. The question was purely perfunctory. To walk out of the room a free man I had merely to say yes. My examiners were sure of my answer. The rosette was leaning forward and smiling encouragingly. The mustache was making little ouis in the air with his pen. And Noyon had given up all hope of making me out a criminal. I might be rash, but I was innocent; the dupe of a superior and malign intelligence. I would probably be admonished to choose my friends more carefully next time and that would be all....

Deliberately, I framed my answer:

"Non. J'aime beaucoup les français."

Agile as a weasel, Monsieur le Ministre was on top of me: "It is impossible to love Frenchmen and not to hate Germans."

I did not mind his triumph in the least. The discomfiture of the rosette merely amused me. The surprise of the mustache I found very pleasant.

Poor rosette! He kept murmuring desperately: "Fond of his friend, quite right. Mistaken of course, too bad, meant well."

With a supremely disagreeable expression on his immaculate face the victorious minister of security pressed his victim with regained assurance: "But you are doubtless aware of the atrocities committed by the boches?"

"I have read about them" I replied very cheerfully.

"You do not believe?"

"Ça se peut."

"And if they are so, which of course they are"(tone of profound conviction) "you do not detest the Germans?"

"Oh, in that case, of course anyone must detest them" I averred with perfect politeness.

And my case was lost, forever lost. I breathed freely once more. All my nervousness was gone. The attempt of the three gentlemen sitting before me to endow my friend and myself with different fates had irrevocably failed.

At the conclusion of a short conference I was told by Monsieur: "I am sorry for you, but due to your friend you will be detained a little while."

I asked: "Several weeks?"

"Possibly" said Monsieur.

This concluded the trial.

Monsieur le Ministre conducted me into room number 1 again. "Since I have taken your cigarettes and shall keep them from you,I will give you some tobacco. Do you prefer English or French?"

Because the French(paquet bleu)are stronger and because he expected me to say English,I said "French."

· With a sorrowful expression Noyon went to a sort of book-case and took down a blue packet. I think I asked for matches,or else he had given back the few which he found on my person.

Noyon,t-d and the grand criminal(alias I)now descended solemnly to the F.I.A.T. The more and more mystified con-ducteur conveyed us a short distance to what was obviously a prison-yard. Monsieur le Ministre watched me descend my volu-minous baggage.

This was carefully examined by Monsieur at the bureau of the prison. Monsieur made me turn everything topsy-turvy and inside-out. Monsieur expressed great surprise at a huge dou-ille:where did I get it?—I said a French soldier gave it to me as a souvenir.—And several têtes d'obus?—Also souvenirs,I assured him merrily. Did Monsieur suppose I was caught in the act of blowing up the French government,or what exactly?—But here are a dozen sketchbooks,what is in them?—Oh,Monsieur,you flatter me:drawings.—Of fortifications?—Hardly;of poilus,chil-dren,and other ruins.—Ummmm.(Monsieur examined the drawings and found that I had spoken the truth.)Monsieur puts all these trifles into a small bag,with which I had been fur-nished(in addition to the huge duffle-bag)by the generous Croix-Rouge. Labels them(in French):"Articles found in the baggage of Cummings and deemed inutile to the case at hand." This leaves in the duffle-bag aforesaid:my fur coat,which I brought from New York,my bed and blankets and bed-roll,my civilian clothes,and about twenty-five pounds of soiled linen. "You may take the bed-roll and the folding bed into your cell"—the rest of my affaires will remain in safe keeping at the bureau.

"Come with me" grimly croaked a lank turnkey-creature.

Bed-roll and bed in hand, I came along.

We had but a short distance to go; several steps in fact. I remember we turned a corner and somehow got sight of a sort of square near the prison. A military band was executing itself to the stolid delight of some handfuls of ragged civils. My new captor paused a moment; perhaps his patriotic soul was stirred. Then we traversed an alley with locked doors on both sides, and stopped in front of the last door on the right. A key opened it. The music could still be distinctly heard.

The opened door showed a room, about sixteen feet short and four feet narrow, with a heap of straw in the further end. My spirits had been steadily recovering from the banality of their examination; and it was with a genuine and never-to-be-forgotten thrill that I remarked, as I crossed what might have been the threshold: "Mais, on est bien ici."

A hideous crash nipped the last word. I had supposed the whole prison to have been utterly destroyed by earthquake, but it was only my door closing....

CHAPTER TWO

En Route

I put the bed-roll down. I stood up.

I was myself.

An uncontrollable joy gutted me after three months of humiliation, of being bossed and herded and bullied and insulted. I was myself and my own master.

In this delirium of relief(hardly noticing what I did)I inspected the pile of straw, decided against it, set up my bed, disposed the roll on it, and began to examine my cell.

I have mentioned the length and breadth. The cell was ridiculously high; perhaps ten feet. The end with the door in it was peculiar. The door was not placed in the middle of this end, but at one side, allowing for a huge iron can waist-high which stood in the other corner. Over the door and across the end, a grating extended. A slit of sky was always visible.

Whistling joyously to myself, I took three steps which brought me to the door end. The door was massively made, all of iron or steel I should think. It delighted me. The can excited my curiosity. I looked over the edge of it. At the bottom reposefully lay a new human turd.

I have a sneaking mania for wood-cuts, particularly when used to illustrate the indispensable psychological crisis of some out-worn romance. There is in my possession at this minute a masterful depiction of a tall bearded horrified man who, clad in an anonymous rig of goatskins, with a fantastic umbrella clasped weakly in one huge paw, bends to examine an indication of humanity in the somewhat cubist wilderness whereof he had fancied himself the owner....

It was then that I noticed the walls. Arm-high they were covered with designs, mottos, pictures. The drawing had all been done in pencil. I resolved to ask for a pencil at the first opportunity.

There had been Germans and Frenchmen imprisoned in this cell. On the right wall, near the door-end, was a long selection from Goethe, laboriously copied. Near the other end of this wall a satiric landscape took place. The technique of this landscape frightened me. There were houses, men, children. And there were trees. I began to wonder what a tree looks like, and laughed copiously.

The back wall had a large and exquisite portrait of a German officer.

The left wall was adorned with a yacht, flying a number—13. "My beloved boat" was inscribed in German underneath. Then came a bust of a German soldier, very idealized, full of unfear. After this, a masterful crudity—a doughnut-bodied rider, sliding with fearful rapidity down the acute back-bone of a totally transparent sausage-shaped horse who was moving simultaneously in five directions. The rider had a bored expression as he supported the stiff reins in one fist. His further leg assisted in his flight. He wore a German soldier's cap and was smoking. I made up my mind to copy the horse and rider at once, so soon that is as I should have obtained a pencil.

Last, I found a drawing surrounded by a scrolled motto. The

drawing was a potted plant with four blossoms. The four blossoms were elaborately dead. Their death was drawn with a fearful care. An obscure deliberation was exposed in the depiction of their drooping petals. The pot tottered very crookedly on a sort of table, as near as I could see. All around ran a funereal scroll. I read: "Mes derniers adieux à ma femme aimée, Gaby." A fierce hand, totally distinct from the former, wrote in proud letters above: "Tombé pour désert. Six ans de prison—dégradation militaire."

It must have been five o'clock. Steps. A vast cluttering of the exterior of the door—by whom? Whang opens the door. Turnkey-creature extending a piece of chocolat with extreme and surly caution. I say "Merci" and seize chocolat. Klang shuts the door.

I am lying on my back, the twilight does mistily bluish miracles thru the slit over the whang-klang. I can just see leaves, meaning trees.

Then from the left and way off, faintly, broke a smooth whistle, cool like a peeled willow-branch, and I found myself listening to an air from Pétrouchka, Pétrouchka, which we saw in Paris at the Châtelet, mon ami et moi...

The voice stopped in the middle—and I finished the air. This code continued for a half-hour.

It was dark.

I had laid a piece of my piece of chocolat on the window-sill. As I lay on my back, a little silhouette came along the sill and ate that piece of a piece, taking something like four minutes to do so. He then looked at me, I then smiled at him, and we parted, each happier than before.

My cellule was cool, and I fell asleep easily.

(thinking of Paris)

...Awakened by a conversation whose vibrations I clearly felt thru the left wall:

Turnkey-creature: "What?"

A moldy moldering molish voice, suggesting putrefying tracts and orifices, answers with a cob-webbish patience so far beyond despair as to be indescribable: "La soupe."

"Well, the soup, I just gave it to you, Monsieur Savy."

"Must have a little something else. My money is chez le directeur. Please take my money which is chez le directeur and give me anything else."

Le Gendarme de Noyon

"All right, the next time I come to see you today I'll bring you a salad, a nice salad, Monsieur."

"Thank you, Monsieur" the voice moldered.

Klang!!—and says the t-c to somebody else; while turning the lock of Monsieur Savy's door; taking pains to raise his voice so that Monsieur Savy will not miss a single word thru the slit over Monsieur Savy's whang-klang:

"That old fool! Always asks for things. When supposest thou will he realize that he's never going to get anything?"

Grubbing at my door. Whang!

The faces stood in the doorway, looking me down. The expression of the faces identically turnkeyish, i.e. stupidly gloating, ponderously and imperturbably tickled. Look who's here, who let that in.

The right body collapsed sufficiently to deposit a bowl just inside.

I smiled and said: "Good morning, sirs. The can stinks."

They did not smile and said "Naturally." I smiled and said: "Please give me a pencil. I want to pass the time." They did not smile and said "Directly."

I smiled and said "I want some water, if you please."

They shut the door, saying "Later."

Klang and footsteps.

I contemplate the bowl which contemplates me. A glaze of greenish grease seals the mystery of its content. I induce two fingers to penetrate the seal. They bring me up a flat sliver of choux and a large, hard, thoughtful, solemn, uncooked bean. To pour the water off (it is warmish and sticky) without committing a nuisance is to lift the cover off Ça Pue. I did.

Thus leaving beans and cabbage-slivers. Which I ate hurryingly, fearing a ventral misgiving.

I pass a lot of time cursing myself about the pencil, looking at my walls, my unique interior.

Suddenly I realize the indisputable grip of nature's humorous hand. One evidently stands on Ça Pue in such cases. Having finished, panting with stink, I tumble on the bed and consider my next move.

The straw will do. Ouch, but it's Dirty.—Several hours elapse…

Stepsandfumble. Klang. Repetition of promise to Monsieur Savy, etc.

Turnkeyish and turnkeyish. Identical expression. One body

collapses sufficiently to deposit a hunk of bread and a piece of water.

Give your bowl.

I gave it, smiled and said : "Well, how about that pencil?"

"Pencil?" T-c looked at t-c.

They recited then the following word: "Tomorrow." Klang-andfootsteps.

So I took matches, burnt, and with just 60 of them wrote the first stanza of a ballade. Tomorrow I will write the second. Day after tomorrow the third. Next day the refrain. After—oh, well.

My whistling of Pétrouchka brought no response this evening.

So I climbed on Ça Pue, whom I now regarded with complete friendliness; the new moon was unclosing sticky wings in dusk, a far noise from near things.

I sang a song the "dirty Frenchmen" taught us, mon ami et moi. The song says Bon soir, Madame la Lune....I did not sing out loud, simply because the moon was like a mademoiselle, and I did not want to offend the moon. My friends: the silhouette and la lune, not counting Ça Pue, whom I regarded almost as a part of me.

Then I lay down, and heard (but could not see) the silhouette eat something or somebody...and saw, but could not hear, the incense of Ça Pue mount gingerly upon the taking air of twilight.

The next day.—Promise to M. Savy. Whang. "My pencil?"—You don't need any pencil, you're going away."—When?"—"Directly."—"How directly?"—"In an hour or two: your friend has already gone before. Get ready."

Klangandsteps.

Everyone very sore about me. Je m'en fous pas mal, however.

One hour I guess.

Steps. Sudden throwing of door open. Pause.

"Come out, American."

As I came out,toting bed and bed-roll,I remarked "I'm sorry to leave you" which made t-c furiously to masticate his unsignificant mustache.

Escorted to bureau,where I am turned over to a very fat gendarme.

"This is the American." The v-f-g eyed me,and I read my sins in his porklike orbs. "Hurry,we have to walk" he ventured sullenly and commandingly.

Himself stooped puffingly to pick up the segregated sack. And I placed my bed,bed-roll,blankets,and ample pelisse under one arm,my 150 lb. duffle-bag under the other;then I paused. Then I said "Where's my cane?"

The v-f-g hereat had a sort of fit,which perfectly became him.

I repeated gently "When I came to the bureau I had a cane."

"Je m'en fous de ta canne" burbled my new captor frothily,his pink evil eyes swelling with wrath.

"I'm staying" I replied calmly,and sat down on a curb,in the midst of my ponderous trinkets.

A foule of gendarmes gathered. One didn't take a cane with one to prison(I was glad to know where I was bound,and thanked this communicative gentleman);or criminals weren't allowed canes;or where exactly did I think I was,in the Tuileries? asks a rube movie-cop personage.

"Very well,gentlemen" I said. "You will allow me to tell you something."(I was beet-coloured.)"En Amérique on ne fait pas comme ça."

This haughty inaccuracy produced an astonishing effect, namely,the prestidigitatorial vanishment of the v-f-g. The v-f-g's numerous confreres looked scared and twirled their whiskers.

I sat on the curb and began to fill a paper with something which I found in my pockets,certainly not tobacco.

Splutter-splutter-fizz-Poop—the v-f-g is back,with my great

oak-branch in his raised hand, slithering opprobria and mostly crying: "Is that huge piece of wood what you call a cane? Is it? It is, is it? What? How? Whatthe—" so on.

I beamed upon him and thanked him, and explained that a "dirty Frenchman" had given it to me as a souvenir, and that I would now proceed.

Twisting the handle in the loop of my sack, and hoisting the vast parcel under my arm, I essayed twice to boost it on my back. This to the accompaniment of HurryHurryHurryHurryHurryHurryHurry... The third time I sweated and staggered to my feet, completely accoutred.

Le Gosse

Down the road. Into the ville. Curious looks from a few pedestrians. A driver stops his wagon to watch the spider and his outlandish fly. I chuckled to think how long since I had washed and shaved. Then I nearly fell, staggered on a few steps, and set down the two loads.

Perhaps it was the fault of the strictly vegetarian diet. At any rate I couldn't move a step farther with my bundles. The sun sent the sweat along my nose in tickling waves. My eyes were blind.

Hereupon I suggested that the v-f-g carry part of one of my bundles with me, and received the answer: "I am doing too much for you as it is. No gendarme is supposed to carry a prisoner's baggage."

I said then "I'm too tired."

He responded: "You can leave here anything you don't care to carry further; I'll take care of it."

I looked at the gendarme. I looked several blocks thru him. My lip did something like a sneer. My hands did something like fists.

At this crisis, along comes a little boy. May God bless all males between seven and ten years of age in France.

The gendarme offered a suggestion, in these words: "Have you any change about you?" He knew of course that the sanitary official's first act had been to deprive me of every last cent. The gendarme's eyes were fine. They reminded me of...never mind. "If you have change" said he, "you might hire this kid to carry some of your baggage." Then he lit a pipe which was made in his own image, and smiled fattily.

But herein the v-f-g had bust his milk-jug. There is a slit of a pocket made in the uniform of his criminal on the right side, and completely covered by the belt which his criminal always wears. His criminal had thus outwitted the gumshoe fraternity.

The gosse could scarcely balance my smaller parcel, but managed after three rests to get it to the station platform; here I tipped him something like two cents(all I had)which with dollar-big eyes he took, and ran.

A strongly-built, groomed apache smelling of cologne and onions greeted my v-f-g with that affection which is peculiar to gendarmes. On me he stared cynically, then sneered frankly.

With a little tooty shriek, the funny train tottered in. My captors had taken pains to place themselves at the wrong end of the platform. Now they encouraged me to HurryHurryHurry.

I managed to get under the load and tottered the length of

the train to a car especially reserved. There was one other crim-
inal,a beautifully-smiling,shortish man,with a very fine blan-
ket wrapped in a water-proof oilskin cover. We grinned at each
other(the most cordial salutation,by the way,that I have ever
exchanged with a human being)and sat down opposite one
another—he,plus my baggage which he helped me lift in,occupy-
ing one seat;the gendarme-sandwich,of which I formed the pièce
de résistance,the other.

The engine got under way after several feints;which pleased
the Germans so that they sent seven scout planes right over the
station,train,us et tout. All the French anti-aircraft guns went
off together for the sake of sympathy;the guardians of the peace
squinted cautiously from their respective windows,and then
began to debate on the number of the enemy while their prison-
ers smiled at each other appreciatively.

"Il fait chaud" said this divine man,prisoner,criminal,or what
not,as he offered me a glass of wine in the form of a huge tin cup
overflowed from the bidon in his slightly unsteady and delicately
made hand. He is a Belgian. Volunteered at beginning of war.
Permission at Paris,overstayed by one day. When he reported to
his officer,the latter announced that he was a deserter—"I said
to him,It is funny. It is funny I should have come back,of my
own free will,to my company. I should have thought that being a
deserter I would have preferred to remain in Paris." The wine was
terribly cold,and I thanked my divine host.

Never have I tasted such wine.

They had given me a chunk of war-bread in place of bless-
ing when I left Noyon. I bit into it with renewed might. But the
divine man across from me immediately produced a sausage,half
of which he laid simply upon my knee. The halving was done with
a large keen poilu's couteau.

I have not tasted a sausage since.

The pigs on my either hand had by this time overcome their respective inertias and were chomping cheek-murdering chunks. They had quite a layout,a regular picnic-lunch elaborate enough for kings or even presidents. The v-f-g in particular annoyed me by uttering alternate chompings and belchings. All the time he ate he kept his eyes half-shut;and a mist overspread the sensual meadows of his coarse face.

His two reddish eyes rolled devouringly toward the blanket in its water-proof roll. After a huge gulp of wine he said thickly(for his huge mustache was crusted with saliva-tinted half-moistened shreds of food)"You will have no use for that machin,là-bas. They are going to take everything away from you when you get there,you know. I could use it nicely. I have wanted such a piece of caoutchouc for a great while,in order to make me an imperméable. Do you see?"(Gulp. Swallow.)

Here I had an inspiration. I would save the blanket-cover by drawing these brigands' attention to myself. At the same time I would satisfy my inborn taste for the ridiculous. "Have you a pencil?" I said. "Because I am an artist in my own country,and will do your picture."

He gave me a pencil. I don't remember where the paper came from. I posed him in a piglike position,and the picture made him chew his mustache. The apache thought it very droll. I should do his picture too,at once. I did my best;though protesting that he was too beautiful for my pencil,which remark he countered by murmuring(as he screwed his mustache another notch)"Never mind,you will try." Oh yes,I would try all right,all right. He objected,I recall,to the nose.

By this time the divine "deserter" was writhing with joy. "If you please,Monsieur" he whispered radiantly,"it would be too great an honour,but if you could—I should be overcome…"

Tears(for some strange reason)came into my eyes.

He handled his picture sacredly, criticized it with precision and care, finally bestowed it in his inner pocket. Then we drank. It happened that the train stopped and the apache was persuaded to go out and get his prisoner's bidon filled. Then we drank again.

He smiled as he told me he was getting ten years. Three years at solitary confinement was it, and seven working in a gang on the road? That would not be so bad. He wishes he was not married, had not a little child. "The bachelors are lucky in this war"— he smiled.

Now the gendarmes began cleaning their beards, brushing their stomachs, spreading their legs, collecting their baggage. The reddish eyes, little and cruel, woke from the trance of digestion and settled with positive ferocity on their prey. "You will have no use..."

Silently the sensitive gentle hands of the divine prisoner undid the blanket-cover. Silently the long, tired, well-shaped arms passed it across to the brigand at my left side. With a grunt of satisfaction the brigand stuffed it in a large pouch, taking pains that it should not show. Silently the divine eyes said to mine: "What can we do, we criminals?" And we smiled at each other for the last time, the eyes and my eyes.

A station. The apache descends. I follow with my numerous affaires. The divine man follows me—the v-f-g him.

The blanket-roll containing my large fur-coat got more and more unrolled; finally I could not possibly hold it.

It fell. To pick it up, I must take the sack off my back.

Then comes a voice "Allow me if you please monsieur"—and the sack has disappeared. Blindly and dumbly I stumbled on with the roll; and so at length we come into the yard of a little prison; and the Divine Man bowed under my great sack...I never thanked him. When I turned, they'd taken him away, and the sack stood accusingly at my feet.

Through the complete disorder of my numbed mind flicker jabbings of strange tongues. Some high boy's voice is appealing to me in Belgian,Italian,Polish,Spanish,and—beautiful English. "Hey,Jack,give me a cigarette,Jack..."

I lift my eyes. I am standing in a tiny oblong space. A sort of court. All around,two-story wooden barracks. Little crude staircases lead up to doors heavily chained and immensely padlocked. More like ladders than stairs. Curious hewn windows,smaller in proportion than the slits in a doll's house. Are these faces behind the slits? The doors bulge incessantly under the shock of bodies hurled against them from within. The whole dirty nouveau business about to crumble.

Glance one.

Glance two: directly before me. A wall with many bars fixed across one minute opening. At the opening a dozen,fifteen,grins. Upon the bars hands,scraggy and bluishly white. Through the bars stretchings of lean arms,incessant stretchings. The grins leap at the window,hands belonging to them catch hold,arms belonging to the hands stretch in my direction...an instant;then new grins leap from behind and knock off the first grins which go down with a fragile crashing like glass smashed: hands wither and break,arms streak out of sight,sucked inward.

In the huge potpourri of misery a central figure clung,shaken but undislodged. Clung like a monkey to central bars. Clung like an angel to a harp. Calling pleasantly in a high boyish voice: "O Jack,give me a cigarette."

A handsome face,dark,Latin smile,musical fingers strong.

I waded suddenly through a group of gendarmes(they stood around me watching with a disagreeable curiosity my reaction to this). Strode fiercely to the window.

Trillions of hands.

Quadrillions of itching fingers.

The angel-monkey received the package of cigarettes politely,disappearing with it into howling darkness. I heard his high boy's voice distributing cigarettes. Then he leapt into sight,poised gracefully against two central bars,saying "Thank you,Jack,good boy" ... "Thanks,merci,gracias..." a deafening din of gratitude reeked from within.

"Put your baggage in here" quoth an angry voice. "No you will not take anything but one blanket in your cell,understand." In French. Evidently the head of the house speaking. I obeyed. A corpulent soldier importantly led me to my cell. My cell is two doors away from the monkey-angel,on the same side. The high boy-voice,centralized in a torrentlike halo of stretchings,followed my back. The head himself unlocked a lock. I marched coldly in. The fat soldier locked and chained my door. Four feet went away. I felt in my pocket,finding four cigarettes. I am sorry I did not give these also to the monkey—to the angel. Lifted my eyes,and saw my own harp.

CHAPTER THREE

A Pilgrim's Progress

Through the bars I looked into that little and dirty lane whereby I had entered;in which a sentinel,gun on shoulder,and with a huge revolver strapped at his hip,monotonously moved. On my right was an old wall overwhelmed with moss. A few growths stemmed from its crevices. Their leaves are of a refreshing colour. I felt singularly happy,and carefully throwing myself on the bare planks sang one after another all the French songs which I had picked up in my stay at the ambulance;sang La Madelon,sang AVec avEC DU,and Les Galiots Sont Lourds Dans L'Sac—concluding with an inspired rendering of La Marseillaise,at which the guard(who had several times stopped his round in what I choose to interpret as astonishment)grounded arms and swore appreciatively. Various officials of the jail passed by me and my lusty songs;I cared no whit. Two or three conferred,pointing in my direction,and I sang a little louder for the benefit of their perplexity. Finally out of voice I stopped.

It was twilight.

As I lay on my back luxuriously I saw through the bars of my twice padlocked door a boy and a girl about ten years old. I saw

them climb on the wall and play together, obliviously and exqui-
sitely, in the darkening air. I watched them for many minutes; till
the last moment of light failed; till they and the wall itself dis-
solved in a common mystery, leaving only the bored silhouette of
the soldier moving imperceptibly and wearily against a still more
gloomy piece of autumn sky.

At last I knew that I was very thirsty; and leaping up began
to clamour at my bars. "Quelque chose à boire, s'il vous plaît."
After a long debate with the sergeant of guards who said very
angrily: "Give it to him", a guard took my request and disap-
peared from view, returning with a more heavily armed guard
and a tin cup full of water. One of these gentry watched the
water and me, while the other wrestled with the padlocks. The
door being minutely opened, one guard and the water painfully
entered. The other guard remained at the door, gun in readiness.
The water was set down, and the enterer assumed a perpendicu-
lar position which I thought merited recognition; accordingly I
said "Merci" politely, without getting up from the planks. Imme-
diately he began to deliver a sharp lecture on the probability of
my using the tin cup to saw my way out; and commended haste
in no doubtful terms. I smiled, asked pardon for my inherent
stupidity (which speech seemed to anger him) and guzzled the
so-called water without looking at it, having learned something
from Noyon. With a long and dangerous look at their prisoner
the gentlemen of the guard withdrew, using inconceivable cau-
tion in the relocking of the door.

I laughed and fell asleep.

After (as I judged) four minutes of slumber, I was awakened
by at least six men standing over me. The darkness was intense, it
was extraordinarily cold. I glared at them and tried to understand
what new crime I had committed. One of the six was repeat-
ing: "Get up, you are going away. Quatre heures." After several

attempts I got up. They formed a circle around me;and together we marched a few steps to a sort of store-room,where my great sac small sac and overcoat were handed to me. A rather agreeably voiced guard then handed me a half-cake of chocolat,saying(but with a tolerable grimness)"Vous en aurez besoin,croyez-moi." I found my stick,at which "piece of furniture" they amused themselves a little until I showed its use,by catching the ring at the mouth of my sac in the curved end of the stick and swinging the whole business unaided on my back. Two new guards—or rather gendarmes—were now officially put in charge of my person;and the three of us passed down the lane,much to the interest of the sentinel,to whom I bade a vivid and unreturned adieu. I can see him perfectly as he stares stupidly at us,a queer shape in the gloom,before turning on his heel.

Toward the very station whereat,some hours since,I had disembarked with the Belgian deserter and my former escorts,we moved. I was stiff with cold and only half awake,but peculiarly thrilled. The gendarmes on either side moved grimly,without speaking;or returning monosyllables to my few questions. Yes,we were to take the train. I was going somewhere,then? "B'en sûr"—"Where?"—"You will know in time."

After a few minutes we reached the station,which I failed to recognize. The yellow flares of lamps,huge and formless in the night mist,some figures moving to and fro on a little platform,a rustle of conversation:everything seemed ridiculously suppressed,beautifully abnormal,deliciously insane. Every figure was wrapped with its individual ghostliness;a number of ghosts each out on his own promenade,yet each for some reason selecting this unearthly patch of the world,this putrescent and uneasy gloom. Even my guards talked in whispers. "Watch him,I'll see about the train." So one went off into the mist. I leaned dizzily against the wall nearest me(having plumped down my baggage)and stared,into the darkness at my elbow,filled with talking shadows. I recognized officiers anglais wandering helplessly up and down,supported with their sticks;French lieutenants talking to each other here and there;the extraordinary sense-bereft station-master at a distance looking like a cross between a jumping-jack and a goblin;knots of permissionnaires cursing wearily or joking hopelessly with one another or stalking back and forth with imprecatory gesticulations. "C'est d'la blague. Sais-tu,il n'y a plus de trains?"—"Le conducteur est mort,j'connais sa sœur."—"J'suis foutu mon vieux."—"Nous sommes tous perdus,dis-donc."—"Quelle heure?"—"Mon cher,il n'y a plus d'heures,le gouvernement français les défend." Suddenly burst out of the loquacious opacity a dozen handfuls of algériens,their feet swaggering with fatigue,their eyes burning apparently by themselves—faceless in the equally black mist. By threes and fives they assaulted the goblin who wailed and shook his withered fist in their faces. There was no train. It had been taken away by the French government. "How do I know how the poilus can get back to their regiments on time? Of course you'll all of you be deserters,but is it my fault?"(I thought of my friend,the Belgian,at this moment lying in a pen at the prison which I had just quitted by some miracle)...One of these fine people from uncivilized ignorant unwarlike Algeria was drunk and knew it,as did two of his very fine friends who announced that as there was no train he should have a good sleep at a farmhouse hard by,which farmhouse one of them claimed to espy through the impenetrable night. The drunk was accordingly escorted into the dark,his friends' abrupt steps correcting his own large slovenly procedure out of earshot.... Some of the Black People sat down near me,and smoked. Their vast gentle hands lay noisily about their knees.

The departed gendarme returned,with a bump,out of the mist. The train for Paris would arrive de suite. We were just in time,our movements had so far been very creditable. All was well. It was cold,eh?

Then with the ghastly miniature roar of an insane toy the train for Paris came fumbling cautiously into the station....

We boarded it,due caution being taken that I should not escape. As a matter of fact I held up the would-be passengers for nearly a minute by my unaided attempts to boost my uncouth baggage aboard. Then my captors and I blundered heavily into a compartment in which an Englishman and two French women were seated. My gendarmes established themselves on either side of the door,a process which woke up the Anglo-Saxon and caused a brief gap in the low talk of the women. Jolt—we were off.

I find myself with a française on my left and an anglais on my right. The latter has already uncomprehendingly subsided into sleep. The former(a woman of about thirty)is talking pleasantly to her friend,whom I face. She must have been very pretty before she put on the black. Her friend is also a veuve. How pleasantly they talk,of la guerre,of Paris,of the bad service;talk in agreeably modulated voices,leaning a little forward to each other,not wishing to disturb the dolt at my right. The train tears slowly on. Both the gendarmes are asleep,one with his hand automatically grasping the handle of the door. Lest I escape. I try all sorts of positions for I find myself very tired. The best is to put my cane between my legs and rest my chin on it;but even that is uncomfortable,for the Englishman has writhed all over me by this time and is snoring creditably. I look him over;an Etonian,as I guess. Certain well-bred-well-fedness. Except for the position— well,c'est la guerre. The women are speaking softly. "And do you know,my dear,that they had raids again in Paris? My sister wrote me."—"One has excitement always in a great city,my dear"—

bump,slowing down. BUMPBUMP.

It is light outside. One sees the world. There is a world still,the gouvernement français has not taken it away,and the air must be beautifully cool. In the compartment it is hot. The gendarmes smell worst. I know how I smell. What polite women.

"Enfin,nous voilà." My guards awoke and yawned pretentiously. Lest I should think they had dozed off. It is Paris.

Some permissionnaires cried "Paris." The woman across from me said "Paris,Paris." A great shout came up from every insane drowsy brain that had traveled with us—a fierce and beautiful cry,which went the length of the train....Paris where one forgets,Paris which is Pleasure,Paris in whom our souls live,Paris the beautiful,Paris enfin.

The Englishman woke up and said heavily to me "I say,where are we?"—"Paris" I answered,walking carefully on his feet as I made my baggage-laden way out of the compartment. It was Paris.

My guards hurried me through the station. One of them(I saw for the first time)was older than the other,and rather handsome with his Van Dyck blackness of curly beard. He said that it was too early for the metro,it was closed. We should take a car. It would bring us to the other Gare from which our next train left. We should hurry. We emerged from the station and its crowds of crazy men. We boarded a car marked something. The conductress,a strong pink-cheeked rather beautiful girl in black,pulled my baggage in for me with a gesture which filled all of me with joy. I thanked her,and she smiled at me. The car moved along through the morning.

We descended from it. We started off on foot. The car was not the right car. We would have to walk to the station. I was faint and almost dead from weariness and I stopped when my overcoat had fallen from my benumbed arm for the second time:"How far is it?" The older gendarme returned briefly "Vingt minutes." I said to him "Will you help me carry these things?"

He thought,and told the younger to carry my small sack filled with papers. The latter grunted "C'est défendu." We went a little farther,and I broke down again. I stopped dead,and said "I can't go any farther." It was obvious to my escorts that I couldn't,so I didn't trouble to elucidate. Moreover I was past elucidation.

The older stroked his beard. "Well" he said,"would you care to take a fiacre?" I merely looked at him. "If you wish to call a fiacre,I will take out of your money which I have here and which I must not give you the necessary sum,and make a note of it,subtracting from the original amount a sufficiency for our fare to the Gare. In that case we will not walk to the Gare,we will in fact ride." "S'il vous plaît" was all I found to reply to this eloquence.

Several libres fiacres had gone by during the peroration of the law,and no more seemed to offer themselves. After some minutes,however,one appeared and was duly hailed. Nervously(he was shy in the big city)the older asked if the cocher knew where the Gare was. "Laquelle?" demanded the cocher angrily. And when he was told—"Naturellement je connais,pourquoi pas?"— we got in;I being directed to sit in the middle,and my two bags and fur coat piled on top of us all.

So we drove through the streets in the freshness of the full morning,the streets full of few divine people who stared at me and nudged one another,the streets of Paris...the drowsy ways wakening at the horse's hoofs,the people lifting their faces to stare.

We arrived at the Gare,and I recognized it vaguely. Was it D'Orléans? We dismounted,and the tremendous transaction of the fare was apparently very creditably accomplished by the older. The cocher gave me a look and remarked whatever it is Paris cochers remark to Paris fiacre-horses,pulling dully at the reins. We entered the station and I collapsed comfortably on a bench;the younger,seating himself with enormous pomposity at my side,adjusted his tunic with a purely feminine gesture expressive at once of pride and nervousness. Gradually my vision gained in focus. The station has a good many people in it. The number increases momently. A great many are girls. I am in a new world—a world of chic femininity. My eyes devour the inimitable details of costume,the inexpressible nuances of pose,the indescribable démarche of the midinette. They hold themselves differently. They have even a little bold colour here and there on skirt or blouse or hat. They are not talking about la guerre. Incredible. They appear very beautiful,these Parisiennes.

And simultaneously with my appreciation of the crisp persons about me comes the hitherto unacknowledged appreciation of my uncouthness. My chin tells my hand of a good quarter inch of beard,every hair of it stiff with dirt. I can feel the dirt-pools under my eyes. My hands are rough with dirt. My uniform is smeared and creased in a hundred thousand directions. My puttees and shoes are prehistoric in appearance....

My first request was permission to visit the vespasienne. The younger didn't wish to assume any unnecessary responsibilities;I should wait till the older returned. There he was now. I might ask him. The older benignly granted my petition,nodding significantly to his fellow-guard,by whom I was accordingly escorted to my destination and subsequently back to my bench. When we got back the gendarmes held a consultation of terrific importance;in substance,the train which should be leaving at that moment(six-something)did not run today. We should therefore wait for the next train,which leaves at twelve-something-else. Then the older surveyed me,and said almost kindly "How would you like a cup of coffee?"—"Much" I replied sincerely enough.—"Come with me" he commanded,resuming instantly his official manner. "And you"(to the younger)"watch his baggage."

Of all the very beautiful women whom I had seen the most very beautiful was the large circular lady who sold a cup of perfectly hot and genuine coffee for deux sous just on the brink of the station,chatting cheerfully with her many customers. Of all the drinks I ever drank,hers was the most sacredly delicious. She wore,I remember,a tight black dress in which enormous and benignant breasts bulged and sank continuously. I lingered over my tiny cup,watching her swift big hands,her round nodding face,her large sudden smile. I drank two coffees,and insisted that my money should pay for our drinks. Of all the treating which I shall ever do,the treating of my captor will stand unique in pleasure. Even he half appreciated the sense of humor involved;though his dignity did not permit a visible acknowledgement thereof.

Madame la vendeuse de café,I shall remember you for more than a little while.

Having thus consummated breakfast,my guardian suggested a wall. Agreed. I felt I had the strength of ten because the coffee was pure. Moreover it would be a novelty me promener sans 150-odd pounds of baggage. We set out.

As we walked easily and leisurely the by this time well peo-

pled rues of the vicinity,my guard indulged himself in pleas-
ant conversation. Did I know Paris much? He knew it all. But
he had not been in Paris for several(eight was it?)years. It was
a fine place,a large city to be sure. But always changing. I had
spent a month in Paris while waiting for my uniform and my
assignment to a section sanitaire? And my friend was with me?
H-mmm-mm.

A perfectly typical runt of a Paris bull eyed us. The older
saluted him with infinite respect,the respect of a shabby rube
deacon for a well-dressed burglar. They exchanged a few well-
chosen words,in French of course. "What ya got there?"—"An
American."—"What'swrongwithhim?"—"H-mmm"—mysterious
shrug of the shoulders followed by a whisper in the ear of the city
thug. The latter contented himself with "Ha-aaa"—plus a look at
me which was meant to wipe me off the earth's face(I pretended
to be studying the morning meanwhile). Then we moved on,
followed by ferocious stares from the Paris bull. Evidently I was
getting to be more of a criminal every minute;I should proba-
bly be shot tomorrow,not(as I had assumed erroneously)the day
after. I drank the morning with renewed vigor,thanking heaven
for the coffee,Paris;and feeling complete confidence in myself. I
should make a great speech(in Midi French). I should say to the
firing squad "Gentlemen,c'est d'la blague,tu sais? Moi,je connais
la sœur du conducteur"....They would ask me when I preferred to
die. I should reply "Pardon me,you wish to ask me when I prefer
to become immortal?" I should answer "What matter? Ça m'est
égal,parce qu'il n'y a plus d'heures—le gouvernement français les
défend."

My laughter surprised the older considerably. He would have
been more astonished had I yielded to the well-nigh irrepressible
inclination,which at the moment suffused me,to clap him heart-
ily upon the back.

Everything was blague. The cocher,the café,the police,the morning,and least and last the excellent French government.

We had walked for a half hour or more. My guide and protector now inquired of an ouvrier the location of the boucheries? "There is one right in front of you" he was told. Sure enough,not a block away. I laughed again. It was eight years all right.

The older bought a great many things in the next five minutes: saucisse,fromage,pain,chocolat,pinard rouge. A bourgeoise with an unagreeable face and suspicion of me written in headlines all over her mouth served us with quick hard laconicisms of movement. I hated her and consequently refused my captor's advice to buy a little of everything(on the ground that it would be a long time till the next meal),contenting myself with a cake of chocolate—rather bad chocolate,but nothing to what I was due to eat during the next three months. Then we retraced our steps,arriving at the station after several mistakes and inquiries to find the younger faithfully keeping guard over my two sacs and overcoat.

The older and I sat down,and the younger took his turn at promenading. I got up to buy a Fantasio at the stand ten steps away,and the older jumped up and escorted me to and from it. I think I asked him what he would read? and he said "Nothing." Maybe I bought him a journal. So we waited,eyed by everyone in the Gare,laughed at by the officers and their marraines,pointed at by sinewy dames and decrepit bonshommes—the center of amusement for the whole station. In spite of my reading I felt distinctly uncomfortable. Would it never be Twelve? Here comes the younger,neat as a pin,looking fairly sterilized. He sits down on my left. Watches are ostentatiously consulted. It is time. En avant. I sling myself under my bags.

"Where are we going now?" I asked the older. Curling the tips of his mustachios,he replied "Mah-say."

Marseilles! I was happy once more. I had always wanted to go to that great port of the Mediterranean, where one has new colours and strange customs, and where the people sing when they talk. But how extraordinary to have come to Paris—and what a trip lay before us. I was much muddled about the whole thing. Probably I was to be deported. But why from Marseilles? Where was Marseilles anyway? I was probably all wrong about its location. Who cared, after all? At least we were leaving the pointings and the sneers and the half-suppressed titters....

Two fat and respectable bonshommes, the two gendarmes, and I, made up one compartment. The former talked an animated stream, the guards and I were on the whole silent. I watched the liquidating landscape and dozed happily. The gendarmes dozed, one at each door. The train rushed lazily across the earth, between farm-houses, into fields, along woods...the sunlight smacked my eye and cuffed my sleepy mind with colour.

I was awakened by a noise of eating. My protectors, knife in hand, were consuming their meat and bread, occasionally tilting their bidons on high and absorbing the thin streams which spurted therefrom. I tried a little chocolat. The bonshommes were already busy with their repast. The older gendarme watched

me chewing away at the chocolat,then commanded "Take some
bread." This astonished me,I confess,beyond anything which had
heretofore occurred. I gazed mutely at him,wondering whether
the gouvernement français had made away with his wits. He had
relaxed amazingly:his cap lay beside him,his tunic was unbut-
toned,he slouched in a completely undisciplined posture—his face
seemed to have been changed from a peasant's,it was almost open
in expression and almost completely at ease. I seized the offered
hunk and chewed vigorously on it. Bread was bread. The older
appeared pleased with my appetite;his face softened still more,as
he remarked:"Bread without wine doesn't taste good" and prof-
fered his bidon. I drank as much as I dared and thanked him:"Ça
va mieux." The pinard went straight to my brain,I felt my mind
cuddled by a pleasant warmth,my thoughts became invested with
a great contentment. The train stopped;and the younger sprang
out carrying the empty bidons of himself and his confrere. When
they and he returned,I enjoyed another coup. From that moment
till we reached our destination at about eight o'clock the older and
I got on extraordinarily well. When the gentlemen descended at
their station he waxed almost familiar. I was in excellent spir-
its;rather drunk;extremely tired. Now that the two guardians and
myself were alone in the compartment,the curiosity which had
hitherto been stifled by etiquette and pride of capture came rap-
idly to light. Why was I here,anyway? I seemed well enough to
them.—Because my friend had written some letters,I told them.—
But I had done nothing myself?—I explained that nous étions tou-
jours ensemble,mon ami et moi;that was the only reason which I
knew of.—It was very funny to see how this explanation improved
matters. The older in particular was immensely relieved.—I would
without doubt,he said,be set free immediately upon my arrival.
The French government didn't keep people like me in prison.—
They fired some questions about America at me,to which I imag-

inatively replied. I think I told the younger that the average height of buildings in America was nine hundred metres. He stared and shook his head doubtfully, but I convinced him in the end. Then in turn I asked questions, the first being: Where was my friend?—It seems that my friend had left Creil (or whatever it was) the morning of the day I had entered it.—Did they know where my friend was going?—They couldn't say. They had been told that he was very dangerous.—So we talked on and on: How long had I studied French? I spoke very well. Was it hard to learn English?—

Yet when I climbed out to relieve myself by the roadside one of them was at my heels.

Finally watches were consulted, tunics buttoned, hats donned. I was told in a gruff voice to prepare myself; that we were approaching the end of our journey. Looking at the erstwhile participants in conversation, I scarcely knew them. They had put on with their caps a positive ferocity of bearing. I began to think that I had dreamed the incidents of the preceding hours.

We descended at a minute, dirty station which possessed the air of having been dropped by mistake from the bung of the gouvernement français. The older sought out the station master, who having nothing to do was taking a siesta in a miniature waiting-room. The general countenance of the place was exceedingly depressing; but I attempted to keep up my spirits with the reflection that after all this was but a junction, and that from here we were to take a train for Marseilles herself. The name of the station, Briouze, I found somewhat dreary. And now the older returned with the news that our train wasn't running today, and that the next train didn't arrive till early morning, and should we walk? I could check my great sac and overcoat. The small sac I should carry along—it was only a step, after all.

With a glance at the desolation of Briouze I agreed to the stroll. It was a fine night for a little promenade; not too cool, and with a promise of a moon stuck into the sky. The sac and coat were accordingly checked by the older;the station-master glanced at me and haughtily grunted(having learned that I was an American);and my protectors and I set out.

I insisted that we stop at the first café and have some wine on me. To this my escorts agreed,making me go ten paces ahead of them,and waiting until I was through before stepping up to the bar—not from politeness,to be sure,but because(as I soon gathered)gendarmes were not any too popular in this part of the world,and the sight of two gendarmes with a prisoner might inspire the habitué to attempt a rescue. Furthermore,on leaving said café(a desolate place if I ever saw one,with a fearful patronne)I was instructed sharply to keep close to them but on no account to place myself between them,there being sundry villagers to be encountered before we struck the high road for Marseilles. Thanks to their forethought and my obedience the rescue did not take place,nor did our party excite even the curiosity of the scarce and soggy inhabitants of the unlovely town of Briouze.

The highroad won,all of us relaxed considerably. The sac full of suspicious letters which I bore on my shoulder was not so light as I had thought,but the kick of the Briouze pinard thrust me forward at a good clip. The road was absolutely deserted;the night hung loosely around it,here and there tattered by attempting moonbeams. I was somewhat sorry to find the way hilly,and in places bad underfoot;yet the unknown adventure lying before me,and the delicious silence of the night(in which our words rattled queerly like tin soldiers in a plush-lined box)boosted me into a condition of mysterious happiness. We talked,the older and I,of strange subjects. As I suspected,he had been not always a gendarme. He had seen service among the Arabs. He had always liked languages and had picked up Arabian with great ease—of this he was very proud. For instance—the Arabian way of saying "Give me to eat" was this;when you wanted wine you said so and so;"Nice day" was something else. He thought I could pick it up inasmuch as I had done so creditably with French. He was absolutely certain that English was much easier to learn than French,and would not be moved. Now what was the American language like? I explained that it was a sort of Argot-English. When I gave him some phrases he was astonished—"It sounds like English!" he cried,and retailed his stock of English phrases for my approval. I tried hard to get his intonation of the Arabian,and he helped me on the difficult sounds. America must be a strange place,he thought....

After two hours walking he called a halt,bidding us rest. We all lay flat on the grass by the roadside. The moon was still battling with clouds. The darkness of the fields on either side was total. I crawled on hands and knees to the sound of silver-trickling water and found a little spring-fed stream. Prone,weight on elbows,I drank heavily of its perfect blackness. It was icy, talkative,minutely alive.

The older presently gave a perfunctory "alors";we got up;I hoisted my suspicious utterances upon my shoulder,which rec-ognized the renewal of hostilities with a neuralgic throb. I banged forward with bigger and bigger feet. A bird,scared,swooped almost into my face. Occasionally some night-noise pricked a futile minute hole in the enormous curtain of soggy darkness. Uphill now. Every muscle thoroughly aching,head spinning,I half-straightened my no longer obedient body;and jumped:face to face with a little wooden man hanging all by itself in a grove of low trees.

—The wooden body clumsy with pain burst into fragile legs with absurdly large feet and funny writhing toes;its little stiff arms made abrupt cruel equal angles with the road. About its stunted loins clung a ponderous and jocular fragment of drap-ery. On one terribly brittle shoulder the droll lump of its neckless head ridiculously lived. There was in this complete silent doll a gruesome truth of instinct, a success of uncanny poignancy, an unearthly ferocity of rectangular emotion.

For perhaps a minute the almost obliterated face and mine eyed one another in the silence of intolerable autumn.

Who was this wooden man? Like a sharp black mechanical cry in the spongy organism of gloom stood the coarse and sudden sculpture of his torment;the big mouth of night carefully spurted the angular actual language of his martyred body. I had seen him before in the dream of some mediaeval saint,with a thief sagging at either side,surrounded by crisp angels. Tonight he was alone;save for myself,and the moon's minute flower pushing between slabs of fractured cloud.

I was wrong,the moon and I and he were not alone....A glance up the road gave me two silhouettes at pause. The gendarmes were waiting. I must hurry to catch up or incur suspicion by my sloth. I hastened forward,with a last look over my shoulder...the wooden man was watching us.

When I came abreast of them,expecting abuse,I was surprised by the older's saying quietly "We haven't far to go",and plunging forward imperturbably into the night.

Nor had we gone a half hour before several dark squat forms confronted us:houses. I decided that I did not like houses— particularly as now my guardians' manner abruptly changed;once more tunics were buttoned,holsters adjusted,and myself directed to walk between and keep always up with the others. Now the road became thoroughly afflicted with houses,houses not however so large and lively as I had expected from my dreams of Marseilles. Indeed we seemed to be entering an extremely small and rather disagreeable town. I ventured to ask what its name was. "Mah-say" was the response. By this I was fairly puzzled. However the street led us to a square,and I saw the towers of a church sitting in the sky;between them the round yellow big moon looked immensely and peacefully conscious...no one was stirring in the little streets,all the houses were keeping the moon's secret.

We walked on.

I was too tired to think. I merely felt the town as a unique unreality. What was it? I knew—the moon's picture of a town. These streets with their houses did not exist,they were but a ludicrous projection of the moon's sumptuous personality. This was a city of Pretend,created by the hypnotism of moonlight.—Yet when I examined the moon she too seemed but a painting of a moon,and the sky in which she lived a fragile echo of colour. If I blew hard the whole shy mechanism would collapse gently with a neat soundless crash. I must not,or lose all.

We turned a corner,then another. My guides conferred concerning the location of something,I couldn't make out what. Then the older nodded in the direction of a long dull dirty mass not a hundred yards away,which(as near as I could see)served either as a church or a tomb. Toward this we turned. All too soon I made out its entirely dismal exterior. Grey long stone walls,surrounded on the street side by a fence of ample proportions and uniformly dull colour. Now I perceived that we made toward a gate,singularly narrow and forbidding,in the grey long wall. No living soul appeared to inhabit this desolation.

The older rang at the gate. A gendarme with a revolver answered his ring;and presently he was admitted,leaving the younger and myself to wait. And now I began to realize that this was the gendarmerie of the town,into which for safe-keeping I was presently to be inducted for the night. My heart sank,I confess,at the thought of sleeping in the company of that species of humanity which I had come to detest beyond anything in hell or on earth. Meanwhile the doorman had returned with the older,and I was bidden roughly enough to pick up my baggage and march.

I followed my guides down a corridor,up a stair-case,and into a dark small room where a candle was burning. Dazzled by the light and dizzied by the fatigue of my ten or twelve mile stroll,I let my baggage go;and leaned against a convenient wall,trying to determine who was now my tormentor.

Facing me at a table stood a man of about my own height,and as I should judge about forty years old. His face was seedy sallow and long. He had bushy semi-circular eyebrows which drooped so much as to reduce his eyes to mere blinking slits. His cheeks were so furrowed that they leaned inward. He had no nose,properly speaking,but a large beak of preposterous widthlessness,which gave his whole face the expression of falling gravely downstairs,and quite obliterated the unimportant chin. His mouth was made of two long uncertain lips which twitched nervously. His cropped black hair was rumpled;his blouse,from which hung a croix de guerre,unbuttoned;and his unputteed shanks culminated in bed-slippers. In physique he reminded me a little of Ichabod Crane. His neck was exactly like a hen's:I felt sure that when he drank he must tilt his head back as hens do in order that the liquid may run down their throats. But his method of keeping himself upright,together with certain spasmodic contractions of his fingers and the nervous "uh-ah,uh-ah" which punctuated his insecure phrases like uncertain commas,combined to offer the suggestion of a rooster;a rather moth-eaten rooster,which took itself tremendously seriously and was showing-off to an imaginary group of admiring hens situated somewhere in the background of his consciousness.

"Vous êtes uh-ah l'am-é-ri-cain?"

"Je suis américain" I admitted.

"Eh-bi-en uh-ah uh-ah—We were expecting you." He surveyed me with great interest.

Behind this seedy and restless personage I noted his abso-
lute likeness, adorning one of the walls. The rooster was faith-
fully depicted à la Rembrandt at half-length in the stirring guise
of a fencer, foil in hand and wearing enormous gloves. The exe-
cution of this masterpiece left something to be desired; but the
whole betokened a certain spirit and verve, on the part of the sit-
ter, which I found difficulty in attributing to the being before me.

"Vous êtes uh-ah KEW-MANGZ?"

"What?" I said, completely baffled by this extraordinary
dissyllable.

"Comprenez vous fran-çais?"

"Un peu."

"Bon. Alors, vous vous ap-pel-lez KEW-MANGZ, n'est-ce-
pas? Edouard KEW-MANGZ."

"Oh" I said, relieved, "yes." It was really amazing, the way he
writhed around the G.

"Comment ça se pronounce en anglais?"

I told him.

He replied benevolently, somewhat troubled "uh-ah uh-ah
uh-ah—Pour-quoi êtes-vous ici, KEW-MANGZ?"

At this question I was for one moment angrier than I had ever
before been in all my life. Then I realized the absurdity of the
situation, and laughed.—"Sais pas."

The questionnaire continued:

"You were in the Red Cross?"—"Surely, in the Norton-Harjes

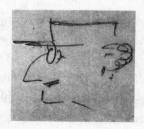

Ambulance,Section Sanitaire Vingt-et-Un."—"You had a friend there?"—"Naturally."—"Il a écrit,votre ami,des bê-tises,n'est-ce-pas?"—"So they told me. N'en sais rien."—"What sort of a person was your friend?"—"He was a magnificent person,always très gentil with me."—(With a queer pucker the fencer remarked)"Your friend got you into a lot of trouble though."—(To which I replied with a broad grin)"N'importe,we are camarades."

A stream of puzzled uh-ahs followed this reply. The fencer or rooster or whatever he might be finally,picking up the lamp and the lock,said:"Alors,venez,avec moi KEW-MANGZ." I started to pick up the sac,but he told me it would be kept in the office(we being in the office). I said I had checked a large sac and my fur overcoat at Briouze,and he assured me they would be sent on by train. He now dismissed the gendarmes,who had been listening curiously to the examination. As I was conducted from the bureau I asked him point-blank:"How long am I to stay here?"—to which he answered "Oh peut-être un jour,deux jours,je ne sais pas."

Two days in a gendarmerie would be enough,I thought. We marched out.

Behind me the bed-slippered rooster uh-ahing shuffled. In front of me clumsily gamboled the huge imitation of myself. It descended the terribly worn stairs. It turned to the right and disappeared....

We were standing in a chapel.

The shrinking light which my guide held had become suddenly minute;it was beating,senseless and futile,with shrill fists upon a thick enormous moisture of gloom. To the left and right through lean oblongs of stained glass burst dirty burglars of moonlight. The clammy stupid distance uttered dimly an uncanny conflict—the mutterless tumbling of brutish shadows. A crowding ooze battled with my lungs. My nostrils fought against the monstrous atmospheric slime which hugged a sweet unpleasant odour. Staring ahead,I gradually disinterred the pale carrion of the darkness—an altar,guarded with the ugliness of unlit candles,on which stood inexorably the efficient implements for eating God.

I was to be confessed,then,of my guilty conscience,before retiring? It boded well for the morrow

...the measured accents of the Fencer said:"Prenez votre paillasse." I turned. He was bending over a formless mass in one corner of the room. The mass stretched half-way to the ceiling. It was made of mattress-shapes. I pulled at one—burlap,stuffed with prickly straw. I got it on my shoulder. "Alors." He lighted me to the door-way by which we had entered.(I was somewhat pleased to leave the place.)

Back,down a corridor,up more stairs;and we are confronted by a small scarred pair of doors from which hung two of the largest padlocks I had ever seen. Being unable to go further,I stopped:he produced a huge ring of keys. Fumbled with the locks. No sound of life:the keys rattled in the locks with surprising loudness;the latter with an evil grace yielded—the two little miserable doors swung open.

Into the square blackness I staggered with my paillasse. There was no way of judging the size of the dark room which uttered no sound. In front of me was a pillar. "Put down by that post,and sleep there for tonight,in the morning nous allons voir" directed the Fencer. "You won't need a blanket" he added;and the doors clanged,the light and Fencer disappeared.

I needed no second invitation to sleep. Fully dressed,I fell on my paillasse with a weariness which I never felt before or since. But I did not close my eyes:for all about me there rose a sea of most extraordinary sound....the hitherto empty and minute room became suddenly enormous;weird cries,oaths,laughter,pulling it sideways and backward, extending it to inconceivable depth and width, telescoping it to frightful nearness. From all directions, by at least thirty voices in eleven languages (I counted as I lay Dutch, Belgian, Spanish, Turkish, Arabian, Polish, Russian, Swedish, German, French—and English) at distances varying from seventy feet to a few inches, for twenty minutes I was ferociously bombarded. Nor was my perplexity purely aural. About five minutes after lying down I saw (by a hitherto unnoticed speck of light which burned near the doors which I had entered) two extraordinary looking figures—one a well-set man with a big, black beard, the other a consumptive with a bald head and sickly mustache, both clad only in their knee-length chemises, hairy legs naked, feet bare—wander down the room and urinate profusely in the corner nearest me. This act accomplished, the figures wandered back, greeted with a volley of ejaculatory abuse from the invisible co-occupants of my new sleeping-apartment; and disappeared in darkness.

I remarked to myself that the gendarmes of this gendarmerie were peculiarly up in languages, and fell asleep.

CHAPTER FOUR

Le Nouveau

"Vous ne voulez pas de café?"

The threatening question recited in a hoarse voice woke me like a shot. Sprawled half on and half off my paillasse, I looked suddenly up into a juvenile pimply face with a red tassel bobbing in its eyes. A boy in a Belgian uniform was stooping over me. In one hand a huge pail a third full of liquid slime. I said fiercely: "Au contraire, je veux bien." And collapsed on the mattress.

"Pas de quart, vous?" the face fired at me.

"Comprends pas" I replied, wondering what on earth the words meant.

"English?"

"American."

At this moment a tin cup appeared mysteriously out of the gloom and was rapidly filled from the pail, after which operation the tassel remarked: "Your friend here" and disappeared.

I decided I had gone completely crazy.

The cup had been deposited near me. Not daring to approach it, I boosted my aching corpse on one of its futile elbows and gazed blankly around. My eyes, wading laboriously through a dank atmosphere,a darkness gruesomely tactile,perceived only here and there lively patches of vibrating humanity. My ears recognized English,something which I took to be low-German and which was Belgian,Dutch,Polish,and what I guessed to be Russian.

Trembling with this chaos,my hand sought the cup. The cup was not warm;the contents,which I hastily gulped,were not even tepid. The taste was dull,almost bitter,clinging,thick,nauseating. I felt a renewed interest in living as soon as the deathful swallow descended to my abdomen,very much as a suicide who changes his mind after the fatal dose. I decided that it would be useless to vomit. I sat up. I looked around.

The darkness was rapidly going out of the sluggish stinking air. I was sitting on my mattress at one end of a sort of room,filled with pillars;ecclesiastical in feeling. I already perceived it to be of enormous length. My mattress resembled an island:all around it,at distances varying from a quarter of an inch to ten feet(which constituted the limit of distinct vision)reposed startling identities. There was blood in some of them. Others consisted of a rind of bluish matter sustaining a core of yellowish froth. From behind me a chunk of hurtling spittle joined its fellows. I decided to stand up.

At this moment,at the far end of the room,I seemed to see an extraordinary vulturelike silhouette leap up from nowhere. It rushed a little way in my direction crying hoarsely "Corvée d'eau!"—stopped,bent down at what I perceived to be a paillasse like mine,jerked what was presumably the occupant by the feet,shook him,turned to the next,and so on up to six. As there seemed to be innumerable paillasses,laid side by side at intervals of perhaps a foot with their heads to the wall on three sides of me,I was wondering why the vulture had stopped at six. On each mattress a crude imitation of humanity,wrapped ear-high in its blanket,lay and drank from a cup like mine and spat long and high into the room. The ponderous reek of sleepy bodies undulated toward me from three directions. I had lost sight of the vulture in a kind of insane confusion which arose from the further end of the room. It was as if he had touched off six high explosives. Occasional pauses in the minutely crazy din were accurately punctuated by exploding bowels;to the great amusement of innumerable somebodies,whose precise whereabouts the gloom carefully guarded.

I felt that I was the focus of a group of indistinct recumbents who were talking about me to one another in many incomprehensible tongues. I noticed beside every pillar(including the one beside which I had innocently thrown down my paillasse the night before)a goodsized pail,overflowing with urine and surrounded by a large irregular puddle. My paillasse was within an inch of the nearest puddle. What I took to be a man,an amazing distance off,got out of bed and succeeded in locating the pail nearest to him after several attempts. Ten invisible recumbents yelled at him in six languages.

All at once a handsome figure rose from the gloom at my elbow. I smiled stupidly into his clear hardish eyes. And he remarked pleasantly:

"Your friend's here,Johnny,and wants to see you."

A bulge of pleasure swooped along my body,chasing aches and numbness,my muscles danced,nerves tingled in perpetual holiday.

B was lying on his camp-cot,wrapped like an Eskimo in a blanket which hid all but his nose and eyes.

"Hello,Cummings" he said smiling. "There's a man here who is a friend of Vanderbilt and knew Cézanne."

I gazed somewhat critically at B. There was nothing particularly insane about him,unless it was his enthusiastic excitement,which might almost be attributed to my jack-in-the-box

B asleep

manner of arriving. He said: "There are people here who speak English, Russian, Arabian. There are the finest people here! Did you go to Creil? I fought rats all night there. Huge ones. They tried to eat me. And from Creil to Paris? I had three gendarmes all the way to keep me from escaping, and they all fell asleep."

I began to be afraid that I was asleep myself. "Please be frank" I begged. "Strictly entre nous: am I dreaming, or is this a bug-house?"

B laughed, and said: "I thought so when I arrived two days ago. When I came in sight of the place a lot of girls waved from the window and yelled at me. I no sooner got inside than a queer looking duck whom I took to be a nut came rushing up to me, and cried: 'Trop tard pour la soupe!'—This is Camp de Triage de La Ferté-Macé, Orne, France, and all these fine people were arrested as espions. Only two or three of them can speak a word of French and that's soupe!"

I said "My God, I thought Marseilles was somewhere on the Mediterranean Ocean, and that this was a gendarmerie."

"But this is M-a-c-é. It's a little mean town, where everybody snickers and sneers at you if they see you're a prisoner. They did at me."

"Do you mean to say we're espions too?"

"Of course!" B said enthusiastically. "Thank God! And in to stay. Every time I think of the section sanitaire,and A. and his thugs,and the whole rotten red-taped Croix Rouge,I have to laugh. Cummings,I tell you this is the finest place on earth!"

A vision of the Chef de Section Sanitaire Vingt-et-Un passed through my mind. The doughy face. Imitation-English-officer swagger. Large calves,squeaking puttees. The daily lecture:"I doughno what's th'matter with you fellers. You look like nice boys. Well-edjucated. But you're so dirty in your habits. You boys are always kickin' because I don't put you on a car together. I'm ashamed to do it,that's why. I doughwanta give this section a black eye. We gotta show these lousy Frenchmen what Americans are. We gotta show we're superior to 'em. Those bastards doughno what a bath means. And you fellers are always hangin' round,talkin' with them dirty frog-eaters that does the cookin' and the dirty work round here. How d'you boys expect me to give you a chance? I'd like to put you fellers on a car,I wanta see you boys happy. But I don't dare to,that's why. If you want me to send you out,you gotta shave and look neat,and *keep away from them dirty Frenchmen*. We Americans are over here to learn them lousy bastards something."

I laughed for sheer joy.

A terrific tumult interrupted my mirth. "Par ici!"—"Get out the way you dam Polak!"—"M'sieu,M'sieu!"—"Over here!"—"Mais non!"—"Gott-ver-dummer" I turned in terror to see my paillasse in the clutches of four men who were apparently rending it in as many directions.

One was a clean-shaved youngish man with lively eyes,alert and muscular,whom I identified as the man who had called me "Johnny". He had hold of a corner of the mattress and was pulling against the possessor of the opposite corner:an incoher-

ent personage enveloped in a buffoonery of amazing rags and
patches,with a shabby head on which excited wisps of dirty hair
stood upright in excitement,and the tall ludicrous extraordi-
nary almost noble figure of a dancing bear. A third corner of
the paillasse was rudely grasped by a six-foot combination of
yellow hair,red hooligan face,and sky-blue trousers;assisted by
the undersized tasseled mucker in Belgian uniform,with a pim-
ply rogue's mug and unlimited impertinence of diction,who had
awakened me by demanding if I wanted coffee. Albeit completely
dazed by the uncouth vocal fracas I realized in some manner
that these hostile forces were contending,not for the possession
of the mattress,but merely for the privilege of presenting the
mattress to myself.

Before I could offer any advice on this delicate topic,a child-
ish voice cried emphatically beside my ear:"Met-tez la pail-lasse
ici! Qu'est-ce que vous al-lez faire? C'est pas la peine de dé-chi-
rer une pail-lasse!"—at the same moment the mattress rushed
with cobalt strides in my direction,propelled by the successful
efforts of the Belgian uniform and the hooligan visage,the clean-
shaven man and the incoherent bear still desperately clutching
their respective corners;and upon its arrival was seized with
surprising strength by the owner of the child's voice—a fluffy
little gnome-shaped man with a sensitive face which had suf-
fered much—and indignantly deposited beside B's bed in a
shape mysteriously cleared for its reception. The gnome imme-
diately kneeled upon it and fell to carefully smoothing certain
creases caused by the recent conflict,exclaiming slowly sylla-
ble by syllable:"Mon Dieu. Main-te-nant,c'est mieux. Il ne faut
pas faire les choses comme ça." The clean-shaven man regarded
him loftily with folded arms,while the tassel and the trousers
victoriously inquired if I had a cigarette?—and upon receiv-
ing one apiece(also the gnome,and the clean-shaven man,who

accepted his with some dignity)sat down without much ado on B's bed—which groaned ominously in protest—and hungrily fired questions at me. The bear meanwhile,looking as if nothing had happened,adjusted his ruffled costume with a satisfied air and(calmly gazing into the distance)began with singularly delicate fingers to stuff a stunted and ancient pipe with what appeared be a mixture of wood and manure.

I was still answering questions,when a gnarled voice suddenly threatened,over our heads:"Balai? Vous. Tout le monde. Surveillant dit. Pas moi,n'est-ce pas?"—I started,expecting to see a parrot.

It was the silhouette.

A vulturelike figure stood before me,a demoralized broom clenched in one claw or fist:it had lean legs cased in shabby trousers,muscular shoulders covered with a rough shirt open at the neck,knotted arms,and a coarse insane face crammed beneath the visor of a cap. The face consisted of a rapid nose,droopy mustache,ferocious watery small eyes,a pugnacious chin,and sunken cheeks hideously smiling. There was something in the ensemble at once brutal and ridiculous,vigorous and pathetic.

Again I had not time to speak;for the hooligan in azure trousers hurled his butt at the bear's feet,exclaiming:"There's another for you Polak!"—jumped from the bed,seized the broom,and poured upon the vulture a torrent of Gott-verdummers,to which the latter replied copiously and in kind. Then the red face bent within a few inches of my own,and for the first time I saw that it had recently been young—"I say I do your sweep for you" it translated pleasantly. I thanked it;and the vulture,exclaiming:"Bon. Bon. Pas moi. Surveillant. Harree faire pour tout le monde. Hee,hee"—rushed off,followed by Harree and the tassel. Out of the corner of my eye I watched the tall ludicrous extraordinary almost proud figure of the bear stoop with quiet dignity,the musical fingers close with a singular delicacy upon the moist indescribable eighth-an-inch of tobacco.

I did not know that this was a Delectable Mountain....

The clean-shaven man (who appeared to have been completely won over by his smoke), and the fluffy gnome, who had completed the arrangement of my paillasse, now entered into conversation with myself and B; the clean-shaven one seating himself in Harree's stead, the gnome declining (on the ground that the bed was already sufficiently loaded) to occupy the place left vacant by the tassel's exit, and leaning against the drab sweating poisonous wall. He managed, however, to call our attention to the shelf at B's head which he himself had constructed, and promised me a similar luxury tout de suite. He was a Russian, and had a wife and gosse in Paris. "Je m'ap-pelle Monsieur Au-guste, à votre service"—and his gentle pale eyes sparkled. The clean-shaven talked distinct and absolutely perfect English. His name was Fritz. He was a Norwegian, a stoker on a ship. "You mustn't mind that feller that wanted you to sweep. He's crazy. They call him John the Baigneur. He used to be the baigneur. Now he's Maître de Chambre. They wanted me to take it—I said 'Fuck it, I don't want it.' Let him have it. That's no kind of a job, everyone complaining and on top of you morning till night. 'Let them that wants the job take it' I said. That crazy Dutchman's been here for two years. They told him to get out and he wouldn't, he was too fond of the booze" (I jumped at the slang) "and the girls. They took it away from John and give it to that little Ree-shar feller, that doctor. That was a swell job he had, baigneur, too. All the bloody liquor you can drink and a girl every time you want one. He ain't never had a girl in his life, that Ree-shar feller." His laughter was hard, clear, cynical. "That Pompom, the little Belgian feller was just here, he's a great one for the girls. He and Harree. Always getting cabinot. I got it twice myself since I been here."

M. Auguste's shelf

All this time The Enormous Room was filling gradually with dirty light. In the further end six figures were brooming furiously, yelling to each other in the dust like demons. A seventh, Harree, was loping to and fro splashing water from a pail and enveloping everything and everybody in a ponderous and blasphemous fog of Gott-verdummers. Along three sides (with the exception that is of the nearer end, which boasted the sole door) were laid, with their lengths at right angles to the walls, at intervals of three or four feet, something like forty paillasses. On each, with half a dozen exceptions (where the occupants had not yet finished their coffee or were on duty for the corvée) lay the headless body of a man smothered in its blanket, only the boots showing.

The demons were working toward our end of the room. Harree had got his broom and was assisting. Nearer and nearer they came;converging,they united their separate heaps of filth in a loudly stinking single mound at the door. Brooms were stacked against the wall in the corner. The men strolled back to their paillasses.

Monsieur Auguste,whose French had not been able to keep pace with Fritz's English,saw his chance,and proposed "Main-te-nant que la Chambre est tout propre,al-lons faire une pe-tite prom-e-nade,tous les trois." Fritz understood perfectly,and rose, remarking as he fingered his immaculate chin "Well,I guess I'll take a shave before the bloody planton comes"—and Monsieur Auguste,B,and I started down the room.

It was in shape oblong,about 80 feet by 40,unmistakably ecclesiastical in feeling—two rows of wooden pillars,spaced at intervals of fifteen feet,rose to a vaulted ceiling 25 or 30 feet above the floor. As you stood with your back to the door,and faced down the room,you had in the near right-hand corner(where the brooms stood)six pails of urine. On the right-hand long wall,a little beyond the angle of this corner,a few boards tacked together in any fashion to make a two-sided screen four feet in height marked the position of a cabinet d'aisance,composed of a small coverless tin pail identical with other six,and a board of the usual design which could be placed on the pail or not as desired. The wooden floor in the neighborhood of the booth and pails was of a dark colour,obviously owing to the continual overflow of their contents.

The right-hand long wall contained something like ten large windows,of which the first was commanded by the somewhat primitive cabinet. There were no other windows in the remaining walls;or they had been carefully rendered useless. In spite of this fact,the inhabitants had contrived a couple of peep-holes—one in the door-end and one in the left-hand long wall;the former commanding the gate by which I had entered,the latter a por-

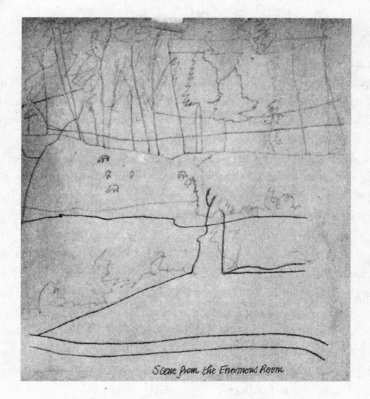

Scene from the Enormous Room

tion of the street by which I had reached the gate. The blocking of all windows on three sides had an obvious significance: les hommes were not supposed to see anything which went on in the world without; les hommes might, however, look their fill on a little washing-shed, on a corner of what seemed to be another wing of the building, and on a bleak lifeless abject landscape of scrubby woods beyond—which constituted the view from the ten windows on the right. The authorities had miscalculated a little in one respect: a merest fraction of the barbed-wire pen which began at the corner of the above-mentioned building was visible from these windows, which windows (I was told) were consequently thronged by fighting men at the time of the girls' promenade. A planton, I was also told, made it his business by keeping les femmes out of this corner of their cour at the point of the bayonet to deprive them of the sight of their admirers. In addition, it was pain sec or cabinot for any of either sex who were caught communicating with each other. Moreover the promenades des hommes et des femmes occurred at roughly speaking the same hour, so that an homme or femme who remained upstairs on the chance of getting a smile or a wave from his or her girl or lover lost the promenade thereby....

We had in succession gazed from the windows, crossed the end of the room, and started down the other side, Monsieur Auguste marching between us—when suddenly B exclaimed in English "Good morning! How are you today?" And I looked across Monsieur Auguste, anticipating another Harree or at least a Fritz. What was my surprise to see a spare majestic figure of manifest refinement, immaculately appareled in a crisp albeit collarless shirt, carefully mended trousers in which the remains of a crease still lingered, a threadbare but perfectly fitting swallow-tail coat, and newly varnished (if somewhat ancient) shoes. Indeed for the first time since my arrival at La Ferté I was confronted by a perfect type: the apotheosis of injured nobility, the humiliated victim of perfectly unfortunate circumstances, the utterly respectable gentleman who has seen better days. There was about him, moreover, something irretrievably English, nay even pathetically Victorian—it was as if a page of Dickens was shaking my friend's hand. "Count Bragard, I want you to meet my friend Cummings"—he saluted me in modulated and courteous accents of indisputable culture, gracefully extending his pale hand. "I have heard a great deal about you from B—, and wanted very much to meet you. It is a pleasure to find a friend of my friend B—,someone congenial and intelligent in contrast to these swine"—he indicated the room with a gesture of complete contempt. "I see you were strolling. Let us take a turn." Monsieur Auguste said tactfully "Je vais vous voir tout à l'heure,mes amis",and left us with an affectionate shake of the hand and a sidelong glance of jealousy and mistrust at B's respectable friend.

"You're looking pretty well today,Count Bragard" B said amiably.

"I do well enough" the Count answered. "It is a frightful strain —you of course realize that—for anyone who has been accustomed to the decencies,let alone the luxuries,of life. This filth"—he pronounced the word with indescribable bitterness—"this herding of men like cattle—they treat us no better than pigs here. The fellows drop their dung in the very room where they sleep. What is one to expect of a place like this? Ce n'est pas une existence"—his French was glib and faultless.

"I was telling my friend that you knew Cézanne" said B. "Being an artist he was naturally much interested."

Count Bragard stopped in astonishment,and withdrew his hands slowly from the tails of his coat. "Is it possible!" he exclaimed,in great agitation. "What an astonishing coincidence! I am myself a painter. You perhaps noticed this badge"—he indicated a button attached to his left lapel,and I bent and read the words: On War Service. "I always wear it" he said with a smile of faultless sorrow,and resumed his walk. "They don't know what it means here,but I wear it all the same. I was a special representative for The London Sphere at the front in this war. I did the trenches and all that sort of thing. They paid me well;I got fifteen pounds a week. And why not? I am an R.A. My specialty was horses. I painted the finest horses in England,among them the King's own entry in the last Derby. Do you know London?" We said no. "If you are ever in London,go to the"(I forget the name)"Hotel—one of the best in town. It has a beautiful large bar, exquisitely furnished in the very best taste. Anyone will tell you where to find the ——. It has one of my paintings over the bar: Straight-jacket" (or some such name) "The Marquis of ——'s horse, who won last time the race was run. I was in America in 1910. You know Cornelius Vanderbilt perhaps? I painted some of his horses. We were the best of friends, Vanderbilt and I. I got handsome prices, you understand, three, five, six thousand pounds. When I left, he gave me this card—I have it here somewhere—" he again stopped, sought in his breast-pocket a moment, and produced a visiting card. On one side I read the name "Cornelius Vanderbilt"—on the other, in bold handwriting—"to my very dear friend Count F.A. de Bragard" and a date. "He hated to have me go."

I was walking in a dream.

"Have you your sketch-books and paints with you? What a pity. I am always intending to send to England for mine, but you know—one can't paint in a place like this. It is impossible—all this dirt and these filthy people—it stinks! Ugh!"

I forced myself to say: "How did you happen to come here?"

He shrugged his shoulders. "How indeed, you may well ask! I cannot tell you. It must have been some hideous mistake. As soon as I got here I spoke to the Directeur and to the Surveillant. The Directeur said he knew nothing about it; the Surveillant told me confidentially that it was a mistake on the part of the French government; that I would be out directly. He's not such a bad sort. So I am waiting: every day I expect orders from the English government for my release. The whole thing is preposterous. I wrote to the Embassy and told them so. As soon as I set foot outside this place, I shall sue the French government for ten thousand pounds for the loss of time it has occasioned me. Imagine it—I had contracts with countless members of The Lords—and the war came. Then I was sent to the front by The

Sphere—and here I am, every day costing me dear, rotting away in this horrible place. The time I have wasted here has already cost me a fortune."

He paused directly in front of the door and spoke with solemnity: "A man might as well be dead."

Scarcely had the words passed his lips when I almost jumped out of my skin, for directly before us on the other side of the wall arose the very noise which announced to Scrooge the approach of Marley's ghost—a dismal clanking and rattling of chains. Had Marley's transparent figure walked straight through the wall and up to the Dickensian character at my side, I would have been less surprised than I was by what actually happened.

The doors opened with an uncanny bang and in the bang stood a fragile minute queer figure, remotely suggesting an old man. The chief characteristic of the apparition was a certain disagreeable nudity which resulted from its complete lack of all the accepted appurtenances and prerogatives of old age. Its little stooping body, helpless and brittle, bore with extraordinary difficulty a head of absurd largeness, yet which moved on the fleshless neck with a horrible agility. Dull eyes sat in the clean-shaven wrinkles of a face neatly hopeless. At the knees a pair of hands hung, infantile in their smallness. In the loose mouth a tiny cigarette had perched and was solemnly smoking itself.

Suddenly the figure darted at me with a spiderlike entirety.

I felt myself lost.

A voice said mechanically from the vicinity of my feet: "Il vous faut prendre des douches"—I stared stupidly. The spectre was poised before me; its averted eyes contemplated the window. "Take your bath" it added as an afterthought, in English—"come with me." It turned suddenly. It hurried to the doorway. I followed. Its rapidly deadly doll-like hands shut and skillfully locked the doors in a twinkling. "Come" its voice said.

It hurried before me down two dirty flights of narrow muti-lated stairs. It turned left,and passed through an open door.

I found myself in the wet sunless air of morning.

To the right it hurried,following the wall of the building. I pursued it mechanically. At the corner,which I had seen from the window upstairs,the barbed-wire fence eight feet in height began. The thing paused,produced a key,and unlocked a gate. The first three or four feet of wire swung inward. He entered,I after him.

In a flash the gate was locked behind me,and I was following along a wall at right angles to the first. I strode after the thing. A moment before I had been walking in a free world:now I was again a prisoner. The sky was still over me,the clammy morning caressed me;but walls of wire and stone told me that my instant of freedom had departed. I was in fact traversing a lane no wider than the gate;on my left,barbed-wire separated me from the famous cour in which les femmes se promènent—a rectangle about 50 feet deep and 200 long,with a stone wall at the further end of it and otherwise surrounded by wire;—on my right,grey sameness of stone,the ennui of the regular and the perpendicu-lar,the ponderous ferocity of silence....

I had taken automatically some six or eight steps in pursuit of the fleeing spectre when,right over my head,the grey stone curdled with a female darkness;the hard and the angular soft-ening in a putrescent explosion of thick wriggling laughter. I started,looked up,and encountered a window stuffed with four savage fragments of crowding Face:four livid,shaggy disks focussing hungrily;four pair of uncouth eyes rapidly smoulder-ing;eight lips shaking in a toothless and viscous titter. Suddenly above and behind these terrors rose a single horror of beauty—a crisp vital head,a young ivory actual face,a night of firm alive icy hair,a white large frightful smile.

...The thing was crying two or three paces in front of me: "Come!" The heads had vanished as by magic.

I dived forward: followed through a little door in the wall into a room about fifteen feet square, occupied by a small stove, a pile of wood, and a ladder. He plunged through another even smaller door, into a bleak rectangular place, where I was confronted on the left by a large tin bath and on the right by ten wooden tubs, each about a yard in diameter, set in a row against the wall. "Undress" commanded the spectre. I did so. "Go into the first one." I climbed into a tub. "You shall pull the string" the spectre said, hurriedly throwing his cigarette into a corner. I stared upward, and discovered a string dangling from a kind of reservoir over my head: I pulled: and was saluted by a stabbing crash of icy water. I leaped from the tub. "Here is your napkin. Make dry yourself"—he handed me a piece of cloth a little bigger than a handkerchief. "Hurree." I donned my clothes, wet and shivering and altogether miserable. "Good. Come now!" I followed him, through the room with the stove, into the barbed-wire lane. A hoarse shout rose from the yard—which was filled with women, girls, children, and a baby or two. I thought I recognized one of the four terrors who had saluted me from the window, in a girl of 18 with a soiled slobby body huddling beneath its dingy dress; her bony shoulders stifled in a shawl upon which excremental hair limply spouted; a huge empty mouth; and a red nose, sticking between the bluish cheeks that shook with spasms of coughing. Just inside the wire a figure reminiscent of Creil, gun on shoulder, revolver on hip, moved monotonously.

The apparition hurried me through the gate and along the wall into the building, where instead of mounting the stairs he pointed down a long gloomy corridor with a square of light at the end of it, saying rapidly "Go to the promenade"—and vanished.

With the laughter of the Five still ringing in my ears, and

no very clear conception of the meaning of existence,I stumbled down the corridor;bumping squarely into a beefy figure with a bull's neck and the familiar revolver who demanded furiously:"Qu'est-ce que vous faites là? Nom de Dieu!"—"Pardon. Les douches" I answered,quelled by the collision.—He demanded in wrathy French "Who took you to the douches?"—For a moment I was at a complete loss—then Fritz's remark about the new baigneur flashed through my mind:"Ree-shar" I answered calmly.—The bull snorted satisfactorily. "Get into the cour and hurry up about it" he ordered.—"C'est par là?" I inquired politely.—He stared at me contemptuously without answering;so I took it upon myself to use the nearest door,hoping that he would have the decency not to shoot me. I had no sooner crossed the threshold when I found myself once more in the welcome air;and not ten paces away I espied B peacefully lounging,with some thirty others,within a cour about one quarter the size of the women's. I marched up to a little dingy gate in the barbed-wire fence,and was hunting for the latch(as no padlock was in evidence)when a scared voice cried loudly "Qu'est-ce que vous faites là?" and I found myself stupidly looking into a rifle. B,Fritz,Harree,Pompom,Monsieur Auguste,The Bear,and last but not least Count de Bragard immediately informed the trembling planton that I was a Nouveau who had just returned from the douches to which I had been escorted by Monsieur Ree-shar,and that I should be admitted to the cour by all means. The cautious watcher of the skies was not however to be fooled by any such fol-de-rol and stood his ground. Fortunately at this point the beefy planton yelled from the doorway "Let him in." And I was accordingly let in,to the gratification of my friends,and against the better judgment of the guardian of the cour,who muttered something about having more than enough to do already.

I had not been mistaken as to the size of the men's yard: it was certainly not more than twenty yards deep and fifteen wide. By the distinctness with which the shouts of les femmes reached my ears I perceived that the two cours adjoined. They were separated by a stone wall ten feet in height, which I had already remarked(while en route to les douches)as forming one end of the cour des femmes. The men's cour had another stone wall slightly higher than the first, and which ran parallel to it; the two remaining sides, which were properly ends, were made by the familiar fil de fer barbelé.

The furniture of the cour was simple: in the middle of the further end, a wooden sentry-box was placed just inside the wire; a curious contrivance, which I discovered to be a sister to the booth upstairs, graced the wall on the left which separated the two cours, while further up on this wall a horizontal iron bar projected from the stone at a height of seven feet and was supported at its other end by a wooden post, the idea apparently being to give the prisoners a little taste of gymnastic; a minute wooden shed filled the right upper corner and served secondarily as a very partial shelter for les hommes and primarily as a stable for an extraordinary water-wagon, composed of a wooden barrel on two wheels with shafts which could not possibly accommodate anything larger than a diminutive donkey(but in which I myself was to walk not infrequently, as it proved); parallel to the second stone wall, but at a safe distance from it, stretched a couple of iron girders serving as a barbarously cold seat for any unfortunate who could not remain on his feet the entire time; on the ground close by the shed lay amusement devices numbers 2 and 3—a huge iron cannon-ball and the six-foot axle of a departed wagon—for testing the strength of the prisoners and beguiling any time which might lie heavily on their hands after they had regaled themselves with the horizontal bar; and finally,a dozen mangy apple-trees,fighting for their very lives in the angry soil,proclaimed to all the world that the cour itself was in reality a verger.

"Les pommiers sont pleins de pommes;
Allons au verger,Simone"....

A description of the cour would be incomplete without an enumeration of the manifold duties of the planton in charge,which were as follows:to prevent the men from using the horizontal bar,except for chinning,since if you swung yourself upon it you could look over the wall into the women's cour;to see that no one threw anything over the wall into said cour;to dodge the cannon-ball which had a mysterious habit of taking advantage of the slope of the ground and bounding along at a prodigious rate of speed straight for the sentry-box;to watch closely anyone who inhabited the cabinet d'aisance,lest he should make use of it to vault over the wall;to see that no one stood on the girders,for a similar reason;to keep watch over anyone who entered the shed;to see that everyone urinated properly against the wall in the general vicinity of the cabinet;to protect the apple-trees into which well-aimed pieces of wood and stone were continually flying and dislodging the sacred fruit;to mind that no one entered or exited by the gate in the upper fence without authority;to report any signs,words,tokens,or other immoralities exchanged by prisoners with girls sitting in the windows of the women's wing(it was from one of these windows that I had recently received my salutation),also names of said girls,it being défendu to exhibit any part of the female person at a window while the males were on promenade;to quell all rixes and especially to prevent people from using the wagon-axle as a weapon of defense or offense;and last,to keep an eye on the balayeur when he and his wheelbarrow

Scene from the cour

made use of a secondary gate situated in the fence at the further end, not far from the sentry-box, to dump themselves.

Having acquainted me with various défendus which limited the activities of a man on promenade, my friends proceeded to enliven the otherwise somewhat tedious morning by shattering one after another all rules and regulations. Fritz, having chinned himself fifteen times, suddenly appeared astride of the bar, evoking a reprimand; Pompom bowled the planton with the cannon-ball, apologizing in profuse and vile French; Harree the Hollander tossed the wagon-axle lightly half the length of the cour, missing The Bear by an inch; The Bear bided his time and cleverly hurled a large stick into one of the holy trees, bringing to the ground a withered apple for which at least twenty people fought for several minutes; and so on. The most open gestures were indulged in for the benefit of several girls who had braved the official wrath and were enjoying the morning at their windows.

The girders were used as a racetrack. The beams supporting the
shed-roof were shinned. The water-wagon was dislocated from its
proper position. The cabinet and urinal were misused. The gate
was continually admitting and emitting persons who said they
were thirsty, and must get a drink at a tub of water which stood
around the corner. A letter was surreptitiously thrown over the
wall into the cour des femmes.

The planton who suffered all these indignities was a solemn
youth with wise eyes situated very far apart in a mealy expres-
sionless ellipse of face, to the lower end of which clung a piece
of down, exactly like a feather sticking to an egg. The rest of him
was fairly normal with the exception of his hands, which were not
mates; the left being considerably larger, and made of wood.

I was at first somewhat startled by this eccentricity; but soon
learned that with the exception of two or three, who formed
the Surveillant's permanent staff and of whom the beefy one
was a shining example, all the plantons were supposed to be
unhealthy; they were indeed réformés whom le gouvernement
français sent from time to time to La Ferté and similar institu-
tions for a little outing, and as soon as they had recovered their
health under these salubrious influences they were shipped back
to do their bit for world-safety, democracy, freedom, etc., in the
trenches. I also learned that of all the ways of attaining cabi-
not by far the simplest was to apply to a planton, particularly
to a permanent planton, say the beefy one (who was reputed to
be peculiarly touchy on this point) the term embusqué. This
method never failed. To its efficacy many of les hommes, and
more of the girls (by whom the plantons, owing to their habit of
taking advantage of the weaker sex at every opportunity, were
even more despised) attested by not infrequent spasms of con-
sumptive coughing, which could be plainly heard from the fur-
ther end of one cour to the other.

In a little over two hours I learned an astonishing lot about La Ferté itself: it was a co-educational receiving station whither were sent from various parts of France(a)males suspected of espionage and(b)females of a well-known type qui se trouvaient dans la zone des armées. It was pointed out to me that the task of finding such members of the human race was pas difficile: in the case of the men,any foreigner would do,provided his country was neutral(e.g. Holland): as for the girls,inasmuch as the armies of the Allies were continually retreating,the zone des armées(particularly in the case of Belgium)was always including new cities,whose petites femmes became automatically subject to arrest. It was not to be supposed that all the women,of La Ferté were putains;there were a large number of femmes honnêtes,the wives of prisoners,who met their husbands at specified times on the floor below the men's quarters whither man and woman were duly and separately conducted by plantons. In this case no charges had been preferred against the women;they were voluntary prisoners,who had preferred to freedom this living in proximity to their husbands. Many of them had children;some babies. In addition there were certain femmes honnêtes whose nationality,as in the case of the men,had cost them their liberty;Marguerite the blanchisseuse,for example,was a German.

La Ferté-Macé was not properly speaking a prison,but a Porte or Camp de Triage: that is to say,persons sent to it were held for a Commission,composed of an official,an avocat,and a capitaine de gendarmerie,which inspected the Camp and passed upon each case in turn for the purpose of determining the guiltiness of the suspected party. If the latter were found guilty by the Commission,he or she was sent off to a regular prison camp pour la durée de la guerre;if not guilty,he or she was(in theory)set free. The Commission came to La Ferté once every three months. It should be added that there were prisonniers who had passed the Commission two,three,four,and even five times,without any appreciable result:there were prisonnières who had remained in La Ferté a year,and even eighteen months.

The authorities at La Ferté consisted of the Directeur,or general overlord,the Surveillant,who had the plantons under him and was responsible to the Directeur for the administration of the Camp,and the Gestionnaire(who kept the accounts). As assistant,the Surveillant had a mail clerk who acted as translator on occasion. Twice a week the Camp was visited by a regular French army doctor(médecin major)who was supposed to prescribe in severe cases and to give the women venereal inspection at regular intervals. The daily routine of attending to minor ailments and injuries was in the hands of Monsieur Ree-shar(Richard),who knew probably less about medicine than any man living and was an ordinary prisonnier like all of us,but whose impeccable conduct merited cosy quarters. A balayeur was appointed from time to time by the Surveillant,acting the Directeur,from the inhabitants of La Ferté;as was also a cook's assistant. The regular Cook was a fixture,and a boche like other fixtures,Marguerite and Richard. This might seem curious were it not that the manner appearance and actions of the Directeur himself proved beyond a shadow of a doubt that he was all which the term Boche could possibly imply.

"He's a son of a bitch" B said heartily. "They took me up to him when I came two days ago. As soon as he saw me he bellowed:'Imbécile et inchrétien!';then he called me a great lot of other things including Shame of my country,Traitor to the sacred cause of liberty,Contemptible coward and Vile sneaking spy. When he got all through I said 'Je ne comprends pas français.' You should have seen him then."

Separation of the sexes was enforced,not,it is true,with suc-

cess, but with a commendable ferocity. The punishments for both
men and girls were pain sec and cabinot.

What on earth is cabinot?" I demanded.

There were various cabinots: each sex had its regular cab-
inot, and there were certain extra ones. B knew all about them
from Harree and Pompon, who spent nearly all their time in the
cabinot. They were rooms about nine feet square and six feet
high. There was no light and no floor, and the ground (three
were on the ground floor) was always wet and often a good many
inches under water. The occupant on entering was searched for
tobacco, deprived of his or her paillasse and blanket, and invited
to sleep on the ground on some planks. One didn't need to
write a letter to a member of the opposite sex to get cabinot, or
even to call a planton embusqué—there was a woman, a for-
eigner, who, instead of sending a letter to her embassy through
the bureau (where all letters were read by the mail clerk to make
sure that they said nothing disagreeable about the authorities
or conditions of La Ferté) tried to smuggle it outside, and attra-
pait vingt-huit jours de cabinot. She had previously written
three times, handing the letters to the Surveillant, as per regu-
lations, and had received no reply. Fritz, who had no idea why he
was arrested and was crazy to get in touch with his embassy, had
likewise written several letters, taking the utmost care to state
the facts only and always handing them in; but he had never
received a word in return. The obvious inference was that letters
from a foreigner to his embassy were duly accepted by the Sur-
veillant, but rarely if ever left La Ferté.

B and I were conversing merrily à propos the God-sent mir-
acle of our escape from Vingt-et-Un, when a benign-faced per-
sonage of about fifty with sparse greyish hair and a Benjamin
Franklin expression appeared on the other side of the fence, from
the direction of the door through which I had passed after

bumping the beefy bull. "Planton" it cried heavily to the wooden handed one, "Deux hommes pour aller chercher l'eau." Harree and Pompom were already at the gate with the archaic water-wagon, the former pushing from behind and the latter in the shafts. The guardian of the cour walked up and opened the gate for them, after ascertaining that another planton was waiting at the corner of the building to escort them on their mission. A little way from the cour, the stone wall which formed one of its boundaries (and which ran parallel to the other stone wall dividing the two cours) met the prison building; and here was a huge double-door, twice padlocked, through which the water-seekers passed on to the street. There was a sort of hydrant up the street a few hundred yards, I was told. The Cook (Benjamin F. that is) required from three to six wagonfuls of water twice a day, and in reward for the labour involved in its capture was in the habit of giving a cup of coffee to the captors. I resolved that I would seek water at the earliest opportunity.

Harree and Pompom had completed their third and final trip and returned from the kitchen, smacking their lips and wiping their mouths with the backs of their hands. I was gazing airily into the muddy sky, when a roar issued from the doorway:

"Montez les hommes!"

It was the beefy-necked. We filed from the cour, through the door, past a little window which I was told belonged to the kitchen, down the clammy corridor, up the three flights of stairs, to the door of The Enormous Room. Padlocks were unlocked, chains rattled, and the door thrown open. We entered. The Enormous Room received us in silence. The door was slammed and locked behind us by the planton, whom we could hear descending the gnarled and filthy stairs.

In the course of a half-hour, which time as I was informed intervened between the just-ended morning promenade and the noon meal which was the next thing on the program, I gleaned considerable information concerning the daily schedule of La Ferté. A typical day was divided by planton-cries as follows:

(1) "Café." At 5.30 every morning a planton or plantons mounted to the room. One man descended to the kitchen, got a pail of coffee, and brought it up.

(2) "Corvée d'eau." From time to time the occupants of the room chose one of their number to be "maître de chambre", or roughly speaking Boss. When the planton opened the door, allowing the coffee-getter to descend, it was the duty of the maître de chamber to rouse a certain number of men (generally six, the occupants of the room being taken in rotation), who forthwith carried the pails of urine and excrement to the door. Upon the arrival of coffee, the maître de chambre and his crew "descended" said pails, together with a few clean pails for water, to the ground floor; where planton was in readiness to escort them to a sort of sewer situated a few yards beyond the cour des femmes. Here the full pails were dumped; with the exception, occasionally, of one or two pails urine which the Surveillant might direct to be thrown

on the Directeur's little garden in which it was rumored he was growing a rose for his daughter. From the sewer the corvée gang were escorted to a pump, where they filled their water pails. They then mounted to the room, where the emptied pails were ranged against the wall beside the door, with the exception of one which was returned to the cabinet. The water pails were placed hard by. The door was now locked, and the planton descended.

While the men selected for corvée had been performing their duties the other occupants had been enjoying coffee. The corvée men now joined them. The maître de chambre usually allowed about fifteen minutes for himself and his crew to consume their breakfast. He then announced:

(3) "Nettoyage de Chambre." Someone sprinkled the floor with water from one of the pails which had been just brought up. The other members of the crew swept the room, fusing their separate piles of filth at the door. This process consumed something like a half hour.

The sweeping completed, the men had nothing more to do till 7.30, at which hour a planton mounted, announcing

(4) "A la promenade les hommes." The corvée crew now carried down the product of their late labours. The other occupants descended or not directly to the cour, according to their tastes; morning promenade being optional. At 9.30 the planton demanded

(5)"Montez les hommes." Those who had taken advantage of the morning stroll were brought upstairs to the room,the corvée men descended the excrement which had accumulated during promenade,and everybody was thereupon locked in for a half hour,or until 10 o'clock,when a planton again mounted and cried:

(6)"A la soupe les hommes." Everyone descended to a wing of the building opposite the cour des hommes,where the noon meal was enjoyed until 10.30 or thereabouts,when the order

(7)"Tout le monde en haut" was given. There was a digestive interval of two and a half hours spent in the room. At 1 o'clock a planton mounted,announcing

(8)"Les hommes à la promenade"(in which case the afternoon promenade was a matter of choice)or "Tout le monde en bas",whereat everyone had to descend,willy-nilly,"éplucher les pommes"—potatoes(which constituted the pièce de resistance of "la soupe")being peeled and sliced on alternate days by the men and the girls. At 3.30

(9)"Tout le monde en haut" was again given,the world mounted,the corvée crew descended excrement,and everyone was then locked in till 4,at which hour a planton arrived to announce

(10)"A la soupe",that is to say the evening meal,or dinner. After dinner anyone who wished might go on promenade for an hour;those who wished might return to the room. At eight o'clock the planton made a final inspection and pronounced:

(11)"Lumières éteintes."

The most terrible cry of all,and which was not included in the regular program of planton-cries,consisted of the words:

"A la douche les hommes"—when all,sick dead and dying not excepted,descended to the baths. Although les douches came only once in quinze jours,such was the terror they inspired that it was necessary for the planton to hunt under paillasses for people who would have preferred death itself.

Upon remarking that corvée d'eau must be excessively disagreeable, I was informed that it had its bright side, viz., that in going to and from the sewer one could easily exchange a furtive signal with the women who always took pains to be at their windows at that moment. Influenced perhaps by this, Harree and Pompom were in the habit of doing their friends' corvées for a consideration. The girls, I was further instructed, had their corvée (as well as their meals) just after the men; and the miraculous stupidity of the plantons had been known to result in the coincidence of the two.

At this point somebody asked me how I had enjoyed my douche?

I was replying in terms of unmeasured opprobrium when I was interrupted by that gruesome clanking and rattling which announced the opening of the door. A moment later it was thrown wide, and the beefy-neck stood in the doorway, a huge bunch of keys in his paw, and shouted:

"A la soupe les hommes."

The cry was lost in a tremendous confusion, a reckless thither-and-hithering of humanity, everyone trying to be at the door, spoon in hand, before his neighbor. B said calmly, extracting his own spoon from beneath his paillasse on which we were seated: "They'll give you yours downstairs and when you get it you want to hide it or it'll be pinched"—and in company with Monsieur Bragard, who had refused the morning promenade, and whose gentility would not permit him to hurry when it was a question of such a low craving as hunger, we joined the dancing roaring throng at the door. I was not too famished myself to be unimpressed by the instantaneous change which had come over The Enormous Room's occupants. Never did Circe herself cast upon men so bestial an enchantment. Among these faces convulsed with utter animalism I scarcely recognized my various acquaintances. The transformation produced by the planton's shout was not merely amazing;it was uncanny,and not a little thrilling. These eyes bubbling with lust,obscene grins sprouting from contorted lips,bodies unclenching and clenching in unctuous gestures of complete savagery,convinced me by a certain insane beauty. Before the arbiter of their destinies some thirty creatures,hideous and authentic,poised,cohering in a sole chaos of desire;a fluent and numerous cluster of vital inhumanity. As I contemplated this ferocious and uncouth miracle,this beautiful manifestation of the sinister alchemy of hunger,I felt that the last vestige of individualism was about utterly to disappear,wholly abolished in a gamboling and wallowing throb.

The beefy-neck bellowed:

"Est-ce que vous êtes tous ici?"

A shrill roar of language answered. He looked contemptuously around him,upon the thirty clamoring faces each of which wanted to eat him—puttees,revolver and all. Then he cried:

"Allez,descendez."

Squirming,jostling,fighting,roaring,we poured slowly through the doorway. Ridiculously. Horribly. I felt like a glorious microbe in huge absurd din irrevocably swathed. B was beside me. A little ahead Monsieur Auguste's voice protested. Count Bragard brought up the rear.

When we reached the corridor nearly all the breath was knocked out of me. The corridor being wider than the stairs allowed me to inhale and look around. B was yelling in my ear:

"Look at the Hollanders and the Belgians! They're always ahead when it comes to food!"

Sure enough:John the Bathman Harree and Pompom were

leading this extraordinary procession. Fritz was right behind them,however,and pressing the leaders hard. I heard Monsieur Auguste crying in his child's voice:

"Si tout-le-monde marche dou-ce-ment nous al-lons ar-ri-ver plus tôt! Il faut pas faire comme ça!"

Then suddenly the roar ceased. The mêlée integrated. We were marching in orderly ranks. B said:

"The Surveillant!"

At the end of the corridor,opposite the kitchen window,there was a flight of stairs. On the third stair from the bottom stood(teetering a little slowly back and forth,his lean hands joined behind him and twitching regularly,a képi tilted forward on his cadaverous head so that its visor almost hid the weak eyes sunkenly peering from under droopy eyebrows,his pompous roosterlike body immaculately attired in a shiny uniform,his puttees sleeked,his croix polished)—the Fencer. There was a renovated look about him which made me laugh. Also his pose was ludicrously suggestive of Napoleon reviewing the armies of France.

Our column's first rank moved by him. I expected it to continue ahead through the door and into the open air,as I had myself done in going from les douches to le cour;but it turned a sharp right and then sharp left,and I perceived a short hall,almost hidden by the stairs. In a moment I had passed the Fencer myself and entered the hall. In another moment I was in a room,pretty nearly square,filled with rows of pillars. On turning into the hall the column had come almost to a standstill. I saw now that the reason for this slowing-down lay in the fact that on entering the room every man in turn passed a table and received a piece of bread from the chef. When B and I came opposite the table the dispenser of bread smiled pleasantly and nodded to B,then selected a hunk and pushed it rapidly into B's hands with an air of doing something which he shouldn't. B introduced me, whereupon the smile and selection was repeated.

"He thinks I'm a German" B explained in a whisper, "and that you are a German too." Then aloud, to the Cook: "My friend here needs a spoon. He just got here this morning and they haven't given him one."

The excellent person at the bread table hereupon said to me: "You shall go to the window and say I tell you to ask for spoon and you will catch one spoon"—and I broke through the waiting line, approaching the kitchen-window, and demanded of a roguish face within.

"Une cuiller, s'il vous plaît."

The roguish face, which had been singing in a high faint voice to itself, replied critically but not unkindly:

"Vous êtes un nouveau?"

I said that I was, that I had arrived late last night.

It disappeared, reappeared and handed me a tin spoon and cup, saying:

"Vous n'avez pas de tasse?"—"Non" I said.

"Tiens. Prends ça. Vite." Nodding in the direction of the Surveillant, who was standing all this time on the stairs behind me.

I expected from the Cook's phrase that something would be thrown at me which I should have to catch, and was accordingly somewhat relieved at the true state of affairs. On reentering the salle à manger I was greeted by many cries and wavings, and looking in their direction perceived tout le monde uproariously seated at wooden benches which were placed on either side of an enormous wooden table. There was a tiny gap in one bench where a place had been saved for me by B, with the assistance of Monsieur Auguste. Count Bragard, Harree and several other fellow-convicts. In a moment I had straddled the bench and was occupying the gap, spoon and cup in hand, and ready for anything.

The din was perfectly terrific. It had a minutely large quality. Here and there,in a kind of sonal darkness,solid sincere unintelligible absurd wisps of profanity heavily flickered. Optically the phenomenon was equally remarkable:seated waggingly swaying corpselike figures,swaggering,pounding with their little spoons,roaring hoarse unkempt. Evidently Monsieur le Surveillant had been forgotten. All at once the roar bulged unbearably. The roguish man,followed by the chef himself,entered with a suffering waddle,each of them bearing a huge bowl of steaming something. At least six people immediately rose,gesturing and imploring:"Ici"—"Mais non,ici"—"Mettez par ici"—

The bearers plumped their burdens carefully down,one at the head of the table and one in the middle. The men opposite the bowls stood up. Every man seized the empty plate in front of him and shoved it into his neighbor's hand;the plates moved toward the bowls,were filled amid uncouth protestations and accusations—"Mettez plus que ça"—"C'est pas juste,alors"—"Donnez-moi encore des pommes"—"Nom de Dieu,il n'y a pas assez"—"Cohon,qu'est-ce qu'il veut?"—"Shut up"—"Gottverdummer"—and returned one by one. As each man received his own,he fell upon it with a sudden guzzle.

Eventually,in front of me,solemnly sat a faintly-smoking urine-coloured circular broth,in which soggily hung half-suspended slabs of raw potato. Following the example of my neighbors,I too addressed myself to La Soupe. I found her lukewarm,completely flavorless. I examined the hunk of bread. It was almost bluish in colour;in taste mouldy,slightly sour. "If you crumb some into the soup" remarked B,who had been studying my reactions from the corner of his eye,"they both taste better." I tried the experiment. It was a complete success. At least one felt as if one were getting nourishment. Between gulps I smelled the bread furtively. It smelled rather much like an old attic in which kites and other toys gradually are forgotten in a gentle darkness.

B and I were finishing our soup together when behind and somewhat to the left there came the noise of a lock being manipulated. I turned and saw in one corner of the salle à manger a little door, shaking mysteriously. Finally it was thrown open, revealing a sort of minute bar and a little closet filled with what appeared to be groceries and tobacco; and behind the bar, standing in the closet, a husky competent-looking lady. "It's the canteen" B said. We rose, spoon in hand and breadhunk stuck on spoon, and made our way to the lady. I had, naturally, no money; but B reassured me that before the day was over I should see the Gestionnaire and make arrangements for drawing on the supply of ready cash which the gendarmes who took me from Creil had confided to the Surveillant's care; eventually I could also draw on my account with Norton-Harjes in Paris; meantime he had quelques sous which might well go into chocolat and cigarettes. The large lady had a pleasant quietness about her, a sort of simplicity, which made me extremely desirous of complying with B's suggestion. Incidentally I was feeling somewhat uncertain in the region of the stomach, due to the unique quality of the lunch which I had just enjoyed, and I brightened at the thought of anything as solid as chocolat. Accordingly we purchased (or rather B did) a paquet jaune and a cake of something which was not Menier. And the remaining sous we squandered on a glass apiece of red acrid pinard, gravely and with great happiness pledging the hostess of the occasion and then each other.

With the exception of ourselves hardly anyone patronized the canteen, noting which I felt somewhat conspicuous. When, however, Harree Pompom and John the Bathman came rushing up and demanded cigarettes my fears were dispelled. Moreover the pinard was excellent.

"Come on! Arrange yourselves!" the bull-neck cried hoarsely as the five of us were lighting up;and we joined the line of fellow-prisoners with their breads and spoons,gaping belching trumpeting fraternally,by the doorway.

"Tout le monde en haut!" the planton roared.

Slowly we filed through the tiny hall,past the stairs(empty now of their Napoleonic burden),down the corridor,up the creaking gnarled damp flights,and(after the inevitable pause in which the escort rattled chains and locks)into The Enormous Room.

This would be about ten thirty.

Just what I tasted,did,smelled,saw,and heard,not to mention touched,between ten thirty and the completion of the evening meal(otherwise the four o'clock soup)I am quite at a loss to say. Whether it was that glass of pinard(plus or rather times the astonishing exhaustion bequeathed me by my journey of the day before)which caused me to enter temporarily the gates of forgetfulness,or whether the sheer excitement attendant upon my ultra-novel surroundings proved too much for an indispensable part of my so-called mind—I do not in the least know. I am fairly certain that I went on afternoon promenade. After which I must surely have mounted to await my supper in The Enormous Room. Whence(after the due and proper interval)I doubtless descended to the clutches of La Soupe Extraordinaire....yes,for I perfectly recall the cry which made me suddenly to reenter the dimension of distinctness....and by Jove I had just finished a glass of pinard....somebody must have treated me....we were standing together,spoon in hand....when we heard—

"A la promenade"....we issued en queue,firmly grasping our spoons and bread,through the dining-room door. Turning right we were emitted,by the door opposite the kitchen,from the building itself into the open air. A few steps and we passed through the little gate in the barbed-wire fence of the cour.

Greatly refreshed by my second introduction to the canteen, and with the digestion of the somewhat extraordinary evening meal apparently assured, I gazed almost intelligently around me. Count Bragard had declined the evening promenade in favor of The Enormous Room, but I perceived in the crowd the now familiar faces of the three Hollanders—John Harree and Pompom—likewise of The Bear, Monsieur Auguste, and Fritz. In the course of the next hour I had become if not personally at least optically acquainted with nearly a dozen others.

Jan

One was a queer-looking almost infantile man of perhaps thirty-five who wore a black vest, a pair of thread-bare pants, a collarless stripped shirt open at the neck with a gold stud therein, a cap slightly too large pulled down so that the visor almost hid his prominent eyebrows if not his tiny eyes, and something approximating sneakers. His expression was imitative and vacant. He stuck to Fritz most of the time, and took pains—when a girl leaned from her window—to betray a manliness of

demeanor which contrasted absurdly with his mentor's natu-
rally athletic bearing. He tried to speak(and evidently thought
he spoke)English,or rather English words;but with the exception
of a few obscenities pronounced in a surprisingly natural man-
ner his vocabulary gave him considerable difficulty. Even when
he and Fritz exchanged views,as they frequently did,in Danish,a
certain linguistic awkwardness persisted;yielding the impression
that to give or receive an idea entailed a tremendous effort of
the intelligence. He was extremely vain,and indeed struck poses
whenever he got a chance. He was also good-natured—stupidly
so. It might be said of him that he never knew defeat;since if,after
staggering a few moments under the weight of the bar which Fritz
raised and lowered with ease fourteen times under the stimu-
lus of a female gaze,the little man fell suddenly to earth with his
burden,not a trace of discomfiture could be seen upon his small
visage—he seemed,on the contrary,well pleased with himself,and
the subsequent pose which his small body adopted demanded
congratulations. When he stuck his chest up or out,he looked a
trifle like a bantam rooster. When he tagged Fritz he resembled
a rather brittle monkey,a monkey on a stick perhaps,capable of
brief and stiff antics. His name was Jan.

On the huge beam of iron,sitting somewhat beautifully all by
himself,I noticed somebody with pink cheeks and blue eyes,in
a dark suit of neatly kept clothes,with a small cap on his head.
His demeanor,in contrast to the other occupants of the cour,was
noticeably inconspicuous. In his poise lived an almost brilliant
quietness. His eyes were remarkably sensitive. They were appar-
ently anxious not to see people and things. He impressed me at
once by a shyness which was completely deerlike. Possibly he
was afraid. Nobody knew him or anything about him. I do not
remember when we devised the name,but B and I referred to him
as The Silent Man.

Silente

Somewhat overawed by the animals Harree and Pom-pom(but nevertheless managing to overawe a goodly portion of his fellow-captives)an extraordinary human being paced the cour. On gazing for the first time directly at him I experienced a feeling of nausea. A figure inclined to corpulence,dressed with care,remarkable only above the neck—and then what a head! It was large,and had a copious mop of limp hair combed back from the high forehead—hair of a disagreeable blond tint,dutch-cut behind,falling over the pinkish soft neck almost to the shoulders. In this pianist's or artist's hair,which shook en masse when the owner walked,two large and outstanding and altogether brutal white ears tried to hide themselves. The face,a cross between classic Greek and Jew,had a Reynard expression,something distinctly wily and perfectly disagreeable. An equally with the hair blond mustache—or rather mustachios projectingly important—waved beneath the prominent nostrils,and served to partially conceal the pallid mouth,weak and large,whose lips assumed from time to time a smile which had something almost foetal about it. Over the even weaker chin was disposed a blond goatee. The cheeks were fatty. The continually perspiring forehead exhibited innumerable pinkish pock-marks. In conversing with a companion this being emitted a disgusting smoothness,his very gestures were oily like his skin. He wore a pair of bloated wristless hands,the knuckles lost in fat,with which he smoothed the air from time to time. He was speaking low and effortless French,completely absorbed in the developing ideas which issued fluently from his mustachios. About him there clung an aura of cringing. His hair whiskers and neck looked as if they were trick neck whiskers and hair,as if they might at any moment suddenly disintegrate,as if the smoothness of his eloquence alone kept them in place.

We called him Judas.

Beside him,clumsily keeping the pace but not the step,was a tallish effeminate person whose immaculate funereal suit hung loosely upon an aged and hurrying anatomy. He wore a black big cap on top of his haggard and remarkably clean-shaven face,the most prominent feature of which was a red nose which sniffed a little now and then as if its owner was suffering from a severe cold. This person emanated age neatness and despair. Aside from the nose which compelled immediate attention,his face consisted of a few large planes loosely juxtaposed and register-ing pathos. His motions were without grace. He had a certain refinement. He could not have been more than forty-five. There was worry on every inch of him. Possibly he thought that he might die. B said "He's a Belgian,a friend of Count Bragard,and his name is Monsieur Pet-airs." From time to time Monsieur Pet-airs remarked something delicately and pettishly in a gen-tle and weak voice. His adam's-apple,at such moments,jumped about in a longish slack wrinkled skinny neck which was like the neck of a turkey. To this turkey the approach of Thanksgiv-ing inspired dread. From time to time M. Pet-airs looked about him sidewise as if he expected to see a hatchet. His hands were claws,kind awkward and nervous. They twitched. The bony and wrinkled things looked as if they would like to close quickly upon a throat.

B called my attention to a figure squatting in the middle of

Judas

the cour with his broad back against one of the more misera-
ble trees. This figure was clothed in a remarkably picturesque
manner: it wore a dark sombrero-like hat with a large drooping
brim, a bright red gipsy shirt of some remarkably fine material
with huge sleeves loosely falling, and baggy corduroy trousers
whence escaped two brown shapely naked feet. On moving a
little I discovered a face—perhaps the handsomest face that
I have ever seen, of a gold brown colour, framed in an amaz-
ingly large and beautiful black beard. The features were finely
formed and almost fluent, the eyes soft and extraordinarily sen-
sitive, the mouth delicate and firm beneath a black mustache
which fused with the silky and wonderful darkness falling upon
the breast. This face contained a beauty and dignity which, as
I first saw it, annihilated the surrounding tumult without an
effort. Around the carefully formed nostrils there was some-
thing almost of contempt. The cheeks had known suns of which
I might not think. The feet had travelled nakedly in countries
not easily imagined. Seated gravely in the mud and noise of the
cour, under the pitiful and scraggly pommier....behind the eyes
lived a world of complete strangeness and silence. The compo-
sure of the body was graceful and Jovelike. This being might
have been a prophet come out of a country nearer to the sun.
Perhaps a god who had lost his road and allowed himself to be

taken prisoner by le gouvernement français. At least a prince of a dark and desirable country, a king over a gold-skinned people, who would return when he wished to his fountains and his houris. I learned upon inquiry that he travelled in various countries with a horse and cart and his wife and children, selling bright colours to the women and men of these countries. As it turned out, he was one of The Delectable Mountains; to discover which I had come a long and difficult way. Wherefore I shall tell you no more about him for the present, except that his name was Josef Demestre.

We called him The Wanderer.

I was still wondering at my good luck in occupying the same miserable yard with this exquisite personage when a hoarse rather thick voice shouted from the gate: "L'américain!"

It was a planton, in fact the chief planton for whom all ordinary plantons had unutterable respect and whom all mere men unutterably hated. It was the planton into whom I had had the distinguished honour of bumping shortly after my visit to le bain.

The Hollanders and Fritz were at the gate in a mob, all shouting "Which" in four languages.

This planton did not deign to notice them. He repeated roughly "L'américain." Then, yielding a point to their frenzied entreaties: "Le nouveau."

B said to me "Probably he's going to take you to the Gestionnaire. You're supposed to see him when you arrive. He's got your money and will keep it for you, and give you an allowance twice a week. You can't draw more than 20 francs. I'll hold your bread and spoon."

"Where the devil is the American" cried the planton.

"Me voici."

"Follow me."

I followed his back and rump and holster through the little

gate in the barbed-wire fence and into the building, at which point he commanded "Proceed."

I asked "Where?"

"Straight ahead" he said angrily.

I proceeded. "Left!" he cried. I turned. A door confronted me. "Entrez" he commanded. I did. An unremarkable looking gentleman in a French uniform, sitting at a sort of table. "Monsieur le médecin, le nouveau." The doctor got up. "Open your shirt." I did. Take down your pants." I did. "All right." Then, as the planton was about to escort me from the room: "English?" he asked with curiosity. "No" I said, "American." "Vraiment"—he contemplated me with attention. "South American are you?" "United States" I explained. "Vraiment"—he looked curiously at me, not disagreeably in the least. "Pourquoi vous êtes ici?" "I don't know" I said smiling pleasantly, "except that my friend wrote some letters which were intercepted by the French censor." "Ah!" he remarked. "C'est tout."

And I departed. "Proceed!" cried the Black Holster. I retraced my steps, and was about to exit through the door leading to the cour, when "Stop! Nom de Dieu! Proceed!"

I asked "Where?" completely bewildered.

"Up" he said angrily.

I turned to the stairs on the left, and climbed.

"Not so fast there" he roared behind me.

I slowed up. We reached the landing. I was sure that the Gestionnaire was a very fierce man—probably a lean slight person who would rush at me from the nearest door saying "Hands up" in French, whatever that may be. The door opposite me stood open. I looked in. There was the Surveillant standing, hands behind back, approvingly regarding my progress. I was asking myself, Should I bow? when a scurrying and a tittering made me look left, along a dark and particularly dirty hall. Women's voices...I almost fell with surprise. Were not these shadows faces peering a little boldly at me from doors? How many girls were there—it sounded as if there were a hundred—

"Qu'est-ce que vous foutez" etc. and the planton gave me a good shove in the direction of another flight of stairs. I obligingly ascended;thinking of the Surveillant as a spider,elegantly poised in the centre of his nefarious web,waiting for a fly to make too many struggles....

At the top of this flight I was confronted by a second hall. A shut door indicated the existence of a being directly over the Surveillant's holy head. Upon this door,lest I should lose time in speculating,was in ample letters inscribed:

GESTIONNAIRE.

I felt unutterably lost. I approached the door. I even started to push it.

"Attends,Nom de Dieu." The planton gave me another shove,faced the door,knocked twice,and cried in accents of profound respect:"Monsieur le Gestionnaire"—after which he gazed at me with really supreme contempt,his neat piglike face becoming almost circular.

I said to myself:This Gestionnaire,whoever he is,must be a very terrible person,a frightful person,a person utterly without mercy.

From within a heavy stupid pleasant voice lazily remarked: "Entrez."

The planton threw the door open,stood stiffly on the threshold,and gave me the look which plantons give to eggs when plantons are a little hungry.

I crossed the threshold,trembling with(let us hope)anger.

Before me,seated at a table,was a very fat personage with a

black skull cap perched upon its head. Its face was possessed of an enormous nose,on which pince-nez precariously roosted;otherwise said face was large whiskered very German and had three chins. Extraordinary creature. Its belly,as it sat,was slightly dented by the table-top,on which table-top rested several enormous tomes similar to those employed by the recording angel on the Day of Judgment,an inkstand or two,innumerable pens and pencils,and some positively fatal looking papers. The person was dressed in worthy and semi-dismal clothes amply cut to afford a promenade for the big stomach. The coat was of that extremely thin black material which occasionally is affected by clerks and dentists and more often by librarians. If ever I looked upon an honest German jowl,or even upon caricature thereof,I looked upon one now. Such a round fat red pleasant beer-drinking face as reminded me only and immediately of huge meerschaum pipes,Deutsche Verein mottos,sudsy seidels of Wurtzburger,and Jacob Wirth's(once upon a time)brachwurst. Such pinlike pink merry eyes as made me think of Kris Kringle himself. Such extraordinarily huge reddish hands as might have grasped six seidels together in the Deutsche Küchen on 13th street. I gasped with pleasurable relief.

Monsieur le Gestionnaire looked as if he was trying very hard,with the aid of his beribboned glasses and librarian's jacket(not to mention a very ponderous gold watch-chain and locket that were supported by his copious equator)to appear possessed of the solemnity necessarily emanating from his lofty and responsible office. This solemnity,however,met its Waterloo in his frank and stupid eyes,not to say his trilogy of cheerful chins—so much so that I felt like crying Wie geht's and cracking him on his huge back. Such an animal! A contented animal,a bulbous animal;the only living hippopotamus in captivity,fresh from the Nile.

He contemplated me with a natural,under the circumstances, curiosity. He even naïvely contemplated me. As if I were hay.

My hay-coloured head perhaps pleased him, as a hippopotamus. He would perhaps eat me. He grunted, exposing tobacco-yellow tusks, and his tiny eyes twittered. Finally he gradually uttered, with a thick accent, the following extremely impressive dictum:

"C'est l'américain."

I felt much pleased, and said "Oui, j'suis américain, Monsieur."

He rolled half over backwards in his creaking chair with wonderment at such an unexpected retort. He studied my face with a puzzled air, appearing slightly embarrassed that before him should stand l'américain and that l'américain should admit it, and that it should all be so wonderfully clear. I saw a second dictum, even more profound than the first, ascending from his black vest. The chain and fob trembled with anticipation. I was wholly fascinated. What vast blob of wisdom would find its difficult way out of him? The bulbous lips wiggled in a pleasant smile.

"Voo parlez français."

This was delightful. The planton behind me was obviously angered by the congenial demeanor of Monsieur le Gestionnaire, and rasped with his boot upon the threshold. The maps to my right and left, maps of France, maps of the Mediterranean, of Europe even were abashed. A little anaemic biped whom I had not previously noted, as he stood in one corner with a painfully deferential expression, looked all at once relieved. I guessed, and correctly guessed, that this little thing was the translator of La Ferté. His weak face wore glasses of the same type as the hippopotamus's, but without a huge black ribbon. I decided to give him a tremor; and said to the hippo "Un peu, Monsieur", at which the little thing looked sickly.

The hippopotamus benevolently remarked "Voo parlez bien", and his glasses fell off. He turned to the watchful planton:

"Voo poovez aller. Je vooz appelerai."

The watchful planton did a sort of salute and closed the door after him. The skullcapped dignitary turned to his papers and began mouthing them with his huge hands, grunting pleasantly. Finally he found one, and said lazily

"De quel endroit que vooz êtes?"

"De Massachusetts" said I.

He wheeled round and stared dumbly at the weak-faced one, who looked at a complete loss, but managed to stammer simperingly that it was a part of the United States.

"UH." The hippopotamus said.

Then he remarked that I had been arrested, and I agreed that I had been arrested.

Then he said "Have you got any money?" and before I could answer clambered heavily to his feet and, leaning over the table before which I stood, punched me gently.

"Uh." Said the hippopotamus, sat down, and put on his glasses.

"I have your money here" he said. "You are allowed to draw a little from time to time. You may draw 20 francs, if you like. You may draw it twice a week."

"I should like to draw 20 francs now" I said, "in order to buy something at the canteen."

"You will give me a receipt" said the hippopotamus. "You want to draw 20 francs now, quite so." He began, puffing and grunting, to make handwriting of a peculiarly large and somewhat loose variety.

The weak face now stepped forward, and asked me gently: "Hugh er a merry can?"—so I carried on a brilliant conversation in pidgin English about my relatives and America until interrupted by

"Uh."

The hip had finished.

"Sign you name, here" he said, and I did. He looked about in one of the tomes and checked something opposite my name, which I enjoyed seeing in the list of inmates. It had been spelled,erased,and re-spelled several times.

Monsieur le Gestionnaire contemplated my signature. Then he looked up,smiled,and nodded recognition to someone behind me. I turned. There stood(having long since noiselessly entered)The Fencer Himself,nervously clasping and unclasping his hands behind his back and regarding me with approval,or as a keeper regards some rare monkey newly forwarded from its habitat by Hagenbeck.

The hip pulled out a drawer. He found,after hunting,some notes. He counted two off,licking his big thumb with a pompous gesture,and having recounted them passed them heavily to me. I took them as a monkey takes a cocoanut.

"Do you wish?"—the Gestionnaire nodded toward me,addressing the Fencer.

"No,no" the Fencer said bowingly. "I have talked to him already."

"Call that planton!" cried Monsieur le Gestionnaire,to the little thing. The little thing ran out dutifully and called in a weak voice "Planton!"

A gruff but respectful "Oui" boomed from below-stairs. In a moment the planton of plantons had respectfully entered.

"The promenade being over,you can take him to the men's room" said the Surveillant,as the hippo(immensely relieved and rather proud of himself)collapsed in his creaking chair.

Feeling like a suit-case in the clutches of a porter,I obediently preceded my escort down two flights,first having bowed to the hippopotamus and said "Merci"—to which courtesy the Hippo paid no attention. As we went along the dank hall on the ground floor I regretted that no whispers and titters had greeted my descent. Probably the furious planton had seen to it that les femmes kept their rooms in silence. We ascended the three

flights at the farther end of the corridor,the planton of all plan-
tons unlocked and unbolted the door at the top landing,and I
was swallowed by The Enormous Room.

I made for B,in my excitement allowing myself to wave the
bank-notes. Instantly a host had gathered at my side. On my way
to my bed—a distance of perhaps thirty feet—I was patted on the
back by Harree Pompom and Bathhouse John,congratulated by
Monsieur Auguste,and saluted by Fritz. Arriving,I found myself
the centre of a stupendous crowd. People who had previously
had nothing to say to me,who had even sneered at my unwashed
and unshaven exterior,now addressed me in terms of more than
polite interest. Judas himself stopped in a promenade of the
room,eyed me a moment,hastened smoothly to my vicinity,and
made a few oily remarks of a pleasant nature. Simultaneously by
Monsieur Auguste Harree and Fritz I was advised to hide my
money and hide it well. There were people,you know...who didn't
hesitate,you understand...I understood,and to the vast disap-
pointment of the clamorous majority reduced my wealth to its
lowest terms and crammed it in my trousers,stuffing several tri-
fles of a bulky nature on top of it. Then I gazed quietly around
with a William S. Hart expression calculated to allay any undue
excitement. One by one the curious and enthusiastic faded from
me,and I was left with the few whom I already considered my
friends;with which few B and myself proceeded to while away the
time remaining before Lumières Eteintes.

Incidentally,I exchanged(in the course of the next two
hours)a considerable mass of two-legged beings for a number of
extremely interesting individuals. Also,in that somewhat limited
period of time,I gained all sorts of highly enlightening informa-
tion concerning the lives habits and likes of half a dozen of as
fine companions as it has ever been my luck to meet or,so far as
I can now imagine,ever will be. In prison one learns several mil-

lion things—if one is l'américain from Mass-a-chu-setts. When
the ominous and awe-inspiring rattle on the further side of the
locked door announced that the captors were come to bid the
captives good night,I was still in the midst of conversation and
had been around the world a number of times. At the clanking
sound our little circle centripetally disintegrated,as if by sheer
magic;and I was left somewhat dizzily to face a renewal of reality.

The door shot wide. The planton's almost indistinguishable
figure in the doorway told me that the entire room was dark.
I had not noticed the darkness. Somebody had placed a can-
dle(which I recalled having seen on a table in the middle of the
room when I looked up once or twice during the conversation)on
a little shelf hard by the cabinet. There had been men playing at
cards by this candle—now everybody was quietly reposing upon
the floor along three sides of The Enormous Room. The planton
entered. Walked over to the light. Said something about every-
body being present,and was answered by a number of voices in a
more or less profane affirmative. Strutted to and fro,kicked the
cabinet,flashed an electric torch,and walked up the room exam-
ining each paillasse to make sure it had an occupant. Crossed
the room at the upper end. Started down on my side. The white
circle was in my eyes. The planton stopped. I stared stupidly and
wearily into the glare. The light moved all over me and my bed.
The rough voice behind the glare said:

"Vous êtes le nouveau?"

Monsieur Auguste,from my left,said quietly:

"Oui,c'est le nouveau."

The holder of the torch grunted,and(after pausing a second
at B's bed to inspect a picture of perfect innocence)banged out
through the door,which whanged to behind him and another
planton of whose presence I had been hitherto unaware. A perfect
symphony of "Bonne-nuit's" "Dormez-bien's" and other affection-

ate admonitions greeted the exeunt of the authorities. They were advised by various parts of the room in divers tongues to dream of their wives, to be careful of themselves in bed, to avoid catching cold, and to attend to a number of personal wants before retiring. The symphony gradually collapsed, leaving me sitting in a state of complete wonderment, dead tired and very happy, upon my paillasse.

"I think I'll turn in" I said to the neighboring darkness.

"That's what I'm doing" B's voice said.

"By God" I said, "this is the finest place I've ever been in my life."

"It's the finest place in the world" said B's voice.

"Thank Heaven, we're out of A.'s way and the—Section Sanitaire" I grunted as I placed my boots where a pillow might have been imagined.

"Amen" B's voice said.

"Si vous met-tez vos chaus-sures au des-sous de la pail-lasse" Monsieur Auguste's voice said, "vous al-lez bien dor-mir."

I thanked him for the suggestion, and did so. I reclined in an ecstasy of happiness and weariness. There could be nothing better than this. To sleep.

"Got a Gottverdummer cigarette?" Harree's voice asked of Fritz.

"No bloody fear" Frit's voice replied coolly.

Snores had already begun in various keys at various distances in various directions. The candle flickered a little; as if darkness and itself were struggling to the death, and darkness were winning.

"I'll get a chew from John" Harree's voice said.

Three or four paillasses away, a subdued conversation was proceeding. I found myself listening sleepily.

"Et puis" a voice said, "je suis réformé...."

CHAPTER FIVE

A Group of Portraits

With the reader's permission I beg, at this point of my narrative, to indulge in one or two extrinsic observations.

In the preceding pages I have described my Pilgrim's Progress from the Slough of Despond, commonly known at Section Sanitaire Vingt-et-Un (then located at Germaine) through the mysteries of Noyon Creil and Paris to the Porte de Triage de La Ferté-Macé, Orne. With the end of my first day as a certified inhabitant of the latter institution a definite progression is brought to a close. Beginning with my second day at La Ferté a new period opens. This period extends to the moment of my departure and includes the discovery of The Delectable Mountains, two of which—The Wanderer and I shall not say the other—have already been sighted. It is like a vast grey box in which are laid helter-skelter a great many toys, each of which is itself completely significant apart from the always unchanging temporal dimension which merely contains it along with the rest. I make this point clear for the benefit of any of my readers who have not had the distinguished privilege of being in jail. To those who have been in jail my meaning is at once apparent; particularly if they have had the highly enlightening experience of being in jail with a perfectly indefinite sentence. How, in such a case, could events occur and be remembered otherwise than as individualities distinct from Time Itself? Or, since one day and the next are the same to such a prisoner, where does Time come in at all? Obviously, once the prisoner is habituated to his environment, once he accepts the fact that speculation as to when he will regain his liberty cannot possibly shorten the hours of his incarceration and may very well drive him into a state of unhappiness (not to say morbidity), events can no longer succeed each other: whatever happens, while it may happen in connection with some other perfectly distinct happening, does not happen in a scale of temporal priorities—each happening is self-sufficient, irrespective of minutes months and the other treasures of freedom.

It is for this reason that I do not purpose to inflict upon the reader a diary of my alternative aliveness and non-existence at La Ferté—not because such a diary would unutterably bore him, but because the diary or time method is a technique which cannot possibly do justice to timelessness. I shall (on the contrary) lift from their grey box at random certain (to me) more or less astonishing toys; which may or may not please the reader, but whose colours and shapes and textures are a part of the actual Present—without future and past—whereof they alone are cognizant who—so to speak—have submitted to an amputation of the world.

I have already stated that La Ferté was a Porte de Triage—that is to say, a place where suspects of all varieties were herded by le gouvernement français preparatory to their being judged as to their guilt by a Commission. If the Commission found that they were wicked persons, or dangerous persons, or undesirable persons, or puzzling persons, or persons in some way insusceptible of analysis, they were sent from La Ferté to a "regular" prison, called

Précigné,in the province of Sarthe. About Précigné the most awful rumors were spread. It was whispered that it had a huge moat about it,with an infinity of barbed-wire fences thirty-feet high,and lights trained on the walls all night to discourage the escape of prisoners. Once in Précigné you were "in" for good and all,pour la durée de la guerre,which durée was a subject of occasional and dismal speculation—occasional for reasons(as I have mentioned)of mental health;dismal for unreasons of diet,privation,filth,and other trifles. La Ferté was,then,a stepping stone either to freedom or to Précigné,the chances in the former case being—no speculation here—something less than the now celebrated formula made famous by the 18th amendment. But the excellent and inimitable and altogether benignant French government was not satisfied with its own generosity in presenting one merely with Précigné—beyond that lurked a cauchemar called by the singularly poetic name:Ile de Groix. A man who went to Ile de Groix was done.

As the Surveillant said to us all,leaning out of a littlish window,and to me personally upon occasion—

"You are not prisoners. Oh,no. No indeed. I should say not. Prisoners are not treated like this. You are lucky."

I had de la chance all right,but that was something which the pauvre M. le Surveillant wot altogether not of. As for my fellow-prisoners,I am sorry to say that he was—it seems to my humble personality—quite wrong. For who was eligible to La Ferté? Anyone whom the police could find in the lovely country of France(a)who was not guilty of treason(b)who could not prove that he was not guilty of treason. By treason I refer to any little annoying habits of independent thought or action which en temps de guerre are put in a hole and covered over,with the somewhat naïve idea that from their cadavers violets will grow whereof the perfume will delight all good men and true

and make such worthy citizens forget their sorrows. Fort Leav-
enworth,for instance,emanates even now a perfume which is
utterly delightful to certain Americans. Just how many La Fertés
France boasted(and for all I know may still boast)God Himself
knows. At least,in that Republic,amnesty has been proclaimed,or
so I hear.—But to return to the Surveillant remark.

J'avais de la chance. Because I am by profession a painter and
a writer. Whereas my very good friends,all of them deeply suspi-
cious characters,most of them traitors,without exception lucky
to have the use of their cervical vertebrae,etc.,etc.,could(with
a few exceptions)write not a word and read not a word;neither
could they faire la photographie as Monsieur Auguste chuck-
lingly called it(at which I blushed with pleasure):worst of all,the
majority of the dark criminals who had been caught in nefar-
ious plots against the honour of France were totally unable to
speak French. Curious thing. Often I pondered the unutterable
and inextinguishable wisdom of the police,who—undeterred by
facts which would have deceived less astute intelligences into
thinking that these men were either too stupid or too simple to
be connoisseurs of the art of betrayal—swooped upon their help-
less prey with that indescribable courage which is the prerogative
of policemen the world over,and bundled same prey into the La
Fertés of that mighty nation upon some,at least,of whose public
buildings it seems to me that I remember reading

LIBERTÉ. EGALITÉ. FRATERNITÉ.

And I wondered that France should have a use for Monsieur
Auguste,who had been arrested(because he was a Russian)when
his fellow munition workers made la grève,and whose wife wanted
him in Paris because she was hungry and because their child was
getting to look queer and white. Monsieur Auguste,that desper-

ate ruffian exactly five feet tall who—when he could not keep from crying(one must think about one's wife or even one's child once or twice,I merely presume,if one loves them—"et ma femme est très gen-tille,elle est fran-çaise et très belle,très,très belle,vrai-ment;elle n'est pas comme moi,un pet-it homme laid,ma femme est grande et belle,elle sait bien lire et é-crire,vrai-ment;et notre fils...vous dev-ez voir notre pet-it fils...")—used to start up and cry out,taking B by one arm and me by the other,

"Al-lons,mes amis! Chan-tons 'Quackquackquack.'"

Whereupon we would join in the following song,which Monsieur Auguste had taught us with great care,and whose renditions gave him unspeakable delight:

"Un canard,déployant ses ailes
                  (Quackquackquack)
Il disait à sa cane fidèle
                  (Quackquackquack)
Il chantait(Quackquackquack)
Il faisait(Quackquackquack)
    Quand"(spelling mine)
  "finiront nos desseins,
            Quack.
               Quack.
                  Quack.
                     Qua-
                       ck."

I suppose I will always puzzle over the ecstasies of That Wonderful Duck. And how Monsieur Auguste,the merest gnome of a man,would bend backwards in absolute laughter at this song's spirited conclusion upon a note so low as to wither us all.

Then too The Schoolmaster.

A little fragile old man. His trousers were terrifically too big for him. When he walked(in an insecure and frightened way)his trousers did the most preposterous wrinkles. If he leaned against a tree in the cour,with a very old and also fragile pipe in his pocket—the stem(which looked enormous in contrast to the owner)protruding therefrom—his three-sizes too big collar would leap out so as to make his wizened neck appear no thicker than the white necktie which flowed upon his two-sizes too big shirt. He wore always a coat which reached below his knees,which coat with which knees perhaps some one had once given him. It had huge shoulders which sprouted,like wings,on either side of his elbows when he sat in The Enormous Room quietly writing at a tiny three-legged table,a very big pen walking away with his weak bony hand. His too big cap had a little button on top which looked like the head of a nail;and suggested that this old doll had once lost its poor grey head and had been repaired by means of tacking its head upon its neck,where it should be and properly belonged. Of what hideous crime was this being suspected? By some mistake he had three mustaches,two of them being eyebrows. He used to teach school in Alsace-Lorraine,and his sister is there. In speaking to you his kind face is peacefully reduced to triangles. And his tie buttons on every morning with a Bang! and off he goes;led about by his celluloid collar,gently worried about himself,delicately worried about the world. At eating time he looks sidelong as he stuffs soup into stiff lips. There are two holes where cheeks might have been. Lessons hide in his wrinkles. Bells ding in the oldness of eyes. Did he,by any chance,tell the children that there are such monstrous things as peace and good will...a corrupter of youth,no doubt...he is altogether incapable of anger,wholly timid and tintinabulous. And he had always wanted so much to know—if there were wild horses in America?

Yes,probably The Schoolmaster was a notorious seditionist.

The Schoolmaster

The all-wise French government has its ways,which like the ways of God are wonderful. But how about Emile?

Emile the Bum. Is the reader acquainted with the cartoons of Mr. F. Opper? If not,he cannot properly relish this personage. Emile the Bum was a man of thought. In chasing his legs,his trousers' seat scoots intriguingly up-and-to-the-side. How often,Emile the Bum,après la soupe,have I ascended behind thee;going slowly up and up and up the miserable stairs behind thy pants' timed slackness. Emile possesses a scarf which he winds about his ample thighs,thereby connecting his otherwise elusively independent trousers with that very important individual—his stomach. His face is unshaven. He is unshorn. Like all Belgians he has a quid in his gums night and day,which quid he buys outside in the town;for in his capacity of Something-orother(perhaps assistant sweeper)he journeys(under proper surveillance)occasionally from the gates which unthoughtful men may not leave. His F. Opper soul peeps from slippery little eyes. Having entered an argument—be its subject the rights of humanity,the price of potatoes,or the wisdom of warfare— Emile the Bum sticks to his theme and his man. He is,curiously enough,above all things sincere. He is almost treacherously sincere. Having argued a man to a standstill and won from him an object admission of complete defeat,Emile stalks rollingly away. Upon reaching a distance of perhaps five metres he suddenly makes a rush at his victim—having turned around with the velocity of lightning,in fact so quickly that no one saw him do it;—his victim writhes anew under the lash of Emile the Bum's insatiate loquacity,—admits,confesses,begs pardon—and off Emile stalks rollingly...to turn again and dash back at his almost weeping opponent,thundering sputteringly with rejuvenated vigour,a vigour which annihilates everything(including reason)before it. Otherwise,considering that he is a Belgian,he is extraordinarily good-natured and minds his business rollingly and sucks his quid happily. Not a tremendously harmful individual,one could say...and why did the French government need him behind lock and key,I wonder? It was his fatal eloquence,doubtless,which betrayed him to the clutches of La Misère. Gendarmes are sensitive in peculiar ways;they do not stand for any misleading information upon the probable destiny of the price of potatoes—since it is their duty and their privilege to resent all that is seditious to The Government,and since The Government includes the Minister of Agriculture(or something),and since the Minister of Something includes,of course,potatoes,and that means that no one is at liberty to in any way(however slightly or insinuatingly)insult a potato. I bet Emile the Bum insulted two potatoes.

We still have,however,the problem of the man in the Orange Cap. The man in the Orange Cap was,optically as well as in every other respect,delightful. Until The Zulu came(of which more later)he was a little and quietly lonely. The Zulu,however,played with him. He was always chasing The Zulu around trees in the cour;dodging,peeping,tagging him on his coat,and sometimes doing something like laughing. Before The Zulu came he was lonely because nobody would have anything to do with the little man in the Orange Cap. This was not because he had done something unpopular;on the contrary,he was perfectly well behaved. It was because he could not speak. Perhaps I should say with more accuracy that he could not articulate. This fact did not prevent the little man in the Orange Cap from being shy. When I asked him,one day,what he had been arrested for,he replied GOO in the shyest manner imaginable. He was altogether delightful. Subconsciously everyone was,of course,fearful that he himself would go nuts—everyone with the exception of those who had already gone nuts,who were in the wholly pleasant situation of having no fear. The still sane were therefore inclined to snub and otherwise affront their luckier fellow-sufferers—unless,as in the case of Bathhouse John,the insane was fully protected by a number of unbeatable gentlemen of his own nationality. The little person was snubbed and affronted at every turn. He didn't care the littlest personal bit,beyond being quietly lonely so far as his big blue expressionless eyes were concerned,and keeping out of the way when fights were on. Which fights he sometimes caught himself enjoying,whereupon he would go sit under a very small apple-tree and ruminate thoroughly upon non-existence until he had sufficiently punished himself. I still don't see how the gouvernement français decided to need him at La Ferté,unless—ah! that's it...he was really a super-intelligent crook who had robbed the cabinet of the greatest cabinet-minister of the greatest cabinet-minister's cabinet papers,a crime involving the remarkable and demoralizing disclosure that President Poincaré had,the night before,been discovered in an unequal hand to hand battle with a défaitistically minded bed-bug...and all the apparent idiocy of the little man with the Orange Cap was a skillfully executed bluff...and probably he was,even when I knew him,gathering evidence of a nature so derogatory as to be well-nigh unpublishable even by the disgusting Défaitiste Organ Itself;evidence about the inno-cent and faithful plantons...yes,now I remember,I asked him in French if it wasn't a fine day(because,as always,it was rain-ing,and he and I alone had dared the promenade together)and he looked me straight in the eyes,and said WOO,and smiled shyly. That would seem to corroborate the theory that he was a master mind,for(obviously)the letters W,O,O,stand for Wil-helm,Ober,Olles,which again is Austrian for Down With Yale. Yes,yes. Le gouvernement français was right,as always. Some-body once told me that the little person was an Austrian,and that The Silent Man was an Austrian,and that—whisper it—they were both Austrians! And that was why they were arrested;just as so-and-so(being a Turk)was naturally arrested,and so-and-so,a Pole,was inevitable naturally and of course(en temps de guerre)arrested. And me,an American;wasn't me arrested? I said Me certainly was,and Me's friend,too.

Once I did see the Orange Cap walk shyly up to The Silent Man. They looked at each other,both highly embarrassed,both perhaps conscious that they ought to say something Austrian to each other. The Silent Man looked away. The little person's face became vacant and lonely,and he tip-toed quietly back to his apple-tree.

"So-and-so,being a Turk" moved in one night,paillasse and all—having arrived from Paris on a very late train,heav-ily guarded by three gendarmes—to a vacant spot temporarily which separated my bed from the next bed on my right. Of the five definite and confirmed amusements which were established at La Ferté—to wit(1)spitting(2)playing cards(3)insulting plan-tons(4)writing the girls,and(5)fighting—I possessed a slight aptitude for the first only. By long practice, leaning with various more accomplished artists from a window and attempting to hit either the sentinel below or a projecting window-ledge or a spot of mud which, after refined and difficult intellectual exercise, we all had succeeded in agreeing upon, I had become not to be sure a master of the art of spitting but a competitor to be reckoned with so far as accuracy was concerned. Spitting in bed was not only amusing, it was—for climatic and other reasons—a necessity. The vacant place to my right made a very agreeable not to say convenient spittoon. Not everyone, in fact only two or three, had my advantage. But everyone had to spit at night. As I lay in bed, having for the third time spit into my spittoon, I was roused by a vision in neatly pressed pajamas which had arisen from the darkness directly beside me. I sat up and confronted a small and as nearly as I could make out Jewish ghost, with sensitive eyes and an expression of mild protest centred in his talking cheeks. The language, said I, is Arabian—but who ever heard of an Arabian in pajamas? So I humbly apologized in French, explaining that his advent was to me as unexpected as it was pleasant. Next morning we exchanged the visiting-cards which prisoners use, that is to say he smoked one of my cigarettes and I one of his, and I learned that he was a Turk whose brother worked in Paris for a confectioner. With a very graceful and polite address he sought in his not over-copious baggage and produced, to my delight and astonishment, the most delicious sweet-meats which I have ever sampled. His generosity was as striking as his refinement. We were fast friends in fifteen minutes. Of an evening, subsequently, he would sit on B's bed or mine and tell us about how he could not imagine that he could have been arrested; tell it with a restrained wonderment which we found extraordinarily agreeable. He was not at all annoyed when we questioned him about the Arabian Turkish and Persian languages, and when pressed he wrote a little for us with a simplicity and elegance that were truly enchanting. I have spent many contented minutes sitting alone copying certain of these rhythmic fragments. We hinted that he might perhaps sing,at which he merely blushed as if he were remembering(or possibly dreaming of)something distant and too pleasant for utterance.

He was altogether too polite not to have been needed at La Ferté.

In supposing that we needed a professor of dancing the French government made,perhaps,one little mistake—I am so bold as to say this because I recall that the extraordinary being in question was with us only a short while. Whither he went the Lord knows,but he left with great cheerfulness. A vain blond boy of perhaps eighteen in blue velvet corduroy pantaloons,who wore a big sash,and exclaimed to us all in confidence

"Moi,j'suis professeur de danse."

Adding that he held at that minute "vingt diplômes". The Hollanders had no use for him but we rather liked him—as you would like a somewhat absurd peacock who,for some reason,lit upon the sewer in which you were living for the eternal nonce. About him I remember nothing else;save that he talked boxing with an air of bravado and addressed everyone as "mon vieux". When he left,clutching his baggage lightly and a little pale,it was as if our dung-heap were minus a butterfly. I imagine that Monsieur Malvy was fond of collecting butterflies—until he got collected himself. Some day I must visit him,at the Santé or whatever health resort he inhabits,and(introducing myself as one of those whom he sent to La Ferté-Macé)question him upon the subject.

I had almost forgot The Bear—number two,not to be confused with the seeker of cigarette-ends. A big,shaggy person,a farmer, talked about "mon petit jardin",an anarchist,wrote practically all the time(to the gentle annoyance of The Schoolmaster)at the

queer-legged table;wrote letters(which he read aloud with evi-
dent satisfaction to himself)addressing "my confreres",stimulat-
ing them to even greater efforts,telling them that the time was
ripe,that the world consisted of brothers,etc. I liked The Bear.
He had a sincerity which,if somewhat startlingly uncouth,was
always definitely compelling. His French itself was both uncouth
and startling. I hardly think he was a dangerous bear. Had I been
the French government I should have let him go berrying,as a
bear must and should,to his heart's content. Perhaps I liked him
best for his great awkward way of presenting an idea—he scooped
it out of its environment with a hearty paw in a way which would
have delighted any one save le gouvernement français. He had,
I think,

VIVE LA LIBERTÉ

tattooed in blue and green on his big hairy chest. A fine bear. A
bear whom no twitchings at his muzzle nor any starvation or yet
any beating could ever teach to dance…but then,I am partial to
bears. Of course none of this bear's letters ever got posted—le
Directeur was not that sort of person;nor did this bear ever expect
that they would go elsewhere than into the official waste-basket
of La Ferté,which means that he wrote because he liked to;which
again means that he was essentially an artist—for which reason I
liked him more than a little. He lumbered off one day—I hope to
his brier-patch,and to his children,and to his confreres,and to all
things excellent and livable and highly desirable to a bruin.

The Young Russian and The Barber escaped while I was enjoy-
ing my little visit at Orne. The former was an immensely tall and
very strong boy of nineteen or under;who had come to our society
by way of solitary confinement,bread and water for months,and
other reminders that to err is human,etc. Unlike Harree,whom if

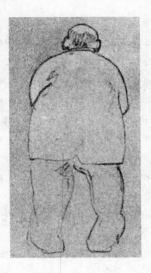

anything he exceeded in strength, he was very quiet. Everyone let him alone. I "caught water" in the town with him several times and found him an excellent companion. He taught me the Russian numerals up to ten, and was very kind to my struggles over 10 and 9. He picked up the cannon-ball one day and threw it so hard that the wall separating the men's cour from the cour des femmes shook, and a piece of stone fell off. At which the cannon-ball was taken away from us (to the grief of its daily wielders, Harree and Fritz) by four perspiring plantons who almost died in the performance of their highly patriotic duty. His friend, The Barber, had a little shelf in The Enormous Room, all tricked out with an astonishing array of bottles atomisers tonics powders scissors, razors and other deadly implements. It has always been a mystère to me that our captors permitted this array of obviously dangerous weapons when we were searched almost weekly for knives. Had I not been in the habit of using B's safety-razor I should probably have become better acquainted with The Barber. It was not his price, nor yet his technique, but the fear of contamination which made me avoid these instruments of hygiene. Not that I shaved to excess. On the contrary,the Surveillant often,nay bi-weekly(so soon as I began drawing certain francs from Norton Harjes)reasoned with me upon the subject of appearance;saying that I was come of a good family,that I had enjoyed(unlike my companions)an education,and that I should keep myself neat and clean and be a shining example to the filthy and ignorant—adding slyly that the "hospital" would be an awfully nice place for me and my friend to live,and that there we could be by ourselves like gentlemen and have our meals served in the room,avoiding the salle à manger;moreover the food would be what we liked,delicious food,especially cooked...all(quoth the Surveillant with the itching palm of a Grand Central Porter awaiting his tip)for a mere trifle or so,which if I liked I could pay him on the spot—whereat I scornfully smiled,being inhibited by a somewhat selfish regard for my own welfare from kicking him through the window. To The Barber's credit be it said:he never once solicited my trade,although the Surveillant's "Soi-même" lectures(as B and I referred to them)were the delight of our numerous friends and must,through them,have reached his alert ears. He was a good-looking quiet man of perhaps thirty,with razor-keen eyes—and that's about all I know of him except that one day The Young Russian and The Barber,instead of passing from the cour directly to the building,made use of a little door in an angle between the stone wall and the kitchen,and that to such good effect that we never saw them again. Nor were the ever-watchful guardians of our safety,the lion-hearted plantons,aware of what had occurred until several hours after;despite the fact that a ten-foot wall had been scaled,some lesser obstructions vanquished,and a run in the open made almost(one unpatriotically-minded might be tempted to say)before their very eyes. But then—who knows? May not the French government deliberately have allowed them

to escape,after—through its incomparable spy system—learning
that The Barber and his young friend were about to attempt the
life of the Surveillant with an atomizer brim-full of T.N.T.? Noth-
ing could after all be more highly probable. As a matter of fact,a
couple of extra-fine razors(presented by the Soi-même-minded
Surveillant.to the wily coiffeur in the interests of public health)as
well as a knife which belonged to the cuisine and had been lent
to The Barber for the purpose of peeling potatoes—he having
complained that the extraordinary safety-device with which,on
alternate days,we were ordinarily furnished for that purpose,was
an insult to himself and his profession—vanished into the rather
thick air of Orne along with The Barber lui-même,I remember
him perfectly in The Enormous Room,cutting apples deliberately
with his knife and sharing them with The Young Russian. The
night of the escape—in order to keep up our morale—we were
helpfully told that both refugees had been snitched ere they had
got well without the limits of the town,and been remanded to
a punishment consisting,among other things,in travaux forcés
à perpetuité—verbum sapientibus,he that hath ears,etc. Also a
nightly inspection was instituted;consisting of our being counted
thrice by a planton,who then divided the total by 3 and vanished.

Soi-même reminds me of a pleasant spirit who graced our lit-
tle company with a good deal of wit and elegance. He was called
by B and myself,after a somewhat exciting incident which I must
not describe but rather outline,by the agreeable title of Même le
Balayeur. Only a few days after my arrival the incident in ques-
tion happened. It seems(I was in la cour promenading for the
afternoon)that certain more virile inhabitants of The Enormous
Room,among them Harree and Pompom bien entendu,declined
se promener and kept their habitat. Now this was in fulfilment of
a little understanding with three or more girls—such as Celina
Lily and Renée—who,having also declined the promenade,man-

aged in the course of the afternoon to escape from their quarters on the second floor, rush down the hall and upstairs, and gain that landing on which was the only and well-locked door to The Enormous Room. The next act of this little comedy (or tragedy, as it proved for the participants, who got cabinet and pain sec—male and female alike—for numerous days thereafter) might well be entitled "Love will find a way." Just how the door was opened, the lock picked, etc., from the inside is (of course) a considerable mystery to anyone possessing a limited acquaintance with the art of burglary. Anyway it was accomplished, and that in several fifths of a second. Now let the curtain fall, and the reader be satisfied with the significant word "Asbestos" which is part of all first-rate performances.

The Surveillant, I fear, distrusted his balayeur. Balayeurs were always being changed because balayeurs were (in shameful contrast to plantons) invariably human beings. For this deplorable reason they inevitably carried notes to and fro between les hommes and les femmes. Upon which ground the balayeur in this case—a well-knit keen-eyed agile man, with a sense of humor and sharp perception of men women and things in particular and in

general—was called before the bar of an impromptu court, held by M. le Surveillant in The Enormous Room after the promenade. I shall not enter in detail into the nature of the charges pressed in certain cases, but confine myself to quoting the close of a peroration which would have done Demosthenes credit:

"Même le balayeur a tiré un coup!"

The individual in question mildly deprecated M. le Surveillant's opinion, while the audience roared and rocked with laughter of a somewhat ferocious sort. I have rarely seen the Surveillant so pleased with himself as after producing this bon mot. Only fear of his superior, the ogrelike Directeur, kept him from letting off entirely all concerned in what after all (from the European point of view) was an essentially human proceeding. As nobody could prove anything about Même, he was not locked up in a dungeon; but he lost his job of sweeper—which was quite as bad, I am sure, from his point of view—and from that day became a common inhabitant of The Enormous Room like any of the rest of us.

His successor, Garibaldi, was a corker.

How the Almighty French Government in its Almighty Wisdom ever found Garibaldi a place among us is more than I understand or ever will. He was a little tot in a faded blue-grey French uniform; and when he perspired he pushed a képi up and back from his worried forehead which a lock of heavy hair threateningly overhung. As I recollect Garibaldi's terribly difficult not to say complicated lineage, his English mother had presented him to his Italian father in the country of France. However this trilogy may be, he had served at various times in the Italian French and English armies. As there was (unless we call Garibaldi Italian, which he obviously was not) nary a subject of King Ponzi or Caruso or whatever be his name residing at La Ferté-Macé, nor yet a suitable citizen of Merry England, Garibaldi was in the habit of expressing himself—chiefly at the card table, be it said—in a curious language which might have been mistaken for French. To B and me he spoke an equally curious language,but a perfectly recognizable one,i.e. Cockney Whitechapel English. He showed us a perfectly authentic mission-card which certified that his family had received a pittance from some charitable organization situated in the Whitechapel neighborhood,and that,moreover,they were in the habit of receiving same pittance;and that,finally,their claim to such pittance was amply justified by the poverty of their circumstances. Beyond this valuable certificate,Garibaldi(which everyone called him)attained great incoherence. He had been wronged. He was always being misunderstood. His life had been a series of mysterious tribulations. I for one have the merest idea that Garibaldi was arrested for the theft of some peculiarly worthless trifle,and sent to the Limbo of La Ferté as a penance. This merest idea is suggested by something which happened when The Clever Man instituted a search for his missing knife—but I must introduce The Clever Man to my reader before describing that rather beguiling incident.

Conceive a tall,well-dressed,rather athletic,carefully kept, clean and neat,intelligent,not for a moment despondent,altogether superior man fairly young(perhaps twenty-nine)and quite bald. He wins enough every night at banque to enable him to pay the less fortunate to perform his corvée d'eau for him. As a consequence he takes his vile coffee in bed every morning,then smokes a cigarette or two lazily,then drops off for a nap,and gets up about the middle of the morning promenade. Upon arising he strops a razor of his own(nobody knows how he gets away with a regular razor),carefully lathers his face and neck—while gazing into a rather classy mirror which hangs night and day over his head,above a little shelf on which he displays at such times a complete toilet outfit—and proceeds to annihilate the inconsiderable growth of beard which his mirror reveals to him. Having completed the annihilation, he performs the most extensive ablutions per one of the three or four pails which The Enormous Room boasts, which pail is by common consent dedicated to his personal and exclusive use. All this time he has been singing loudly and musically the following sumptuously imaginative ditty:

"mEEt me tonIght in DREAmland,
Under the SIL-v'ry mOOn,
Meet me in DREAmland
Sweet dreamy DREAmland
There all my DRE-ams come trUE."

His English accent is excellent. He pronounces his native language, which is the language of the Hollanders, crisply and firmly. He is not given to Gottverdummering. In addition to Dutch and English he speaks French clearly and Belgian distinctly. I daresay he knows half a dozen languages in all. He gives me the impression of a man who would never be at a loss, in whatever circumstances he might find himself. A man capable of extricating himself from the most difficult situation; and that with the greatest ease. A man who bides his time; and improves the present by separating, one after one, his monied fellow-prisoners from their bank-notes. He is, by all odds, the coolest player that I have ever watched. Nothing worries him. If he loses two-hundred francs tonight, I am sure he will win it and fifty in addition tomorrow. He accepts opponents without distinction—the stupid, the wily, the vain, the cautious, the desperate, the hopeless. He had not the slightest pity, not the least fear. In one of my numerous note-books I have this perfectly direct paragraph:

Card table: 4 stares play banque with 2 cigarettes (1 dead) &
A pipe the clashing faces yanked by a leanness of one candle

bottle-stuck(Birth of X)where sits The Clever Man who pyr-
amids,sings(mornings)"Meet Me..."
which specimen of telegraphic technique,being interpreted,
means Judas,Garibaldi,and The Holland Skipper(whom the
reader will meet de suite)—Garibaldi's cigarette having gone out,
so greatly is he absorbed—play banque with four intent and highly
focussed individuals who may or may not be The Schoolmas-
ter,Monsieur Auguste,The Barber,and Même;with The Clever
Man(as nearly always)acting as banker. The candle by whose
somewhat uncorpulent illumination the various physiognomies
are yanked into ferocious unity is stuck into the mouth of a bot-
tle. The lighting of the whole,the rhythmic disposition of the fig-
ures,construct a sensuous integration suggestive of The Birth of
Christ by one of the Old Masters. The Clever Man,having had
his usual morning warble,is extremely quiet. He will win,he
pyramids—and he pyramids because he had the cash and can
afford to make every play a big one. All he needs is the rake of a
croupier to complete his disinterested and wholly nerveless poise.
He is a born gambler,is The Clever Man—and I dare say that to
play cards in time of war constituted a heinous crime and I am
certain that he played cards before he arrived at La Ferté;more-
over,I suppose that to win at cards in time of war is an unut-
terable crime,and I know that he has won at cards before in his
life—so now we have a perfectly good and valid explanation of
the presence of The Clever Man in our midst. The Clever Man's
chief opponent was Judas. It was a real pleasure to us whenever
of an evening Judas sweated and mopped and sweated and lost
more and more and was finally cleaned out.

But The Skipper,I learned from certain prisoners who
escorted the baggage of The Clever Man from The Enormous
Room when he left us one day(as he did for some reason,to enjoy
the benefits of freedom),paid the master-mind of the card table

150 francs at the gare—poor Skipper! upon whose vacant bed lay down luxuriously the Lobster, immediately to be wheeled fiercely all around The Enormous Room by the Garde Champêtre and Judas, to the boisterous plaudits of tout le monde—but I started to tell about the afternoon when the master-mind lost his knife; and tell it I will forthwith. B and I were lying prone upon our respective beds when—presto, a storm arose at the further end of The Enormous Room. We looked, and beheld The Clever Man, thoroughly and efficiently angry, addressing threatening and frightening generally a constantly increasing group of fellow-prisoners. After dismissing with a few sharp linguistic cracks of the whip certain theories which seemed to be advanced by bolder auditors with a view to palliating persuading and tranquilizing his just wrath, he made for the nearest paillasse, turned it topsy-turvy, slit it neatly and suddenly from stem to stern with a jack-knife, banged the hay about, and then went with careful haste through the pitifully minute baggage of the paillasse's owner. Silence fell. No one, least of all the owner, said anything. From this bed The Clever Man turned to the next, treated it in the same fashion, searched it thoroughly, and made for the third.

His motions were those of a perfectly oiled machine. He proceeded up the length of the room, varying his procedure only by sparing an occasional mattress, throwing paillasses about, tumbling sacs and boxes inside out; his face somewhat paler than usual but otherwise immaculate and expressionless. B and I waited with some interest to see what would happen to our belongings. Arriving at our beds he paused, seemed to consider a moment, then, not touching our paillasses proper, proceeded to open our duffle-bags and hunt half-heartedly, remarking that "somebody might have put it in"; and so passed on. "What in hell is the matter with that guy?" I asked of Fritz, who stood near us with a careless air, some scorn and considerable amusement in his eyes. "The bloody fool's lost his knife" was Fritz's answer. After completing his rounds The Clever Man searched almost everyone except ourselves and Fritz, and absolutely subsided on his own paillasse muttering occasionally "if he found it" what he'd do. I think he never did find it. It was a "beautiful" knife, John the Baigneur said. "What did it look like?" I demanded with some curiosity. "It had a naked woman on the handle" Fritz said, his eyes sharp with amusement.

And everyone agreed that it was a great pity that The Clever Man had lost it, and everyone began timidly to restore order and put his personal belongings back in place and say nothing at all.

But what amused me was to see the little tot in a bluish-grey French uniform, who—about when the search approached his paillasse—suddenly hurried over to B(his perspiring forehead more perspiring than usual, his képi set at an angle of insanity)and hurriedly presented B with a long-lost German silver folding camp-knife, purchased by B from a fellow-member of Vingt-et-Un who was known to us as "Lord Algie"—a lanky, effeminate, brittle, spotless creature who was en route to becoming an officer and to whose finicky tastes the fat-jowled A. tirelessly pandered for, doubtless, financial considerations—which knife according to the trembling and altogether miserable Garibaldi had "been found" by him that day in the cour; which was eminently and above all things curious, as the treasure had been lost weeks before.

Which again brings us to The Skipper, whose elaborate couch has already been mentioned—he was a Hollander and one of the strongest most gentle and altogether most pleasant of men, who used to sit on the water-wagon under the shed in the cour and smoke his pipe quietly of an afternoon. His stocky even tightly-knit person, in its heavy trousers and jersey sweater, culminated in a bronzed face which was at once as kind and firm a piece of supernatural work as I think I ever knew. His voice was agreeably modulated. He was utterly without affectation. He had three sons. One evening a number of gendarmes came to his house and told him that he was arrested, "so my three sons and I threw them all out the window into the canal."

I can still see the opening smile, squared kindness of cheeks, eyes like cool keys—his heart always with the Sea.

The little Machine-Fixer(le petit bonhomme avec le bras

cassé as he styled himself,referring to his little paralyzed left arm)was so perfectly different that I must let you see him next. He was slightly taller than Garibaldi,about of a size with Monsieur Auguste. He and Monsieur Auguste together were a fine sight,a sight which made me feel that I came of a race of giants. I am afraid it was more or less as giants that B and I pitied the Machine-Fixer—still this was not really our fault,since the Machine-Fixer came to us with his troubles much as a very minute and helpless child comes to a very large and omnipotent one. And God knows we did not only pity him,we liked him—and if we could in some often ridiculous manner assist the Machine-Fixer I think we nearly always did. The assistance to which I refer was wholly spiritual;since the minute Machine-Fixer's colossal self-pride eliminated any possibility of material assistance. What we did,about every other night,was to entertain him(as we entertained our other friends)chez nous;that is to say,he would come up late every evening or every other evening,after his day's toil—for he worked as co-balayeur with Garibaldi and he was a tremendous worker;never have I seen a man who took his work so seriously and made so much of it—to sit,with great care and very respectfully,upon one or the other of our beds at the upper end of The Enormous Room,and smoke a black small pipe,talking excitedly and strenuously and fiercely about La Misère and himself and ourselves,often crying a little but very bitterly,and from time to time striking matches with a short angry gesture on the sole of his big almost square boot. His little abrupt conscientious relentless difficult self lived always in a single dimension—the somewhat beautiful dimension of Sorrow. He was a Belgian,and one of two Belgians in whom I have ever felt the least or slightest interest;for the Machine-Fixer might have been a Polak or an Idol or an Eskimo so far as his nationality affected his soul. By and large,that was the trouble—the Machine-Fixer had a soul. Put the bracelets on an ordinary man,tell him he's a bad egg,treat him rough,shove him into the jug or its equivalent(you see I have regard always for M. le Surveillant's delicate but no doubt necessary distinction between La Ferté and Prison),and he will become one of three animals—a rabbit,that is to say timid;a mole,that is to say stupid;or a hyena,that is to say Harree the Hollander. But if,by some fatal,some incomparably fatal accident,this man has a soul—ah,then we have and truly have and have most horribly what is called in La Ferté-Macé by those who have known it:La Misère. Monsieur Auguste's valiant attempts at cheerfulness and the natural buoyancy of his gentle disposition in a slight degree protected him from La Misère. The Machine-Fixer was lost. By nature he was tremendously sensible,he was the very apotheosis of l'âme sensible in fact. His sensibilité made him shoulder not only the inexcusable injustice which he had suffered but the incomparable and overwhelming total injustice which everyone had suffered and was suffering en masse day and night in The Enormous Room. His woes,had they not sprung from perfectly real causes,might have suggested a persecution complex. As it happened there was no possible method of relieving them— they could be relieved in only one way:by Liberty. Not simply by his personal liberty,but by the liberation of every single fellow-captive as well. His extraordinarily personal anguish could not be selfishly appeased by a merely partial righting,in his own case,of the Wrong—the ineffable and terrific and to be perfectly avenged Wrong—done to those who ate and slept and wept and played cards within that abominable and unyielding Symbol which enclosed the immutable vileness of our common life. It was necessary,for its appeasement,that a shaft of bright lightning suddenly and entirely should wither the human and material structures which stood always between our filthy and pitiful selves and the unspeakable cleanness of Liberty.

Machine-Fixer

B recalls that the little Machine-Fixer said or hinted that he had been either a socialist or an anarchist when he was young. So that is doubtless why we had the privilege of his society. After all, it is highly improbable that this poor socialist suffered more at the hands of the great and good French government than did many a C.O. at the hands of the great and good American government; or—since all great governments are per se good and vice versa—than did many a man in general who was cursed with a talent for thinking during the warlike moments recently passed; during that is to say an epoch when the g. and g. nations demanded of their respective peoples the exact antithesis to thinking; said antithesis being vulgarly called Belief. Lest which statement prejudice some members of the American Legion in the disfavor of the Machine-Fixer or rather of myself—awful thought—I hasten to assure everyone that the Machine-Fixer was a highly moral person. His morality was at times almost gruesome: as when he got started on the inhabitants of the women's quarters. Be it understood that the Machine-Fixer was human,that he would take a letter—provided he liked the sender—and deliver it to the sender's adorée without a murmur. That was simply a good deed done for a friend;it did not imply that he approved of the friend's choice,which for strictly moral reasons he invariably and to the friend's very face violently deprecated. To this little man of perhaps forty-five,with a devoted wife waiting for him in Belgium(a wife whom he worshipped and loved more than he worshipped and loved anything in the world,a wife whose fidelity to her husband and whose trust and confidence in him echoed in letters which—when we three were alone—the little Machine-Fixer tried always to read to us,never getting beyond the first sentence or two before he broke down and sobbed from his feet to his eyes),to such a little person his reaction to les femmes was more than natural. It was in fact inevitable.

Women,to him at least,were of two kinds and two kinds only. There were les femmes honnêtes and there were les putains. In La Ferté,he informed us—and as balayeur he ought to have known whereof he spoke—there were as many as three ladies of the former variety. One of them he talked with often. She told him her story. She was a Russian,of a very fine education,living peacefully in Paris up to the time that she wrote to her relatives a letter containing the following treasonable sentiment:

"Je m'ennuie pour les neiges de la Russie."

The letter had been read by the French censor,as had B's letter and her arrest and transference from her home in Paris to La Ferté-Macé promptly followed. She was as intelligent as she was virtuous and had nothing to do with her frailer sisters,so the Machine-Fixer informed us with a quickly passing flash of joy. Which sisters(his little forehead knotted itself and his big bushy eyebrows plunged together wrathfully)were wicked and indecent and utterly despicable disgraces to their sex—and this relentless

Joseph fiercely and jerkily related how only the day before he had repulsed the painfully obvious solicitations of a Madame Potiphar by turning his back, like a good Christian, upon temptation and marching out of the room, broom tightly clutched in virtuous hand.

"M'sieu'Jean"(meaning myself)"savez-vous"—with a terrific gesture which consisted in snapping his thumb-nail between his teeth—"ÇA PUE!"

Then he added: And what would my wife say to me, if I came home to her and presented her with that which this creature had presented to me? They are animals—cried the little Machine-Fixer—all they want is a man, they don't care who he is, they want a man. But they won't get me!—and he warned us to beware.

Especially interesting, not to say valuable, was the Machine-Fixer's testimony concerning the more or less regular "inspections"(which were held by the very same doctor who had "examined" me in the course of my first day at La Ferté)for les femmes; presumably in the interests of public safety. Les femmes, quoth the Machine-Fixer, who had been many times an eye-witness of this proceeding, lined up talking and laughing and—crime of crimes—smoking cigarettes, outside the bureau of M. le Médecin Major. "Une femme entre. Elle se lève les jupes jusqu'au menton et se met sur le banc. Le médecin major la regarde. Il dit de suite 'Bon. C'est tout.' Elle sort. Une autre entre. La même chose. 'Bon. C'est fini'...M'sieu'Jean: prenez garde!"

And he struck a match fiercely on the black almost square boot which lived on the end of his little worn trouser-leg, bending his small body forward as he did so, and bringing the flame upward in a violent curve. And the flame settled on his little black pipe. And his cheeks sucked until they must have met, and a slow unwilling noise arose, and with the return of his cheeks a small colourless wisp of possible smoke came upon the air.—

That's not tobacco. Do you know what it is? It's wood! And I sit here smoking wood in my pipe when my wife is sick with worrying..."M'sieu'Jean"—leaning forward with jaw protruding and a oneness of bristly eyebrows,"Ces grands messieurs qui ne se foutent pas mal si l'on CREVE de faim,savez-vous ils croient chacun qu'il est Le Bon Dieu LUI-Même. Et M'sieu'Jean,savez-vous,ils sont tous"—leaning right in my face,the withered hand making a pitiful fist of itself—"Ils. Sont. Des. CRAPULES!"

And his ghastly and toylike wizened and minute arm would try to make a pass at their lofty lives. O Gouvernement Français,I think it was not very clever of You to put this terrible doll in La Ferté;I should have left him in Belgium with his little doll-wife if I had been You;for when Governments are found dead there is always a little doll on top of them,pulling and tweaking with his little hands to get back the microscopic knife which sticks firmly in the quiet meat of their hearts.

One day only did I see him happy or nearly happy—when a Belgian baroness for some reason arrived,and was bowed and fed and wined by the delightfully respectful and perfectly behaved Official Captors—"and I know of her in Belgium,she is a great lady,she is very powerful and she is generous;I fell on my knees before her,and implored her in the name of my wife and Le Bon Dieu to intercede in my behalf;and she made a note of it,and she told me she would write the Belgian King and I will be free in a few weeks,FREE!"

The little Machine-Fixer,I happen to know,did finally leave La Ferté—for Précigné.

...In the kitchen worked a very remarkable person. Who wore sabots. And sang continuously in a very subdued way to himself as he stirred the huge black kettles. We,that is to say B and I,became acquainted with Afrique very gradually. You did not know Afrique suddenly. You became cognizant of Afrique gradually. You were in the cour,staring at ooze and dead trees,when a figure came striding from the cuisine lifting its big wooden feet after it rhythmically,unwinding a parti-coloured scarf from its waist as it came,and singing to itself in a subdued manner a jocular and I fear unprintable ditty concerning Paradise. The figure entered the little gate to the cour in a businesslike way,unwinding continuously,and made stridingly for the cabinet situated up against the stone-wall which separated the promenading sexes—dragging behind it on the ground a tail of ever-increasing dimensions. The cabinet reached,tail and figure parted company;the former fell inert to the limitless mud,the latter disappeared into the contrivance with a Jack-in-the-box rapidity. From which contrivance the continuing ditty

"le paradis est une maison..."

—Or again,it's a lithe pausing poise,intensely intelligent,certainly sensitive,delivering dryingly a series of sure and rapid hints that penetrate the fabric of stupidity accurately and whisperingly;dealing one after another brief and poignant instupidities,distinct and uncompromising,crisp and altogether arrowlike. The poise has a cigarette in its hand,which cigarette it has just pausingly rolled from material furnished by a number of carefully saved butts(whereof Afrique's pockets are invariably full). Its neither old nor young but rather keen face hoards a pair of greyish-blue witty eyes,which face and eyes are directed upon us through the open door of a little room. Which little room is in the rear of the cuisine;a little room filled with the inexpressibly clean and soft odour of newly-cut wood. Which wood we are pretending to split and pile for kindling. As a matter of fact we are enjoying Afrique's conversation,escaping from the bleak and profoundly muddy cour,and(under the watchful auspices of the Cook,who plays sentinel)drinking something approximating coffee with something approximating sugar therein. All this because the Cook thinks we're boches and being the Cook and a boche lui-même is consequently peculiarly concerned for our welfare.

Afrique is talking about les journaux,and to what prodigous pains they go to not tell the truth;or he is telling how a native stole up on him in the night armed with a spear two metres long,once on a time in a certain part of the world;or he is predicting that the Germans will march upon the French by way of Switzerland;or he is teaching us to count and swear in Arabic;or he is having a very good time in the Midi as a tinker,sleeping under a tree outside of a little town...

And le Chef is grunting,without lifting his old eyes from the dissection of an obstreperous cabbage,

"Dépêches-toi,voici le planton"

and we are something like happy. For it is singularly and pleasantly warm in the cuisine. And Afrique's is an alert kind of mind,which has been and seen and observed and penetrated and known—a bit there,somewhat here,chiefly everywhere. Its specialty being politics,in which case Afrique has had the inestimable advantage of observing without being observed—until La Ferté;whereupon Afrique goes on uninterruptedly observing,recognizing that a significant angle of observation has been presented to him gratis. Les journaux and politics in general are topics upon which Afrique can say more,without the slightest fatigue,than a book as big as my two thumbs—

"Mais oui,ils ont cherché de l'eau et puis je leur donne du café"

Monsieur or more properly Mynheer le Chef is expostulating;the planton protesting that we are supposed to be upstairs;Afrique is busily stirring a huge black pot,winking gravely at us and singing softly

"Le Bon Dieu,soûl comme un cochon..."

Now that I have mentioned the pleasures of the kitchen,it is perhaps à propos that I say a word upon the displeasures of Brown Bread. He was a Belgian,and therefore chewed and spat juice night and day from the unutterably stolid face of an overgrown farmer. The only words in English which he was able to articulate were "Me too"—when cigarettes were handed round by somebody who had got some money from somewhere. I hasten to say that the name which we gave him is a contraction of an occult sound,or rather rumbling shout,uttered by the Surveillant when he leaned from a little window which faced the cour and announced the names of those fortunate for whom letters(duly opened,read,and their contents approved by the Secrétaire,alias the weak-eyed biped)had somehow emanated from the mystère of the outer world. The Surveillant,his glasses having tremulously inspected a letter or a carte postale—while all les hommes breathlessly attended,in the mud,upon his slightest murmur—successfully would(to the great disappointment of everyone else)pronounce

"boo-r-OWNbread"

whereat this ten-foot personage would awkwardly advance in his squeaky black puttees,shifting his quid with a violent effort in order to reply simperingly

"Oui,Monsieur le Surveillant."

For the rest,he was perfectly stupid,inclined to be morose,and had friends very much like himself who shared his nationality and whose moroseness and stupidity I do not particularly care to remember. He was a Belgian,and that's all. By which I mean that I am uncharitable enough to not care what happened to him or for what stupid and morose crime he was doing penance at La Ferté under the benignant auspices of the French government.

Just as well perhaps,since my search for causes in this con-
nection has proved futile;a fact which by this time the reader
realizes. Better to have let a sleeping mystère lie,I suppose—or
no I don't,for The Man Who Played Too Late did that very thing
and thereby shrouded the inexplicable in a nimbus of inaccu-
racy. Perhaps because he felt,in his blond hungrily cadaverous
way,that to have been arrested for functioning(as a member of
an orchestra)after closing time in Paris was a humiliation too
obvious to require analysis. Be that as it may,I conclude this
particular group of portraits with his own remark,which frames
them after all rather nicely:

"Everyone is here for something."

CHAPTER SIX

Apollyon

The inhabitants of The Enormous Room whose portraits I have attempted in the preceding chapter were, with one or two exceptions, inhabiting at the time of my arrival. Now the thing which above all things made death worth living and life worth dying at La Ferté-Macé was the kinetic aspect of that institution; the arrivals, singly or in groups, of nouveaux of sundry nationalities whereby our otherwise more or less simple existence was happily complicated, our putrescent placidity shaken by a fortunate violence. Before, however, undertaking this aspect I shall attempt to represent for my own benefit as well as the reader's certain more obvious elements of that stasis which greeted the candidates for disintegration upon their admittance to our select, not to say distinguished, circle. Or: I shall describe, briefly, Apollyon and the instruments of his power, which instruments are three in number: Fear Women and Sunday.

By Apollyon I mean a very definite fiend. A fiend who, secluded in the sumptuous and luxurious privacy of his own personal bureau (which as a rule no one of lesser rank than the Surveillant was allowed, so far as I might observe—and I observed—to enter)compelled to the unimaginable meanness of his will,by means of the three potent instruments in question,all,within the sweating walls of La Ferté,that was once upon a time human. I mean a very complete Apollyon,a Satan whose word is dreadful not because it is painstakingly unjust but because it is incomprehensibly omnipotent. I mean,in short,Monsieur le Directeur.

I shall discuss first of all Monsieur le Directeur's most obvious weapon.

Fear was instilled by three means into the erstwhile human entities whose presence at La Ferté gave Apollyon his job. The three means were:his subordinates,who being one and all fearful of his power directed their energies to but one end—the production in ourselves of a similar emotion;two forms of punishment,which supplied said subordinates with a weapon over any of us who refused to find room for this desolating emotion in his heart of hearts;and,finally,direct contact with his unutterable personality.

Beneath the Demon was the Surveillant. I have already described the Surveillant. I wish to say,however,that in my opinion the Surveillant was the most decent official at La Ferté. I pay him this tribute gladly and honestly. To me,at least,he was kind:to the majority he was inclined to be lenient. I honestly and gladly believed that the Surveillant was incapable of that quality whose innateness,in the case of his superior,rendered that gentleman a(to my mind)perfect representative of the Almighty French Government:I believe that the Surveillant did not enjoy being cruel,that he was not absolutely without pity or understanding. As a personality I therefore pay him my respects. I am myself incapable of caring whether,as a tool of the Devil,he will find the bright fire-light of Hell too warm for him or no.

Beneath the Surveillant were the Secrétaire,Monsieur Richard the Cook,and the plantons. The first I have described sufficiently since he was an obedient and negative—albeit peculiarly responsible—cog in the machine of decomposition. Of Monsieur Richard,whose portrait is included in the account of my first day at La Ferté,I wish to say that he had a very comfortable room of his own filled with primitive and otherwise imposing medicines;the walls of this comfortable room being beauteously adorned by some fifty magazine-covers representing the female form in every imaginable state of undress,said magazine-covers being taken chiefly from such amorous periodicals as Le Sourire and that old stand-by of indecency,La Vie Parisienne. Also Monsieur Richard kept a pot of geraniums upon his window-ledge,which haggard and aged-looking symbol of joy he doubtless(in his spare moments)peculiarly enjoyed watering. The Cook is by this time familiar to my reader. I beg to say that I highly approve of the Cook;exclusive of the fact that the coffee,which went up to The Enormous Room tous les matins,was made every day with same grounds plus a goodly injection of checker-berry—for the simple reason that the Cook had to supply our captors and especially Apollyon with real coffee whereas what he supplied to les hommes made no difference. The same is true of sugar : our morning coffee,in addition to being a water-thin black muddy stinking liquid,contained not the smallest suggestion of sweetness,whereas the coffee which went to the officials—and the coffee which B and I drank in recompense for "catching water"—had all the sugar you could possibly wish for. The poor Cook was fined one day as a result of his economies,subsequent to a united action on the part of the fellow-sufferers. It was a day when a gent immaculately dressed appeared—after duly warning the Fiend that he was about to inspect the Fiend's ménage—an I think public official of Orne. Judas(at the time chef de chambre)supported by the sole and

unique indignation of all his fellow-prisoners save two or three
out of whom Fear had made rabbits or moles,early carried the
pail(which by common agreement not one of us had touched
that day)downstairs,along the hall,and up one flight—where
he encountered the Directeur Surveillant and Handsome
Stranger all amicably and pleasantly conversing. Judas set the
pail down;bowed;and begged,as spokesman for the united
male gender of La Ferté-Macé,that the quality of the coffee
be examined. "We won't any of us drink it,begging your par-
don,Messieurs" he claims that he said. What happened then is
highly amusing. The petit balayeur,an eye-witness of the pro-
ceeding,described it to me as follows:

"The Directeur roared 'COMMENT?' He was horribly
angry. 'Oui,Monsieur' said the maître de chambre humbly—
'Pourquoi?' thundered the Directeur—'Because it's undrink-
able' the maître de chambre said quietly.—'Undrinkable? Non-
sense!' cried the Directeur furiously.—'Be so good as to taste
it,Monsieur le Directeur.'—'I taste it? Why should I taste it? The
coffee is perfectly good,plenty good for you men. This is ridic-
ulous—'—'Why don't we all taste it?' suggested the Surveillant
ingratiatingly.—'Why,yes' said the Visitor mildly.—'Taste it? Of
course not. This is ridiculous and I shall punish—'—'I should
like,if you don't mind,to try a little' the Visitor said.—'Oh
well,of course,if you like' the Directeur mildly agreed. 'Give me
a cup of that coffee,you!'—'With pleasure,sir' said the maître
de chambre. The Directeur—M'sieu'Jean,you would have burst
laughing—seized the cup,lifted it to his lips,swallowed with a
frightful expression(his eyes almost popping out of his head)
and cried fiercely 'DELICIOUS!' The Surveillant took a cup-
ful;sipped;tossed the coffee away,looking as if he had been hit in
the eyes,and remarked 'Ah.' The maître de chambre—M'sieu'Jean
he is clever—scooped the third cupful from the very bottom of

the pail, and very politely, with a big bow, handed it to the Visitor; who took it, touched it to his lips, turned perfectly green, and cried out 'Impossible!' M'sieu'Jean, we all thought—the Directeur and the Surveillant and the maître de chambre and myself—that he was going to vomit. He leaned against the wall a moment, quite green; then recovering said faintly—'The Kitchen.' The Directeur looked very nervous and shouted, trembling all over, 'Yes indeed! We'll see the Cook about this perfectly impossible coffee. I had no idea that my men were getting such coffee. It's abominable! That's what it is, an outrage!'—And they all tottered downstairs to the Cook; and M'sieu'Jean, they searched the kitchen; and what do you think? They found ten pounds of coffee and twelve pounds of sugar all neatly hidden away, that the Cook had been saving for himself out of our allowance. He's a beast, the Cook!"

I must say that, although the morning coffee improved enormously for as much as a week, it descended afterwards to its original level of excellence.

The Cook, I may add, officiated three times a week at a little table to the left as you entered the dining-room. Here he stood and threw at everyone (as everyone entered) a hunk of the most extraordinary viande which I have ever had the priv-

Les Platons

ilege of trying to masticate—it could not be tasted. It was pale and leathery. B and myself often gave ours away in our hungriest moments;which statement sounds as if we were generous to others,whereas the reason for these donations was that we couldn't eat,let alone stand the sight of,this staple of diet. We had to do our donating on the sly since the Chef always gave us choice pieces and we were anxious not to hurt the Chef's feelings. There was a good deal of spasmodic protestation à propos la viande,but the Cook always bullied it down—nor was the meat his fault;since,from the miserable carcasses which I have often seen carried into the kitchen from without,the Cook had to select something which would suit the meticulous stomach of the Lord of Hell,as also the less meticulous digestive organs of his minions;and it was only after every planton had got a piece of viande to his plantonic taste that the captives,female and male,came in for consideration.

On the whole,I think I never envied the Cook his strange and difficult,not to say gruesome,job. With the men en masse he was bound to be unpopular. To the good-will of those above he was necessarily more or less a slave. And on the whole I liked the Cook very much,as did B—for the very good and sufficient reason that he liked us both.

About the plantons I have something to say,something which it gives me huge pleasure to say. I have to say,about the plantons,that as a bunch they struck me at the time and will always impress me as the next to the lowest species of human organism;the lowest,in my experienced estimation,being the gendarme proper. The plantons were,with one exception—he of the black holster with whom I collided on the first day—changed from time to time. Again with this one exception,they were(as I have noted)apparently réformés who were enjoying a vacation from the trenches in the lovely environs of Orne. Nearly all of them were witless. Every one of them had something the matter with him physically as well. For instance, one planton had a large wooden hand. Another was possessed of a long unmanageable left leg made, as nearly as I could discover, of tin. A third had a huge glass eye.

These peculiarities of physique, however, did not inhibit the plantons from certain essential and normal desires. On the contrary. The plantons probably realized that, in competition with the male world at large, their glass legs and tin hands and wooden eyes would not stand a Chinaman's chance of winning the affection and admiration of the fair sex. At any rate they were always on the alert for opportunities to triumph over the admiration and affection of les femmes at La Ferté, where their success was not endangered by competition. They had the bulge on everybody; and they used what bulge they had to such good advantage that one of them, during my stay, was pursued with a revolver by their sergeant, captured, locked up, and shipped off for court-martial on the charge of disobedience and threatening the life of a superior officer. He had been caught with the goods—that is to say, in the girl's cabinot—by said superior: an incapable strutting undersized bepimpled person in a bright uniform who spent his time assuming the poses of a general for the benefit of the ladies; of his admiration for whom and his intentions toward whom he made no secret. By all means one of the most disagreeable petty bullies whom I ever beheld. This arrest of a planton was, so long as I inhabited La Ferté, the only case in which abuse of the weaker sex was punished. That attempts at abuse were frequent I know from allusions and direct statements made in the letters which passed by way of the balayeur from the girls to their captive admirers. I might say that the senders of these letters, whom I shall attempt to portray presently, have my unmitigated and unqualified admiration. By all odds they possessed the most terrible vitality and bravery of any human beings,women or men,whom it has ever been my extraordinary luck to encounter,or ever will be(I am absolutely sure)in this world.

The duties of the plantons were those simple and obvious duties which only very stupid persons can perfectly fulfill,namely:to take turns guarding the building and its inhabitants;to not accept bribes,whether in the form of matches cigarettes or conversation,from their prisoners;to accompany any one who went anywhere outside the walls(as did occasionally the balayeurs,to transport baggage;the men who did corvée;and the catchers of water for the Cook,who proceeded as far as the hydrant situated on the outskirts of the town—a momentous distance of perhaps five hundred feet);and finally to obey any and all orders from all and any superiors without thinking. Plantons were supposed—but only supposed—to report any schemes for escaping which they might overhear during their watch upon les femmes et les hommes en promenade. Of course they never overheard any,since the least intelligent of the watched was a paragon of wisdom by comparison with the watchers. B and I had a little ditty about plantons,of which I can quote(unfortunately)only the first line and refrain,

"A planton loved a lady once
(Cabbages and cauliflowers!)"

It was a very fine song. In concluding my remarks upon plantons I must,in justice to my subject,mention the three prime plantonic virtues—they were(1)beauty,as regards face and person and bearing(2)chivalry,as regards women(3)heroism,as regards males.

The somewhat unique and amusing appearance of the plantons rather militated against than served to inculcate Fear—it was therefore not wonderful that they and the desired emotion were supported by two strictly enforced punishments, punishments which were meted out with equal and unflinching severity to both sexes alike. The less undesirable punishment was known as pain sec—which Fritz, shortly after my arrival, got for smashing a windowpane by accident; and which Harree and Pompom, the incorrigibles, were getting most of the time. This punishment consisted in denying to the culprit all nutriment save two stone-hard morsels of dry bread per diem. The culprit's intimate friends, of course, made a point of eating only a portion of their own morsels of soft heavy sour bread (we got two a day, with each soupe) and presenting the culprit with the rest. The common method of getting pain sec was also a simple one—it was for a man to wave shout or make other signs audible or visible to an inhabitant of the women's quarters; and, for a girl, to be seen at her window by the Directeur at any time during the morning and afternoon promenades of the men. The punishment for sending a letter to a girl might possibly be pain sec, but was more often—I pronounce the word even now with a sinking of the heart, though curiously enough I escaped that for which it stands—cabinot.

There were (as already mentioned) a number of cabinots, sometimes referred to as cachots by persons of linguistic propensities. To repeat myself slightly: at least three were situated on the ground floor; and these were used whenever possible in preference to the one or ones upstairs, for the reason that they were naturally more damp and chill and dark and altogether more dismal and unhealthy. Dampness and cold were considerably increased by the substitution, for a floor, of two or three planks resting in mud. I am now describing what my eyes saw, not what was shown to the inspectors on their rare visits to the Directeur's little shop for making criminals. I know what these occasional visitors beheld,because it,too,I have seen with my own eyes: seen the two balayeurs staggering downstairs with a bed(consisting of a high iron frame,a huge mattress of delicious thickness,spotless sheets,warm blankets,and a sort of quilt neatly folded overall);seen this bed placed by the panting sweepers in the thoroughly cleaned and otherwise immaculate cabinot at the foot of the stairs and opposite the cuisine,the well-scrubbed door being left wide open. I saw this done as I was going to dinner. While les hommes were upstairs recovering from la soupe,the gentlemen-inspectors were invited downstairs to look at a specimen of the Directeur's kindness—a kindness which he could not restrain even in the case of those who were guilty of some terrible wrong.(The little Belgian with the Broken Arm,alias the Machine-Fixer,missed not a word nor a gesture of all this;and described the scene to me with an indignation which threatened his sanity.)—Then,while les hommes were in the cour for the afternoon,the balayeurs were rushed to The Enormous Room,which they cleaned to beat the band with the fear of Hell in them;after which,the Directeur led his amiable guests leisurely upstairs and showed them the way the men kept their quarters;kept them without dictation on the part of the officials,so fond were they of what was to them one and all more than a delightful temporary residence—was in fact a home. From The Enormous Room the procession wended a gentle way to the women's quarters(scrubbed and swept in anticipation of their arrival)and so departed;conscious—no doubt—that in the Directeur France had found a rare specimen of whole-hearted and efficient generosity.

Upon being sentenced to cabinot,whether for writing an intercepted letter,fighting,threatening a planton,or committing some minor offense for the nth time,a man took one blanket from his bed,carried it downstairs to the cachot,and disappeared therein for a night or many days and nights as the case might be. Before entering he was thoroughly searched and temporarily deprived of the contents of his pockets,whatever they might include. It was made certain that he had no cigarettes or tobacco in any other form upon his person,and no matches. The door was locked behind him and double and triple locked—to judge by the sound—by a planton,usually the Black Holster,who on such occasions produced a ring of enormous keys suggestive of a burlesque jailor. Within the stone walls of his dungeon(into which a beam of light no bigger than a ten-cent piece,and in some cases no light at all penetrated)the culprit could shout and scream his or her heart out if he or she liked,without serious annoyance to His Majesty King Satan. I wonder how many times,en route to la soupe or The Enormous Room or promenade,I have heard the unearthly smouldering laughter of girls or of men entombed within the drooling greenish walls of La Ferté-Macé. A dozen times,I suppose,I have seen a friend of the entombed stoop adroitly and shove a cigarette or a morceau of chocolat under the door,to the girls or the men or the girl or man screaming,shouting,and pommelling faintly behind that very door—but,you would say by the sound,a good part of a mile away...Ah well,more of this later,when we come to les femmes on their own account.

The third method employed to throw Fear into the minds of his captives lay,as I have said,in the sight of the Captor Himself. And this was by far the most efficient method.

He loved to suddenly dash upon the girls when they were carrying their slops along the hall and downstairs,as(in common with the men)they had to do at least twice every morning and twice every afternoon. The corvée of girls and men were of course arranged so as not to coincide;yet somehow or other they managed to coincide on the average about once a week,or if not coincide,at any rate approach coincidence. On such occasions,as often as not under the planton's very stupid nose,a kiss or an embrace would be stolen—provocative of much fierce laughter and some scurrying. Or else,while the moneyed captives(including B and Cummings)were waiting their turn to enter the bureau de M. le Gestionnaire,or even were ascending the stairs with a planton behind them,en route to Mecca,along the hall would come five or six women staggering and carrying huge pails full to the brim of everyone knew what;five or six heads lowered,ill-dressed bodies tense with effort,free arms rigidly extended from the shoulder downward and outward in a plane at right angles to their difficult progress and thereby helping to balance the disconcerting load—all embarrassed,some humiliated,others desperately at ease—along they would come under the steady sensual gaze of the men,under a gaze which seemed to eat them alive...and then one of them would laugh with the laughter which is neither pitiful nor terrible,but horrible...

And BANG! would a door fly open,and ROAR! a well-dressed animal about five feet six inches in height,with prominent cuffs and a sportive tie,the altogether decently and neatly clothed thick-built figure squirming from top to toe with anger,the large-head trembling and whitefaced beneath a flourishing mane of coarse blackish bristly perhaps hair,the arm crooked at the elbow and shaking a huge fist of pinkish well-manicured flesh,the distinct cruel brightish eyes sprouting from their sockets under bushily enormous black eyebrows,the big weak coarse mouth extended almost from ear to ear and spouting invective,the soggy brutal lips clinched upward and backward showing the huge horse-like teeth to the frothshot gums—

And I saw once a little girl eleven years old scream in terror and drop her pail of slops,spilling most of it on her feet;and seize it in a clutch of frail child's fingers,and stagger,sobbing and

shaking,past the Fiend—one hand held over her contorted face to shield her from the Awful Thing of Things—to the head of the stairs;where she collapsed,and was half-carried half-dragged by one of the older ones to the floor below while another older one picked up her pail and lugged this and her own hurriedly downward.

And after the last head had disappeared,Monsieur le Directeur continued to rave and shake and tremble for as much as ten seconds,his shoe-brush mane crinkling with black anger—then,turning suddenly upon les hommes(who cowered up against the wall as men cower up against a material thing in the presence of the supernatural)he roared and shook his pinkish fist at us till the gold stud in his immaculate cuff walked out upon the wad of clenching flesh:

"ET VOUS—PRENEZ GARDE—SI JE VOUS ATTRAPE AVEC LES FEMMES UNE AUTRE FOIS JE VOUS FOUS AU CABINOT POUR QUINZE, JOURS, TOUS—TOUS—"

for as much as half a minute;then turning suddenly his round-shouldered big back he adjusted his cuffs,muttering PROSTI-TUTES and WHORES and DIRTY FILTH OF WOMEN, crammed his big fists into his trousers,pulled in his chin till his

fattish jowl rippled along the square jaws,panted,grunted,very completely satisfied,very contented,rather proud of himself,took a strutting stride or two in his expensive shiny boots,and shot all at once through the open door which he SLAMMED after him.

A propos the particular incident described for purposes of illustration,I wish to state that I believe in miracles:the miracle being that I did not knock the spit-covered mouthful of teeth and jabbering brutish outthrust jowl(which certainly were not far-ther than eighteen inches from me)through the bullneck bulging in its spotless collar. For there are times when one almost decides not to merely observe...besides which,never in my life before had I wanted to kill to thoroughly extinguish and to entirely murder. Perhaps some day. Unto God I hope so.

Amen.

Now I will try to give the reader a glimpse of the Women of La Ferté-Macé.

The little Machine-Fixer,as I said in the preceding chap-ter,divided them into Good and Bad. He said there were as much as three Good ones,of which three he had talked to one and knew her story. Another of the three Good Women obvi-ously was Margherite—a big,strong female who did wash-ing,and who was a permanent resident because she had been careless enough to be born of German parents. I think I spoke with number three on the day I waited to be examined by the Commission—a Belgian girl,whom I shall mention later along with that incident. Whereat,by process of elimination,we arrive at les putains,whereof God may know how many there were at La Ferté,but I certainly do not. To les putains in general I have already made my deep and sincere bow. I should like to speak here of four individuals. They are Celina,Lena,Lily,Renée.

Celina Tek was an extraordinary beautiful animal. Her firm girl's body emanated a supreme vitality. It was neither tall nor short,its movements neither graceful nor awkward. It came and went with a certain sexual velocity,a velocity whose health and vigour made everyone in La Ferté seem puny and old. Her deep sensual voice had a coarse richness. Her face,dark and young,annihilated easily the ancient and greyish walls. Her wonderful hair was shockingly black. Her perfect teeth,when she smiled,reminded you of an animal. The cult of Isis never worshipped a more deep luxurious smile. This face,framed in the night of its hair,seemed(as it moved at the window overlooking the cour des femmes)inexorably and colossally young. The body was absolutely and fearlessly alive. In the impeccable and altogether admirable desolation of La Ferté and the Normandy Autumn Celina,easily and fiercely moving,was a kinesis.

The French government must have already recognized this;it called her incorrigible.

Lena,also a Belgian,always and fortunately just missed being a type which in the American language(sometimes called "Slang")has a definite nomenclature. Lena had the makings of an ordinary broad. And yet,thanks to La Misère,a certain indubitable personality became gradually rescued. A tall hard face about which was loosely pitched some haycoloured hair. Strenuous and mutilated hands. A loose,raucous way of laughing,which contrasted well with Celina's definite gurgling titter. Energy rather than vitality. A certain power and roughness about her laughter. She never smiled. She laughed loudly and obscenely and always. A woman.

Lily was a German girl,who looked unbelievably old,wore white or once white dresses,had a sort of drawling scream in her throat besides a thick deadly cough,and floundered leanly under the eyes of men. Upon the skinny neck of Lily a face had been set for all the world to look upon and be afraid. The face itself was made of flesh green and almost putrescent. In each cheek a bloody spot. Which was not rouge, but the flower which consumption plants in the cheek of its favorite. A face vulgar and vast and heavy-featured, about which a smile was always slopping uselessly. Occasionally Lily grinned, showing several monstrously decayed and perfectly yellow teeth, which teeth usually were smoking a cigarette. Her bluish hands were very interestingly dead; the fingers were nervous, they lived in cringing bags of freckled skin, they might almost be alive.

She was perhaps eighteen years old.

Renée, the fourth member of the circle, was always well-dressed and somehow chic. Her silhouette had character, from the waved coiffure to the enormously high heels. Had Renée been able to restrain a perfectly toothless smile she might possibly have passed for a jeune gonzesse. She was not. The smile was ample and black. You saw through it into the back of her neck. You felt as if her life was in danger when she smiled, as it probably was. Her skin was not particularly tired. But Renée was old, older than Lena by several years; perhaps twenty-five, which for a lady of her profession is very old. Also about Renée there was a certain dangerous fragility, the fragility of unhealthy. And yet Renée was hard, immeasurably hard. And accurate. Her exact movements were the movements of a mechanism. Including her voice, which had a purely mechanical timbre. She could do two things with this voice and two only—screech and boom. At times she tried to chuckle and almost fell apart. Renée was in fact dead. In looking at her for the first time, I realized that there may be something stylish about death.

This first time was interesting in the extreme. It was Lily's birthday. We looked out of the windows which composed one side of the otherwise windowless Enormous Room; looked down, and saw—just outside the wall of the building—Celina Lena Lily and a new girl who was Renée. They were all individually intoxicated.

Celina was joyously tight. Renée was stiffly bunnied. Lena was raucously pickled. Lily,floundering and staggering and tumbling and whirling,was utterly soused. She was all tricked out in an erstwhile dainty dress,white,and with ribbons. Celina(as always)wore black. Lena had on a rather heavy striped sweater and skirt. Renée was immaculate in tightfitting satin or something of the sort;she seemed to have somehow escaped from a doll's house overnight. About the group were a number of plantons,roaring with laughter,teasing,insulting,encouraging,from time to time attempting to embrace the ladies. Celina gave one of them a terrific box on the ear. The mirth of the others was redoubled. Lily spun about and fell down,moaning and coughing,and screaming about her fiancé in Belgium:what a handsome young fellow he was,how he had promised to marry her ...shouts of enjoyment from the plantons. Lena had to sit down or else fall down,so she sat down with a good deal of dignity,her back against the wall,and in that position attempted to execute a kind of dance. Les plantons rocked and applauded. Celina smiled beautifully at the men who were staring from every window of The Enormous Room and,with a supreme effort,went over and dragged Renée(who had neatly and accurately folded up with machinelike rapidity in the mud)through the doorway and into the house. Eventually Lena followed her example,capturing Lily en route. The scene must have consumed all of twenty minutes. The plantons were so mirth-stricken that they had to sit down and rest under the washing-shed. Of all the inhabitants of The Enormous Room,Fritz and Harree and Pompom and Bathhouse John enjoyed it most. I should include Jan,whose chin nearly rested on the window-sill with the little body belonging to it fluttering in an ugly interested way all the time. That Bathhouse John's interest was largely cynical is evidenced by the remarks which he threw out between spittings—"Une section mesdames!" "A la gare!" "Aux armes tout le monde!" etc. With the exception of these enthusiastic watchers, the other captives evidenced vague amusement—excepting Count Bragard who said with lofty disgust that it was "no better than a bloody knocking 'ouse, Mr. Cummings" and Monsieur Pet-airs whose annoyance amounted to agony. Of course these twain were, comparatively speaking, old men...

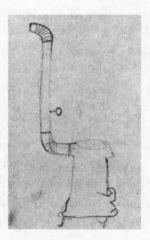

Le Poêle

The four female incorrigibles encountered less difficulty in attaining cabinot than any four specimens of incorrigibility among les hommes. Not only were they placed in dungeon vile with a frequency which amounted to continuity; their sentences were far more severe than those handed out to the men. Up to the time of my little visit to La Ferté I had innocently supposed that in referring to women as "the weaker sex" a man was strictly within his rights. La Ferté, if it did nothing else for my intelligence, rid it of this overpowering error. I recall, for example, a period of sixteen days and nights spent (during my stay) by the woman Lena in the cabinot. It was either toward the latter part of October or the early part of November that this occurred, I will not be sure

which. The dampness of the autumn was as terrible,under nor-
mal conditions—that is to say in The Enormous Room—as any
climatic eccentricity which I have ever experienced. We had a
wood-burning stove in the middle of the room,which antiquated
apparatus was kept going all day to the vast discomfort of eyes
and noses not to mention throats and lungs—the pungent smoke
filling the room with an atmosphere next to unbreathable,but
tolerated for the simple reason that it stood between ourselves
and death. For even with the stove going full blast the walls never
ceased to sweat and even trickle,so overpowering was the damp-
ness. By night the chill was to myself—fortunately bedded at least
eighteen inches from the floor and sleeping in my clothes;bed-
roll,blankets,and all,under and over me and around me—not
merely perceptible but desolating. Once my bed broke,and I
spent the night perforce on the floor with only my paillasse under
me;to awake finally in the whitish dawn perfectly helpless with
rheumatism. Yet with the exception of my bed and B's bed and
a wooden bunk which belonged to Bathhouse John,every pail-
lasse lay directly on the floor;moreover the men who slept thus
were three-quarters of them miserably clad,nor had they any-
thing beyond their light-weight blankets—whereas I had a com-
plete outfit including a big fur coat,which I had taken with me(as
previously described)from the Section Sanitaire. The morning
after my night spent on the floor I pondered,having nothing
to do and being unable to move,upon the subject of my phys-
ical endurance—wondering just how the men about me,many
of them beyond middle age,some extremely delicate,in all not
more than five or six as rugged constitutionally as myself,lived
through the nights in The Enormous Room. Also I recollected
glancing through an open door into the women's quarters,at the
risk of being noticed by the planton in whose charge I was at the
time(who,fortunately,was stupid even for a planton,else I should

have been well punished for my curiosity)and beholding pail-
lasses identical in all respects with ours reposing on the floor;and
I thought,if it is marvellous that old men and sick men can stand
this and not die,it is certainly miraculous that girls of eleven
and fifteen,and the baby which I saw once being caressed out in
the women's cour with unspeakable gentleness by a little putain
whose name I do not know,and the dozen or so oldish females
whom I have often seen on promenade—can stand this and not
die. These things I mention not to excite the reader's pity nor yet
his indignation;I mention them because I do not know of any
other way to indicate—it is no more than indicating—the signif-
icance of the torture perpetrated under the Directeur's direction
in the case of the girl Lena. If incidentally it throws light on the
personality of the torturer I shall be gratified.

Lena's confinement in the cabinot—which dungeon I have
already attempted to describe but to whose filth and slime no
words can begin to do justice—was in this case solitary. Once
a day,of an afternoon and always at the time when all the men
were upstairs after the second promenade(which gave the
writer of this history an exquisite chance to see an atrocity at
first-hand),Lena was taken out of the cabinot by three plantons
and permitted a half-hour promenade just outside the door of
the building,or in the same locality—delimited by barbed-wire
on one side and the washing-shed on another—made famous by
the scene of inebriety above described. Punctually at the expi-
ration of thirty minutes she was shoved back into the cabinot
by the plantons. Every day for sixteen days I saw her;noted the
indestructible bravado of her gait and carriage,the unchanging
timbre of her terrible laughter in response to the salutation of
an inhabitant of The Enormous Room(for there were at least six
men who spoke to her daily,and took their pain sec and their
cabinot in punishment therefor with the pride of a soldier who

takes the médaille militaire in recompense for his valor);noted the increasing pallor of her flesh;watched the skin gradually assume a distinct greenish tint(a greenishness which I cannot describe save that it suggested putrefaction);heard the coughing to which she had been always subject grow thicker and deeper till it doubled her up every few minutes,creasing her body as you crease a piece of paper with your thumb-nail,preparatory to tearing it in two—and I realized fully and irrevocably and for perhaps the first time the meaning of civilization. And I realized that it was true—as I had previously only suspected it to be true—that in finding us unworthy of helping to carry forward the banner of progress,alias the tricolour,the inimitable and excellent French government was conferring upon B and myself—albeit with other intent—the ultimate compliment.

And the Machine-Fixer,whose opinion of this blond putain grew and increased and soared with every day of her martyrdom till the Machine-Fixer's former classification of les femmes exploded and disappeared entirely—the Machine-Fixer who would have fallen on his little knees to Lena had she given him a chance,and kissed the hem of her striped skirt in an ecstasy of adoration—told me that Lena on being finally released walked upstairs herself,holding hard to the banister without a look for anyone,"having eyes as big as tea-cups." He added,with tears in his own eyes

"M'sieu'Jean,a woman."

I recall perfectly being in the kitchen one day,hiding from the eagle-eye of the Black Holster and enjoying a talk on the economic consequences of war,said talk being delivered by Afrique. As a matter of fact,I was not in the cuisine proper but in the little room which I have mentioned previously. The door into the cuisine was shut. The sweetly soft odour of newly-cut wood was around me. And all the time that Afrique was talking I heard clearly,through the shut door and through the kitchen wall and through the locked door of the cabinot situated directly across the hall from la cuisine,the insane gasping voice of a girl singing and yelling and screeching and laughing. Finally I interrupted my speaker to ask what on earth was the matter in the cabinot?—"C'est la femme allemande qui s'appelle Lily" Afrique briefly answered. A little later BANG went the cabinot door,and ROAR went the familiar coarse voice of the Directeur. It disturbs him,the noise,Afrique said. The cabinot door slammed. There was silence. Heavily steps ascended. Then the song began again,a little more insane than before;the laughter a little wilder...You can't stop her,Afrique said admiringly. A great voice Mademoiselle has,eh? So,as I was saying,the national debt being conditioned—

But the experience,à propos les femmes,which meant and will always mean more to me than any other,the scene which is a little more unbelievable than perhaps any scene that it has ever been my privilege to witness,the incident which(possibly more than any other)revealed to me those unspeakable foundations upon which are builded with infinite care such at once ornate and comfortable structures as La Gloire and Le Patriotisme— occurred in this wise.

Les hommes,myself among them,were leaving la cour for The Enormous Room under the watchful eye(as always)of a planton. As we defiled through the little gate in the barbed-wire fence we heard,apparently just inside the building whither we were pro- ceeding on our way to The Great Upstairs,a tremendous sound of mingled screams curses and crashings. The planton of the day was not only stupid—he was a little deaf;to his ears this hideous racket had not,as nearly as one could see,penetrated. At all events he marched us along toward the door with utmost plantonic sat- isfaction and composure. I managed to insert myself in the fore of the procession,being eager to witness the scene within;and reached the door almost simultaneously with Fritz Harree and two or three others. I forget which of us opened it. I will never forget what I saw as I crossed the threshold.

The hall was filled with stifling smoke;the smoke which straw makes when it is set on fire,a peculiarly nauseous choking whitish-blue smoke. This smoke was so dense that only after some moments could I make out,with bleeding eyes and wounded lungs,anything whatever. What I saw was this:five or six plantons were engaged in carrying out of the nearest cabinot two girls,who looked perfectly dead. Their bodies were absolutely limp. Their hands dragged foolishly along the floor as they were carried. Their upward white faces dangled loosely upon their necks. Their crumpled figures sagged in the plantons' arms. I recognized Lily and Renée. Lena I made out at a little distance tottering against the door of the cuisine opposite the cabinot,her haycoloured head drooping and swaying slowly upon the open breast of her shirt-waist,her legs far apart and propping with difficulty her hinging body,her hands spasmodically searching for the knob of the door. The smoke proceeded from the open cabinot in great ponderous murdering clouds. In one of these clouds,erect and tense and beautiful as an angel—her wildly shouting face framed in its huge night of dishevelled hair,her deep sexual voice,hoarsely strident above the din and smoke,shouting fiercely through the darkness—stood,triumphantly and colossally young,Celina. Facing her,its clenched pinkish fists raised high above its savagely bristling head in a big brutal gesture of impotence and rage and anguish—the Fiend Himself paused,quivering,on the fourth stair from the bottom of the flight leading to the women's quarters. Through the smoke the great bright voice of Celina rose at him,hoarse and rich and sudden and intensely luxurious,a quick throaty accurate slaying deepness:

CHIEZ,SI VOUS VOULEZ,CHIEZ

and over and beneath and around the voice I saw frightened faces of women hanging in the smoke,some screaming with their lips apart and their eyes closed,some staring with wide eyes;and among the women's faces I discovered the large placid interested expression of the Gestionnaire and the nervous clicking eyes of the Surveillant. And there was a shout—it was the Black Holster shouting at us as we stood transfixed—

"Who the devil brought les hommes in here? Get up with you where you belong,you..."

—And he made a rush at us,and we dodged in the smoke and passed slowly up the hall,looking behind us,speechless to a man with the admiration of Terror,till we reached the further flight of stairs;and mounted slowly with the din falling below us,ringing in our ears,beating upon our brains—mounted slowly with quickened blood and pale faces—to the peace of The Enormous Room.

I spoke with both balayeurs that night. They told me,independently,the same story:the four incorrigibles had been locked in the cabinot ensemble. They made so much noise,particularly Lily,that the plantons were afraid the Directeur would be disturbed. Accordingly the plantons got together and stuffed the contents of a paillasse in the cracks around the door,and particularly in the crack under the door wherein cigarettes were commonly inserted by friends of the entombed. This process made the cabinot air-tight. But the plantons were not taking any chances on disturbing Monsieur le Directeur. They carefully lighted the paillasse at a number of points and stood back to see the results of their efforts. So soon as the smoke found its way inward the singing was supplanted by coughing;then the coughing stopped. Then nothing was heard. Then Celina began crying out within—"Open the door,Lily and Renée are dead"—and

the plantons were frightened. After some debate they decided
to open the door—out poured the smoke, and in it Celina, whose
voice in a fraction of a second roused everyone in the building.
The Black Holster wrestled with her and tried to knock her down
by a blow on the mouth; but she escaped, bleeding a little, to the
foot of the stairs—simultaneously with the advent of the Direc-
teur who for once had found someone beyond the power of his
weapon—Fear, someone in contact with whose indescribable
Youth the puny threats of death withered between his lips, some-
one finally completely and unutterably Alive whom the Lie upon
his slavering tongue could not kill.

I do not need to say that, as soon as the girls who had fainted
could be brought to, they joined Lena in pain sec for many days
to come; and that Celina was overpowered by six plantons—at
the order of Monsieur le Directeur—and reincarcerated in the
cabinot adjoining that from which she had made her veloci-
tous exit—reincarcerated without food for twenty-four hours.
"Mais, M'sieu' Jean" the Machine-Fixer said trembling, "Vous savez
elle est forte. She gave the six of them a fight, I tell you. And three
of them went to the doctor as a result of their efforts, including le
vieux (the Black Holster). But of course they succeeded in beat-
ing her up, six men upon one woman. She was beaten badly I tell
you before she gave in. M'sieu' Jean, ils sont tous—les plantons
et le Directeur Lui-Même et le Surveillant et le Gestionnaire et
tous—ils sont des—" and he said very nicely what they were, and
lit his little black pipe with a crisp curving upward gesture, and
shook like a blade of grass.

With which specimen of purely mediaeval torture I leave
the subject of Women, and embark upon the quieter if no less
enlightening subject of Sunday.

Sunday, it will be recalled, was Monsieur le Directeur's third
weapon. That is to say: lest the ordinarily tantalizing proxim-

ity of les femmes should not inspire les hommes to deeds which placed the doers automatically in the clutches of himself, his subordinates, and la punition, it was arranged that once a week the tantalizing proximity aforesaid should be supplanted by a positively maddening approach to coincidence. Or in other words, les hommes and les femmes might for an hour or less enjoy the same exceedingly small room; for purposes of course of devotion—it being obvious to Monsieur le Directeur that the representatives of both sexes at La Ferté-Macé were inherently of a strongly devotional nature. And lest the temptation to err in such moments be deprived, through a certain aspect of compulsion, of its complete force, the attendance of such strictly devotional services was made optional.

The uplifting services to which I refer took place in that very room which (the night of my arrival) had yielded me my paillasse under the Surveillant's direction. It may have been thirty feet long and twenty wide. At one end was an altar at the top of several wooden stairs, with a large candle on each side. To the right as you entered a number of benches were placed to accommodate les femmes. Les hommes upon entering took off their caps and stood over against the left wall so as to leave between them and les femmes an alley perhaps five feet wide. In this alley stood the Black Holster with his képi firmly resting upon his head, his arms folded, his eyes spying to left and right in order to intercept any signals exchanged between the sheep and goats. Those who elected to enjoy spiritual things left the cour and their morning promenade after about an hour of promenading, while the materially minded remained to finish the promenade; or if one declined the promenade entirely (as frequently occurred owing to the fact that weather conditions on Sunday were invariably more indescribable than usual) a planton mounted to The Enormous Room and shouted

"La Messe!"

several times;whereat the devotees lined up and were carefully conducted to the scene of spiritual operations.

The priest was changed every week. His assistant(whom I had the indescribable pleasure of seeing only upon Sundays)was always the same. It was his function to pick the priest up when he fell down after tripping upon his robe,to hand him things before he wanted them,to ring a huge bell,to interrupt the peculiarly divine portions of the service with a squeaking of his shoes,to gaze about from time to time upon the worshippers for purposes of intimidation,and finally—most important of all—to blow out the two big candles at the very earliest opportunity,in the interests(doubtless)of economy. As he was a short fattish ancient strangely soggy creature and as his longish black suit was somewhat too big for him,he executed a series of profound efforts in extinguishing the candles. In fact he had to climb part way up the candles before he could get at the flames;at which moment,he looked very much like a weakly and fat boy(for he was obviously in his second or fourth childhood)climbing a flag-pole. At moments of leisure he abased his fatty whitish jowl and contemplated with watery eyes the floor in front of his highly polished boots,having first placed his ugly chubby hands together behind his most ample back.

Dimanche: green murmurs in coldness. Surplice fiercely fearful,praying on his bony both knees,crossing himself...The Fake French Soldier,alias Garibaldi,beside him,a little face filled with terror...the Bell cranks the sharp-nosed curé on his knees...titter from bench of whores—

and that reminds me of a Sunday afternoon on our backs spent with the wholeness of a hill in Chevincourt,discovering a great apple pie,B and Jean Stahl and Maurice le Menuisier and myself;and the sun falling roundly before us.

—And then One Dimanche a new high old man with a sharp violet face and green hair—"Vous êtes libres,mes enfants,de faire l'immortalité—Songez,songez donc—L'Eternité est une existence sans durée—Toujours le Paradis,toujours l'Enfer"(to the silently roaring whores)"Le ciel est fait pour vous"—and the Belgian ten-foot farmer spat three times and wiped them with his foot,his nose dripping;and the nigger shot a white oyster into a far-off scarlet handkerchief—and the Man's strings came untied and he sidled crablike down the steps—the two candles wiggle a strenuous softness...

In another chapter I will tell you about the nigger.

And another Sunday I saw three tiny old females stumble forward,three very formerly and even once bonnets perched upon three wizened skulls,and flop clumsily before the Man,and take the wafer hungrily into their leathery faces.

CHAPTER SEVEN

An Approach to
The Delectable Mountains

"Sunday(says Mr. Pound,with infinite penetration)is a
    dreadful day,
Monday is much pleasanter.
Then let us muse a little space
Upon fond Nature's morbid grace."

It is a great and distinct pleasure to have penetrated and arrived
upon the outside of Le Dimanche. We may now—Nature's mor-
bid grace being a topic whereof the reader has already heard
much and will necessarily hear more—turn to the "much pleas-
anter",the in fact "Monday",aspect of La Ferté;by which I mean
les nouveaux whose arrivals and reactions constituted the actual
or kinetic aspect of our otherwise merely real Nonexistence. So
let us tighten our belts(everyone used to tighten his belt at least
twice a day at La Ferté,but for another reason—to follow and
keep track of his surely shrinking anatomy)seize our staffs into
our hands,and continue the ascent begun with the first pages of
the story.

   One day I found myself expecting La Soupe Number 1 with

something like avidity. My appetite faded,however,upon per-
ceiving a vision en route to the empty place at my left. It slightly
resembled a tall youth not more than sixteen or seventeen years
old,having flaxen hair,a face whose whiteness I have never seen
equalled,and an expression of intense starvation which might
have been well enough in a human being but was somewhat
unnecessarily uncanny in a ghost. The ghost,floatingly and slen-
derly,made for the place beside me,seated himself suddenly and
gently like a morsel of white wind,and regarded the wall before
him. La soupe arrived. He obtained a plate(after some protest
on the part of certain members of our table to whom the advent
of a newcomer meant only that everyone would get less for
lunch),and after gazing at his portion for a second in apparent
wonderment at its size caused it gently and suddenly to disap-
pear. I was no sluggard as a rule,but found myself outclassed by
minutes—which,said I to myself,is not to be worried over since
'tis sheer vanity to compete with the supernatural. But(even
as I lugged the last spoonful of luke-warm greasy water to my
lips)this ghost turned to me for all the world as if I too were a
ghost,and remarked softly

"Voulez-vous me prêter dix sous? Je vais acheter du tabac à la
cantine."

One has no business crossing a spirit,I thought;and produced
the sum cheerfully—which sum disappeared,the ghost arose slen-
derly and soundlessly,and I was left with emptiness beside me.

Later I discovered that this ghost was called Pete.

Pete was a Hollander,and therefore found firm and staunch
friends in Harree John O'The Bathhouse and the other Hollander.
In three days Pete discarded the immateriality which had con-
stituted the exquisite definiteness of his advent,and donned the
garb of flesh-and-blood. This change was due equally to La Soupe
and the canteen,and to the finding of friends. For Pete had been

in solitary confinement for three months and had had nothing to eat but bread and water during that time, having been told by the jailors (as he informed us, without a trace of bitterness) that they would shorten his sentence provided he did not partake of La Soupe during his incarceration—that is to say, le gouvernement français had a little joke at Pete's expense. Also he had known nobody during that time but the five fingers which deposited said bread and water with conscientious regularity on the ground beside him. Being a Hollander neither of these things killed him—on the contrary, he merely turned into a ghost, thereby fooling the excellent French government within an inch of its foolable life. He was a very excellent friend of ours—I refer as usual to B and myself—and from the day of his arrival until the day of his departure to Précigné along with B and three others I never ceased to like and to admire him. He was naturally sensitive, extremely the antithesis of coarse (which "refined" somehow does not imply), had not in the least suffered from a "good", as we say, education, and possessed an at once frank and unobstreperous personality. Very little that had happened to Pete's physique had escaped Pete's mind. This mind of his quietly and firmly had expanded in proportion as its owner's trousers had become too big around the waist—altogether not so extraordinary as was the fact that, after being physically transformed as I have never seen a human being transformed by food and friends, Pete thought and acted with exactly the same quietness and firmness as before. He was a rare spirit, and I salute him where he is.

Mexique was a good friend of Pete's, as he was of ours. He had been introduced to us by a man we called One Eyed David, who was married and had a wife downstairs, with which wife he was allowed to live all day—being conducted to and from her society by a planton. He spoke Spanish well and French passably; had black hair, bright Jewish eyes, a dead-fish expression, and a both amiable and courteous disposition. One Eyed Dah-veed(as it was pronounced of course)had been in prison at Noyon during the German occupation,which he described fully and without hyperbole—stating that no one could have been more considerate or just than the commander of the invading troops. Dah-veed had seen with his own eyes a French girl extend an apple to one of the common soldiers as the German army entered the outskirts of the city:"Prenez,elle dit,vous êtes fatigué.—Madame,répondit le soldat allemand en français,je vous remercie—et il cherchait dans la poche et trouvait dix sous. Non,non,dit la jeune fille,je ne veux pas d'argent;je vous donne de bonne volonté—Pardon,madame,dit le soldat,il vous faut savoir qu'il est défendu pour un soldat allemand de prendre quelque chose sans payer."—And before that,One Eyed Dah-veed had talked at Noyon with a barber whose brother was an aviator with the French army:"Mon frère,me dit le coiffeur,m'a raconté une belle histoire il y a quelques jours. Il volait au-dessus des lignes,et s'étonnait,un jour,de remarquer que les canons français ne tiraient pas sur les boches mais sur les français eux-mêmes. Précipitamment il atterissait,sautait de l'appareil,allait de suite au bureau du général. Il donnait le salut,et criait,bien excité:Mon général,vous tirez sur les français! Le général le regardait sans intérêt,sans bouger,puis il disait tout simplement:On a commencé,il faut finir." Which is why perhaps,said One Eyed Dah-veed,looking two ways at once with his uncorrelated eyes,the Germans entered Noyon...But to return to Mexique.

One night we had a soirée,as Dah-veed called it,à propos a pot of hot tea which Dah-veed's wife had given him to take upstairs,it being damnably damp and cold(as usual)in The Enormous Room. Dah-veed,cautiously and in a low voice,invited us to his paillasse to enjoy this extraordinary pleasure;and we accepted,B and I,with huge joy;and sitting on Dah-veed's paillasse we found somebody who turned out to be Mexique—to whom, by his right name, our host introduced us with all the poise and courtesy vulgarly associated with a French salon.

For Mexique I cherish and always will cherish unmitigated affection. He was perhaps nineteen years old, very chubby, extremely good-natured; and possessed of an unruffled disposition which extended to the most violent and obvious discomforts a subtle and placid illumination. He spoke beautiful Spanish, had been born in Mexico, and was really called Philippe Burgos. He had been in New York. He criticized some one for saying "Yes" to us, one day, stating that no American said "Yes" but "Yuh"; which—whatever the reader may think—is to my mind a very profound observation. In New York he had worked nights as a fireman in some big building or other and slept days, and this method of seeing America he had enjoyed extremely. Mexique had one day taken ship (being curious to see the world) and worked as chauffeur—that is to say in the stoke-hole. He had landed in, I think, Havre; had missed his ship; had inquired something of a gendarme in French (which he spoke not at all, with the exception of a phrase or two like "quelle heure qu'il est?"); had been kindly treated and told that he would be taken to a ship de suite—had boarded a train in the company of two or three kind gendarmes, ridden a prodigious distance, got off the train finally with high hopes, walked a little distance, come in sight of the grey perspiring wall of La Ferté, and—"So, I ask them: Where is the Ship? He point to here and tell me, There is the ship. I say: This is a God Dam Funny Ship"—quoth Mexique, laughing.

Mexique played dominoes with us (B having devised a set from cardboard), strolled The Enormous Room with us, telling of his father and brother in Mexico, of the people, of the customs; and—when we were in the cour—wrote the entire conjugation of tengo in the deep mud with a little stick, squatting and chuckling and explaining. He and his brother had both participated in the revolution which made Carranza president. His description of which affair was utterly delightful.

"Every-body run a-round with guns" Mexique said. "And bye-and-bye no see to shoot everybody,so everybody go home." We asked if he had shot anybody himself. "Sure. I shoot everybody I do'no" Mexique answered laughing. "I t'ink every-body no hit me" he added,regarding his stocky person with great and quiet amusement. When we asked him once what he thought about the war,he replied "I t'ink lotta bullshit" which,upon copious reflection,I decided absolutely expressed my own point of view.

Mexique was generous,incapable of either stupidity or despondency,and mannered as a gentleman is supposed to be. Upon his arrival he wrote almost immediately to the Mexican or is it Spanish consul—"He know my fader in Mexico"—stating in perfect and unambiguous Spanish the facts leading to his arrest;and when I said good-bye to La Misère Mexique was expecting a favorable reply at any moment,as indeed he had been cheerfully expecting for some time. If he reads this history I hope he will not be too angry with me for whatever injustice it does to one of the altogether pleasantest companions I have ever had. My note-books,one in particular,are covered with conjugations which bear witness to Mexique's ineffable good-nature. I also have a somewhat superficial portrait of his back sitting on a bench by the poêle. I wish I had another of Mexique out in le jardin with a man who worked there,who was a Spaniard,and whom the Surveillant had considerately allowed Mexique to assist;with the perfectly correct idea that it would be pleasant for Mexique to talk to someone who could speak Spanish—if not as well as he,Mexique,could,at least passably well. As it is,I must be content to see my very good friend sitting with his hands in his pockets by the stove with Bill the Hollander beside him. And

I hope it was not many days after my departure that Mexique went free. Somehow I feel that he went free...and if I am right, I will only say about Mexique's freedom what I have heard him slowly and placidly say many times concerning not only the troubles which were common property to us all but his own peculiar troubles as well

"That's fine."

The Young Skipper

The Young(or Holland)Skipper—not to be confused with The Skipper whom I have already tried to describe—was a real contribution to our midst. On his own part he contributed his mate—a terribly tall rather round-shouldered individual, of whom I said to myself immediately: By Jove, here's a crook a tough guy and a murderer all in one. Of course I was wrong; I say "of course", since to judge an arrival by the arrival's exterior was(as I discovered in practically every case)equivalent to judging a motor by its horse-power instead of by what it did when confronted by a hill. As it turned out, the mate was a taciturn and very gentle youth who had committed no greater crime than that of being a member of The Young Skipper's crew. That this was far from a crime was proved by The Young Skipper himself,than whom I have never met a jollier more open-hearted and otherwise both generous and genuine man in my life. He wore a collarless shirt gayly striped,a vest and trousers calculated to withstand the ravages of time,a jaunty cap,a big signet ring on his fourth finger,and a pair of seaworthy boots which were the envy and admiration of everyone including myself. He used to sit on an extraordinarily small wooden stool by the stove,thereby exaggerating his almost round five-feet exactly of bone and muscle. The Hollanders,especially John,made a great deal of him. He was ready without being rough,had a pair of frank,good-humoured eyes,a tiny happy nose somewhat uppish and freckled,and large strong hard hands which seemed always rather embarrassed to find themselves on land. He told us confidentially that Pete had run away to sea;that Pete came of a very good family in Holland,who were worried to death about Pete's whereabouts;that Pete was too proud to let them know he had been arrested;and that he,The Young Skipper,if and when he got back to Holland,would make a point of going immediately to Pete's parents and telling them where Pete was,which would make them move earth and heaven for their son's liberty. Of a Sunday,The Young or Holland Skipper got himself up to beat the cars and joined the immaculate Holland Delegation at la messe—being,from the instant of his arrival,assoted upon a fair lady who invariably attended all functions of a religious nature. I must add(for the benefit of the highly moral readers of this chronicle)that this admiration served merely to while away the moments of The Young Skipper's captivity—add that The Young Skipper never seriously deviated from an intense devotion to "my girl" as he called her,whose photograph he always carried over his heart. A large faced and plump person,with apparently a very honest heart of her own—I wish I could say more for her...but then,photographs are always untrustworthy. He told us some very vivid incidents in his voyages,which(the war being on)were accomplished with some danger and a great deal of excitement. I remember how his eyes twinkled when he said his ship passed directly under a huge Zeppelin:"And the fellers waved to us,and we gave 'em a cheer and waved too,and all the fellers in the Zeppelin keeked"—due to which word in particular I conceived a great fondness for The Young Skipper. He told about the multitudinous English deserters in Holland,how "The girls were crazy about 'em,and if a Hollander comes up and asks 'em to go skating with him on the canal they won't,for the English soldiers don't know how to skate"—and later,when the haughty misses had been "left" by their flames,"Up we'd come and give 'em the laugh."...He spoke first-rate English,clear rousing Dutch,some I should say faulty but fluent German,and no French. "This language is too bloody much for me" said The Young Skipper with perfect candor,smiling. "The john-darmz ask me a lotta questions and I say no parlezvous so they take me and my mate"—with a gesture toward the mild and monumental youth by the stove—"and puts us on trains and everywhere and where the Gottverdummer bloody Hell are we all agoing I don't know till we gets here"—at which he laughed heartily. "Thanks" he said when I offered a Scarferlati Jaune,"I'll get some myself tonight at the canteen and pay you back"—for in common with Pete he shared a great conscientiousness in respect to receiving favors. "They're made of bloody dust,these" he said smiling pleasantly after the first inhalation. I asked him what did he carry in way of cargo? "Coal" he replied with great emphasis. And he told me they got it clear from Norway,and that it was a good business bringing it(for the French needed it and would pay anything)—"Provided you can stand the excitement." His utter and absolute contempt for the john-darmz was,to B and myself in particular,considerably more than delightful. "Them fellers with their swords and little "coats capelike" were not to be spoken of in the same breath with a man. As B says, one of the nicest things anyone ever did in La Ferté (I almost said in prison) was done by The Young Skipper one night: who came up to our beds where we were cooking cocoa or rather chocolate (for we sliced up a cake of imitation Menier purchased at the canteen, added water, and heated the ensemble in a tin cup suspended by a truly extraordinary series of wires (B fecit) directly above a common bougie) and said to us, with a sticking of his thumb behind him—"There's a poor feller lying sick over there and I wonder will you give me a bit o'hot chocolate for him, he wouldn't ask for it himself." Naturally we were peculiarly happy to give it—happier when we saw The Young Skipper stride over to the bed of The Silent Man, to whom he spoke very gently and persuadingly in (as I guess) German—happiest, when we saw The Silent Man half-rise from his paillasse and drink, with The Young Skipper standing over him smiling from ear to ear. Anyone who could with utmost ease conquer the irrevocable diffidence of The Silent Man is insusceptible of portraiture. I hereby apologize to The Young Skipper, and wish him well with his girl in Holland, where I hope with all my heart he is. And maybe some day we'll all of us go skating on the canals; and maybe we'll talk about what happens when the dikes break, and about the houses and the flowers and the windmills.

Here let me introduce the Garde Champêtre, whose name I have already taken more or less in vain. A little sharp hungry-looking person who subsequent to being a member of a rural police force (of which membership he seemed rather proud) had served his patrie—otherwise known as La Belgique—in the capacity of motor-cyclist. As he carried dispatches from one end of the line to the other his disagreeably big eyes had absorbed certain peculiarly inspiring details of civilized warfare. He had, at one time, seen a bridge hastily constructed by les alliés over the Yser River, the cadavers of the faithful and the enemy alike being thrown in helter-skelter to make a much needed foundation for the timbers. This little procedure had considerably outraged the Garde Champêtre's sense of decency. The Yser, said he, flowed perfectly red for a long time. "We were all together: Belgians, French, English...we Belgians did not see any good reason for continuing the battle. But we continued. O indeed we continued. Do you know why?"

I said that I was afraid I didn't.

"Because in front of us we had les obus allemands, en arrière les mitrailleuses françaises, toujours les mitrailleuses françaises, mon vieux."

"Je ne comprends pas bien" I said in confusion, recalling all the high-falutin rigmarole which Americans believed—(little martyred Belgium protected by the allies from the inroads of the aggressor etc.)—"why should the French put machine-guns behind you?"

The Garde Champêtre lifted his big empty eyes nervously. The vast hollows in which they lived darkened. His little rather hard face trembled within itself. I thought for a second he was going to throw a fit at my feet—instead of doing which he replied pettishly, in a sunken bright whisper

"To keep us going forward. At times a company would drop its guns and turn to run. Pupupupupupupupup..." his short unlovely arm described gently the swinging of a mitrailleuse..."finish. The Belgian soldiers to left and right of them took the hint. If they did not—pupupupupupupupup...O we went forward. Yes. Vive le patriotisme."

And he rose with a gesture which seemed to brush away these painful trifles from his memory, crossed the end of the room with short rapid steps, and began talking to his best friend

Judas, who was at that moment engaged in training his wobbly mustachios...Toward the close of my visit to La Ferté the Garde Champêtre was really happy for a period of two days—during which time he moved in the society of a rich intelligent mistakenly arrested and completely disagreeable youth in bone spectacles copious hair and spiral puttees, whom B and I named Jo Jo the Lion Faced Boy, thereby partially contenting ourselves. Had the charges against Jo Jo been stronger my tale would have been longer—fortunately for tout le monde they had no basis; and back went Jo Jo to his native Paris, leaving the Garde Champêtre with Judas and attacks of only occasionally interesting despair.

Jo Jo

The reader may suppose that it is about time another Delectable Mountain appeared upon his horizon. Let him keep his eyes wide open, for here one comes...

Whenever our circle was about to be increased, a bell from somewhere afar(as a matter of fact the gate which had admitted my weary self to La Ferté upon a memorable night, as already has

been faithfully recounted)tanged audibly—whereat up jumped
the more strenuous inhabitants of The Enormous Room and
made pell-mell for the common peep-hole,situated at the door
end or nearer end of our habitat and commanding a somewhat
fragmentary view of the gate together with the arrivals,male
and female,whom the bell announced. In one particular case the
watchers appeared almost unduly excited,shouting "four!"—"big
box"—"five gendarmes!" and other incoherencies with a loudness
which predicted great things. As nearly always,I had declined
to participate in the mêlée;and was still lying comfortably on
my bed(thanking God that it had been well and thoroughly
mended by a fellow prisoner whom we called The Frog and Le
Coiffeur—a tremendously keen-eyed man with a large droop-
ing black mustache,whose boon companion,chiefly on account
of his shape and gait,we knew as The Lobster)when the usual
noises attendant upon the unlocking of la porte began with
exceptional violence. I sat up. The door shot open,there was a
moment's pause,a series of grunting remarks uttered by two
rather terrible voices;then in came four nouveaux of a decidedly
interesting appearance. They entered in two ranks of two each.
The front rank was made up of an immensely broad shouldered
hipless and consequently triangular man in blue trousers belted
with a piece of ordinary rope,plus a thick-set ruffianly person-
age the most prominent part of whose accoutrements were a
pair of hideous whiskers. I leaped to my feet and made for the
door,thrilled in spite of myself. By the,in this case,shifty blue
eyes,the pallid hair,the well-knit form of the rope's owner I knew
instantly a Hollander. By the coarse brutal features half-hidden
in the piratical whiskers,as well as by the heavy mean wandering
eyes,I recognized with equal speed a Belgian. Upon its shoulders
the front rank bore a large box,blackish,well-made,obviously
very weighty,which box it set down with a grunt of relief hard by

the cabinet. The rear rank marched behind in a somewhat asymmetrical manner:a young stupid-looking clear-complexioned fellow(obviously a farmer,and having expensive black puttees and a handsome cap with a shiny black leather visor)slightly preceded a tall gliding thinnish unjudgable personage who peeped at everyone quietly and solemnly from beneath the visor of a somewhat large slovenly cloth cap,showing portions of a lean long incognizable face upon which sat or rather drooped a pair of mustachios identical in character with those which are sometimes pictorially attributed to a Chinese dignitary—in other words,the mustachios were exquisitely narrow,homogeneously downward,and made of something like black corn-silk. Behind les nouveaux staggered four paillasses motivated mysteriously by two pair of small legs belonging(as it proved)to Garibaldi and the little Machine-Fixer;who,coincident with the tumbling of the paillasses to the floor,perspiringly emerged to sight.

The first thing the shifty-eyed triangular Hollander did was to exclaim Gottverdummer. The first thing the whiskery Belgian did was to grab his paillasse and stand guard over it. The first thing the youth in the leggings did was to stare helplessly about him,murmuring something whimperingly in Polish. The first thing the fourth nouveau did was pay no attention to anybody;lighting a cigarette in an unhurried manner as he did so,and puffing silently and slowly as if in all the universe nothing whatever save the taste of tobacco existed.

A bevy of Hollanders were by this time about the triangle,asking him all at once Was he from so and so,What was in his box,How long had he been in coming,were on the point of trying the lock—when suddenly with incredible agility the unperturbed smoker shot a yard forward,landing quietly beside them;and exclaimed rapidly and briefly through his nose

"Mang."

He said it almost petulantly,or as a child says "Tag! You're it."

The onlookers recoiled,completely surprised. Whereat the frightened youth in black puttees sidled over and explained with a pathethically at once ingratiating and patronizing accent

"Il n'est pas méchant. C'est un bonhomme. C'est mon ami. Il veut dire que c'est à lui,la caisse. Il parle pas français."

"It's the Gottverdummer Polak's box" said the Triangular Man exploding in Dutch—"They're a pair of Polakers;and this man"(with a twist of his pale blue eyes in the direction of the Bewhiskered One)"and I had to carry it all the Gottverdummer way to this Gottverdummer place."

All this time the incognizable nouveau was smoking slowly and calmly,and looking at nothing at all with his black button-like eyes. Upon his face no faintest suggestion of expression could be discovered by the hungry minds which focused unanimously upon its almost stern contours. The deep furrows in the cardboardlike cheeks(furrows which resembled slightly the gills of some extraordinary fish,some unbreathing fish)moved not an atom. The mustache drooped in something like mechanical tranquility. The lips closed occasionally with a gesture at once abstracted and sensitive upon the lightly and carefully held cigarette;whose curling smoke accentuated the poise of the head,at once alert and uninterested.

Monsieur Auguste broke in,speaking as I thought Russian—and in an instant he and the youth in puttees and the Unknowable's cigarette and the box and the Unknowable had disappeared through the crowd in the direction of Monsieur Auguste's paillasse,which was also the direction of the paillasse belonging to the Cordonnier as he was sometimes called—a diminutive man with immense mustachios of his own who promenaded with Monsieur Auguste,speaking sometimes French and as a general rule Russian or Polish.

Which was my first glimpse,and is the reader's,of the Zulu;he being one of The Delectable Mountains. For which reason I shall have more to say of him later,when I ascend The Delectable Mountains in a separate chapter or chapters;till when the reader must be content with the above however unsatisfactory description....

One of the most utterly repulsive personages whom I have met in my life—perhaps(and on second thought I think certainly)the most utterly repulsive—was shortly after this presented to our midst by the considerate French government. I refer to The Fighting Sheeney. Whether or no he arrived after the Spanish Whoremaster I cannot say. I remember that Bill The Hollander—which was the name of the triangular rope-belted man with shifty blue eyes(co-arrivé with the whiskery Belgian;which Belgian,by the way,from his not to be exaggerated brutal look,B and myself called The Babysnatcher)—upon his arrival told great tales of a Spanish millionaire with whom he had been in prison just previous to his discovery of La Ferté. "He'll be here too in a couple o'days" added Bill The Hollander,who had been fourteen years in These United States,spoke the language to a T,talked about "The America Lakes" and was otherwise amazingly well acquainted with The Land of The Free. And sure enough in less than a week one of the fattest men whom I have ever laid eyes on,over-dressed much beringed and otherwise wealthy-looking,arrived—and was immediately played up to by Judas(who could smell cash almost as far as le gouvernement français could smell sedition)and,to my somewhat surprise,by the utterly respectable Count Bragard. But most emphatically NOT by Mexique,who spent a half-hour talking to the nouveau in his own tongue,then drifted placidly over to our beds and informed us

"You see dat feller over dere,dat fat feller? I speak Spanish to him. He no good. Tell me he make fifty-tousand franc last year runnin' whore-house in"(I think it was)"Brest. Son of bitch!"

Dat fat feller lived in a perfectly huge bed which he contrived to have brought up for him immediately upon his arrival. The bed arrived in a knock-down state and with it a mechanician from la ville who set about putting it together,meanwhile indulging in many glances expressive not merely of interest but of amazement and even fear. I suppose the bed had to be of a special size in order to accommodate the circular millionaire,and being an extraordinary bed required the services of a skilled artisan—at all events,dat fat feller's couch put The Skipper's altogether in the shade. As I watched the process of construction it occurred to me that after all here was the last word in luxury—to call forth from the metropolis not only a special divan but with it a special slave,the Slave of the Bed....Dat fat feller had one of the prisoners perform his corvée for him. Dat fat feller bought enough at the canteen twice every day to stock a transatlantic liner for seven voyages,and never ate with the prisoners. I will mention him again à propos the Mecca of respectability,the Great White Throne of purity,Three rings Three—alias Count Bragard,to whom I have long since introduced my reader.

So we come,willy-nilly,to The Fighting Sheeney.

The Fighting Sheeney arrived carrying the expensive suit-case of a livid strangely unpleasant looking Roumanian gent,who wore a knit sweater of a strangely ugly red hue,impeccable clothes,and an immaculate velour hat which must have been worth easily fifty francs. We called this gent Rockyfeller. His personality might be faintly indicated by the adjective Disagreeable. The porter was a creature whom Ugly does not even slightly describe. There are some specimens of humanity in whose presence one instantly and instinctively feels a profound revulsion,a revulsion which—perhaps because it is profound—cannot be analyzed. The Fighting Sheeney was one of these specimens. His face(or to use the good American idiom,his mug)was exceedingly coarse-featured and had an indefatigable expression of sheer brutality—yet the impression which it gave could not be traced to any particular plane or line. I can and will say,however,that this face was most hideous—perhaps that is the word—when it grinned. When The Fighting Sheeney grinned you felt that he desired to eat you,and was prevented from eating you only by a superior desire to eat everybody at once. He and Rockyfeller came to us from I think it was the Santé;both accompanied B to Précigné. During the weeks which The Fighting Sheeney spent at La Ferté-Macé,the non-existence of the inhabitants of The Enormous Room was rendered something more than miserable. It was rendered well-nigh unbearable.

The night Rockyfeller and his slave arrived was a night to be remembered by everyone. It was one of the wildest and strangest and most perfectly interesting nights I,for one,ever spent. Rockyfeller had been corralled by Judas,and was enjoying a special bed to our right at the upper end of The Enormous Room. At the canteen he had purchased a large number of candles in addition to a great assortment of dainties which he and Judas were busily enjoying—when the planton came up,counted us thrice,divided by three,gave the order "Lumières éteintes",and descended locking the door behind him. Everyone composed himself for miserable sleep. Everyone except Judas,who went on talking to Rockyfeller,and Rockyfeller,who proceeded to light one of his candles and begin a pleasant and conversational evening. The Fighting Sheeney lay stark-naked on a paillasse between me and his lord. The Fighting Sheeney told everyone that to sleep stark-naked was to avoid bugs(whereof everybody including myself had a goodly portion). The Fighting Sheeney was,however,quieted by the planton's order;whereas Rockyfeller continued to talk and munch to his heart's content. This began to get on everybody's nerves. Protests in a number of languages arose from all parts of The Enormous Room. Rockyfeller gave a contemptuous look around him and proceeded with his conversation. A curse emanated from the darkness. Up sprang The Fighting Sheeney,stark-naked;strode over to the bed of the curser,and demanded ferociously

"Boxe? Vous!"

The curser was apparently fast asleep,and even snoring. The Fighting Sheeney turned away disappointed,and had just reached his paillasse when he was greeted by a number of uproariously discourteous remarks uttered in all sorts of tongues. Over he rushed,threatened,received no response,and turned back to his place. Once more ten or twelve voices insulted him from the darkness. Once more The Fighting Sheeney made for them,only to find sleeping innocents. Again he tried to go to bed. Again the shouts arose,this time with redoubled violence and in greatly increased number. The Fighting Sheeney was at his wits' end. He strode about challenging everyone to fight,receiving not the slightest recognition,cursing,reviling,threatening,bullying. The darkness always waited for him to resume his paillasse,then burst out in all sorts of maledictions upon his head and the sacred head of his lord and master. The latter was told to put out his candle,go to sleep,and give the rest a chance to enjoy what pleasure they might in forgetfulness of their woes. Whereupon he appealed to The Sheeney to stop this. The Sheeney(almost weeping)said he had done his best,that everyone was a pig,that nobody would fight,that it was disgusting. Roars of applause. Protests from the less strenuous members of our circle against the noise in general:Let him have his foutue candle,Shut up,Go to sleep yourself,etc. Rockyfeller kept on talking(albeit visibly annoyed by the ill-breeding of his fellow-captives)to the smooth and oily Judas. The noise or rather noises increased. I was for some reason angry at Rockyfeller—I think I had a curious notion that if I couldn't have a light after "lumières éteintes",and if my very good friends were none of them allowed to have one,then by God neither should Rockyfeller. At any rate I passed a few remarks calculated to wither the by this time a little nervous Übermensch;got up,put on some enormous sabots(which I had purchased from a horrid little boy whom the French government had arrested with his parent,for some cause unknown—which horrid little boy told me that he had "found" the sabots "in a train" on the way to La Ferté)shook myself into my fur coat,and banged as noisemakingly as I knew how over to One Eyed Dah-veed's paillasse,where Mexique joined us. "It is useless to sleep" said One Eyed Dah-veed in French and Spanish. "True" I agreed,"therefore let's make all the noise we can."

Steadily the racket bulged in the darkness. Human cries quips and profanity had now given place to wholly inspired imitations of various not to say sundry animals. Afrique exclaimed—with great pleasure I recognized his voice through the impenetrable gloom—

"Agahagahagahagahagah"

—perhaps,said I,he means a machine gun;it sounds like either that or a monkey. The Wanderer crowed beautifully. Monsieur Auguste's bosom friend,le Cordonnier,uttered an astonishing

"meeee-ooooooOW!"

which provoked a tornado of laughter and some applause. Mooings chirpings cacklings—there was a superb hen—neighings he-hawings roarings bleatings growlings quackings peepings screamings bellowings,and—something else,of course—set The Enormous Room suddenly and entirely alive. Never have I imagined such a ménagerie as had magically instated itself within the erstwhile soggy and dismal four walls of our chambre. Even such staid characters as Count Bragard set up a little bawling.

Monsieur Pet-airs uttered a tiny aged crowing, to my immense astonishment and delight. The dying, the sick, the ancient, the mutilated, made their contributions to the common pandemonium. And then, from the lower left darkness, sprouted one of the very finest noises which ever fell on human ears—the noise of a little dog with floppy ears who was tearing after something on very short legs and carrying his very fuzzy tail straight up in the air as he tore; a little dog who was busier than he was wise, louder than he was big; a red-tongued foolish breathless intent little dog with black eyes and a great smile and woolly paws—which noise, conceived and executed by The Lobster, sent The Enormous Room into an absolute and incurable hysteria.

The Fighting Sheeney was at a stand-still. He knew not how to turn. At last he decided to join with the insurgents, and wailed brutally and dismally. That was the last straw: Rockyfeller, who could no longer (even by shouting to Judas) make himself heard, gave up conversation and gazed angrily about him; angrily yet fearfully, as if he expected some of these numerous bears lions tigers and baboons to leap upon him from the darkness. His livid super-disagreeable face trembled with the flickering cadence of the bougie. His lean lips clenched with mortification and wrath. "Vous êtes chef de chambre" he said fiercely to Judas—"why don't you make the men stop this? C'est emmerdant." "Ah" replied Judas smoothly and insinuatingly—"They are only men, and boors at that; you can't expect them to have any manners." A tremendous group of Something Elses greeted this remark together with cries insults groans and linguistic trumpetings. I got up and walked the length of the room to the cabinet (situated as always by this time of night in a pool of urine which was in certain places six inches deep, from which pool my sabots somewhat protected me) and returned, making as loud a clattering as I was able. Suddenly the voice of Monsieur Auguste leaped through the din in an

"Alors! c'est as-sez."

The next thing we knew he had reached the window just below the cabinet(the only window,by the way,not nailed up with good long wire nails for the sake of warmth)and was shouting in a wild high gentle angry voice to the sentinel below—

"Plan-ton! C'est im-possi-ble de dor-mir!"

The Lobster

A great cry "OUI!JE VIENS!" floated up—every single noise dropped—Rockyfeller shot out his hand for the candle,seized it in terror,blew it out as if blowing it out were the last thing he would do in this life—and The Enormous Room hung silent;enormously dark,enormously expectant...

BANG! Open flew the door. "Alors,qui m'appelle? Qu'est-ce qu'on fout ici." And the Black Holster,revolver in hand,flashed his torch into the inky stillness of the chambre. Behind him stood two plantons white with fear;their trembling hands clutching revolvers,the barrels of which shook ludicrously.

"C'est moi,plan-ton!"—Monsieur Auguste explained that no one could sleep because of the noise,and that the noise was because "ce monsieur là" would not extinguish his bougie when everyone wanted to sleep. The Black Holster turned to the room at large and roared: "You children of Merde don't let this happen again or I'll fix you every one of you."—Then he asked if anyone wanted to dispute this assertion(he brandishing his revolver the while)and was answered by peaceful snorings. Then he said by X Y and Z he'd fix the noisemakers in the morning and fix them good—and looked for approbation to his trembling assistants. Then he swore twenty or thirty times for luck,turned,and thundered out on the heels of his fleeing confreres who almost tripped over each other in their haste to escape from The Enormous Room. Never have I seen a greater exhibition of bravery than was afforded by the Black Holster,revolver in hand,holding at bay the snoring and weaponless inhabitants of The Enormous Room. Vive les plantons. He should have been a gendarme.

Of course Rockyfeller,having copiously tipped the officials of La Ferté upon his arrival,received no slightest censure nor any hint of punishment for his deliberate breaking of an established rule—a rule for the breaking of which any one of the common scum(e.g. thank God,myself)would have got cabinot de suite. No indeed. Several of les hommes,however,got pain sec—not because they had been caught in an act of vociferous protestation by the Black Holster,which they had not—but just on principle,as a warning to the rest of us and to teach us a wholesome respect for(one must assume)law and order. One and all,they heartily agreed that it was worth it. Everyone knew,of course,that the Spy had peached. For,by Jove,even in The Enormous Room there was a man who earned certain privileges and acquired a complete immunity from punishments by squealing on his fellow-sufferers at each and every opportunity. A really ugly person,with a hard knuckling face and treacherous hands,whose daughter lived downstairs in a separate room apart from les putains(against which "dirty" "filthy" "whores" he could not say enough—"Hi'd rather die than 'ave my daughter with them stinkin' 'ores" remarked once to me this strictly moral man, in Cockney English)and whose daughter(aged thirteen)was generally supposed to serve the Directeur in a pleasurable capacity. One did not need to be warned against the Spy(as both B and I were warned, upon our arrival)—a single look at that phiz was enough for anyone partially either intelligent or sensitive. This phiz or mug had, then, squealed. Which everyone took as a matter of course and admitted among themselves that hanging was too good for him.

But the vast and unutterable success achieved by the Ménagerie was this—Rockyfeller, shortly after, left our ill-bred society for "l'hôpital"; the very same "hospital" whose comforts and seclusion Monsieur le Surveillant had so dextrously recommended to B and myself. Rockyfeller kept The Fighting Sheeney in his pay, in order to defend him when he went on promenade : otherwise our connection with him was definitely severed, his new companions being Muskowitz the Cock-eyed Millionaire, and The Belgian Song Writer—who told everyone to whom he spoke that he was a government official("de la blague" cried the little Machine-Fixer, "c'est un menteur!" Adding that he knew of this person in Belgium and that this person was a man who wrote popular ditties). Would to Heaven we had got rid of the slave as well as the master—but unfortunately The Fighting Sheeney couldn't afford to follow his lord's example. So he went on making a nuisance of himself, trying hard to curry favor with B and me, getting into fights, and bullying everyone generally.

Also this lion-hearted personage spent one whole night shrieking and moaning on his paillasse after an injection by Monsieur Richard—for syphilis. Two or three men were, in the course of a few days, discovered to have had syphilis for some time. They had it in their mouths. I don't remember them particularly, except that at least one was a Belgian. Of course they and The Fighting Sheeney had been using the common dipper and drinking-water pail. Le gouvernement français couldn't be expected to look out for a little thing like venereal disease among prisoners: didn't it have enough to do curing those soldiers who spent their time on permission trying their best to infect themselves with both gonorrhea and syphilis? Let not the reader suppose I am day-dreaming: let him rather recall that I had had the honour of being a member of Section Sanitaire Vingt-et-Un, which helped evacu-ate the venereal hospital at Ham, with whose inhabitants (in odd moments) I talked and walked and learned several things about la guerre. Let the reader—if he does not realize it already—realize that This Great War For Humanity etc., did not agree with some people's ideas, and that some people's ideas made them prefer to the glories of the front line the torments (I have heard my friends at Ham screaming a score of times) attendant upon venereal dis-eases. Or as one of my aforesaid friends told me—after discover-ing that I was, in contrast to les américains, not bent upon making France discover America but rather upon discovering France and les français myself—

"Mon vieux, c'est tout-à-fait simple. Je m'en vais en permission. Je demande à aller à Paris, parce qu'il y a des gonzesses là-bas qui sont toutes malades! J'attrape le syphilis, et, quand il est possi-ble, la gonnorrhée aussi. Je reviens. Je pars pour la première ligne. Je suis malade. L'hôpital. Le médecin me dit: il ne faut pas fumer ni boire, comme ça vous serez bientôt guéri. 'Merci, monsieur le médecin!' Je fume toujours et je bois toujours et je ne suis pas guéri. Je reste cinq, six, sept semaines. Peut-être des mois. Enfin, je suis guéri. Je rejoins mon régiment. Et maintenant, c'est mon tour d'aller en permission. Je m'en vais. Encore la même chose. C'est joli ça, tu sais."

But about the syphilitics at La Ferté: they were, somewhat tardily to be sure,segregated in a very small and dirty room—for a matter of,perhaps two weeks. And the Surveillant actually saw to it that during this period they ate la soupe out of individual china bowls.

I scarcely know whether The Fighting Sheeney made more of a nuisance of himself during his decumbiture or during the period which followed it—which period houses an astonishing number of fights rows bullyings,etc. He must have had a light case for he was guéri in no time,and on everyone's back as usual. Well,I will leave him for the nonce;in fact I will leave him until I come to The Young Pole,who wore black puttees and spoke of The Zulu as "mon ami"—The Young Pole whose troubles I will recount in connection with the second Delectable Mountain Itself. I will leave The Sheeney with the observation that he was almost as vain as he was vicious;for with that ostentation,one day when we were in the kitchen,did he show me a post-card received that afternoon from Paris,whereon I read "Comme vous êtes beau" and promises to send more money as fast as she earned it and,hoping that he had enjoyed her last present,the signature(in a big,adoring hand)

"Ta môme. Alice"

and when I had read it—sticking his map up into my face,The Fighting Sheeney said with emphasis:

"No travailler moi. Femme travaille,fait les noces,tout le temps. Toujours avec officiers anglais. Gagne beaucoup,cent francs,deux cent francs,trois cent francs,toutes les nuits. Anglais riches. Femme me donne tout. Moi no travailler. Bon,eh?"

A charming fellow,The Fighting Sheeney.

Now I must tell you what happened to the poor Spanish Whoremaster. I have already noted the fact that Count Bragard conceived an immediate fondness for this roly-poly individual,whose belly—as he lay upon his back of a morning in bed—

rose up with the sheets blankets and quilts as much as two feet above the level of his small stupid head studded with chins. I have said that this admiration on the part of the admirable Count and R.A. for a personage of the Spanish Whoremaster's profession somewhat interested me. The fact is, a change had recently come in our own relations with Vanderbilt's friend. His cordiality toward B and myself had considerably withered. From the time of our arrivals the good nobleman had showered us with favors and advice. To me, I may say, he was even extraordinarily kind. We talked painting for example: Count Bragard folded a piece of paper, tore it in the centre of the folded edge, unfolded it carefully, exhibiting a good round hole, and remarking—"Do you know this trick? It's an English trick, Mr. Cummings"—held the paper before him and gazed profoundly through the circular aperture at an exceptionally disappointing section of the altogether gloomy landscape, visible thanks to one of the ecclesiastical windows of The Enormous Room. "Just look at that, Mr. Cummings" he said with quiet dignity. I looked. I tried my best to find something to the left—"No, no, straight through" Count Bragard corrected me. "There's a lovely bit of landscape" he said sadly. "If I only had my paints here. I thought, you know, of asking my housekeeper to send them on from Paris—but how can you paint in a bloody place like this with all these bloody pigs around you? It's ridiculous to think of it. And it's tragic, too" he added grimly, with something like tears in his grey tired eyes.

Or we were promenading The Enormous Room after supper—the evening promenade in the cour having been officially eliminated owing to the darkness and the cold of the autumn twilight—and through the windows the dull bloating colours of sunset pouring faintly; and the Count stops dead in his tracks and regards the sunset without speaking for a number of seconds. Then—"it's glorious, isn't it?" he asks quietly. I say "Glorious indeed." He resumes his walk with a sigh, and I accompany him. "Ce n'est pas difficile à peindre, un coucher du soleil, it's not hard" he remarks gently. "NO?" I say with deference. "Not hard a bit" the Count says beginning to use his hands. "You only need three colours, you know. Very simple." "Which colours are they?" I inquire ignorantly. "Why, you know of course" he says surprised. "Burnt sienna, cadmium yellow, and—er—there! I can't think of it. I know it as well as I know my own face. So do you. Well, that's stupid of me."

Or, his worn eyes dwelling benignantly upon my duffle-bag, he warns me (in a low voice) of Prussian Blue.

"Did you notice the portrait hanging in the bureau of the Surveillant?" Count Bragard inquired one day. "That's a pretty piece of work, Mr. Cummings. Notice it when you get a chance. The green mustache, particularly fine. School of Cézanne."—"Really?" I said in surprise.—"Yes, indeed" Count Bragard said, extracting his tiredlooking hands from his tiredlooking trousers with a cultured gesture. "Fine young fellow painted that, I knew him. Disciple of the master. Very creditable piece of work."—"Did you ever see Cézanne?" I ventured.—"Bless you, yes, scores of times" he answered almost pityingly.—"What did he look like?" I asked, with great curiosity.—"Look like? His appearance, you mean?" Count Bragard seemed at a loss. "Why he was not extraordinary looking. I don't know how you could describe him. Very difficult in English. But you know a phrase we have in French, 'l'air pesant'; I don't think there's anything in English for it; il avait l'air pesant, Cézanne, if you know what I mean.

"I should work, I should not waste my time" the Count would say almost weepingly. "But it's no use, my things aren't here. And I'm getting old too; couldn't concentrate in this stinking hole of a place you know."

I did some hasty drawings of Monsieur Pet-airs washing and

rubbing his bald head with a great towel in the dawn. The R.A. caught me in the act and came over shortly after, saying "Let me see them." In some perturbation(the subject being a particular friend of his)I showed one drawing. "Very good, in fact excellent"; the R.A. smiled whimsically. "You have a real talent for caricature, Mr. Cummings, and you should exercise it. You really got Peters. Poor Peters, he's a fine fellow, you know; but this business of living in the muck and filth, c'est malheureux. Besides, Peters is an old man. It's a dirty bloody shame, that's what it is. A bloody shame that all of us here should be forced to live like pigs with this scum!

"I tell you what, Mr. Cummings" he said with something like fierceness, his weary eyes flashing, "I'm getting out of here shortly, and when I do get out(I'm just waiting for my papers to be sent on by the English consul)I'll not forget my friends. We've lived together and suffered together and I'm not a man to forget it. This hideous mistake is nearly cleared up, and when I go free I'll do anything for you and Mr. B—. Anything I can do for you I'd be only too glad to do it. If you want me to buy you paints when I'm in Paris, nothing would give me more pleasure. I know French as well as I know my own language"(he most certainly did)"and whereas you might be cheated, I'll get you everything you need à bon marché. Because you see they know me there, and I know just where to go. Just give me the money for what you need and I'll get you the best there is in Paris for it. You needn't worry"—I was protesting that it would be too much trouble—"my dear fellow, it's no trouble to do a favour for a friend."

And to B and myself ensemble he declared, with tears in his eyes, "I have some marmalade at my house in Paris; real marmalade, not the sort of stuff you buy these days. We know how to make it. You can't get an idea how delicious it is. In big crocks"— the Count said simply—"well, that's for you boys." We protested that he was too kind. "Nothing of the sort" he said, with a delicate smile. "I have a son in the English army" and his face clouded with worry,"and we send him some now and then,and he's crazy about it. I know what it means to him. And you shall share in it too. I'll send you six crocks." Then,suddenly looking at us with a pleasant expression,"By Jove" the Count said "do you like whiskey? Real Bourbon whiskey? I see by your look that you know what it is. But you never tasted anything like this. Do you know London?" I said no,as I had said once before. "Well,that's a pity" he said,"for if you did you'd know this bar. I know the bar-keeper well,known him for thirty years. There's a picture of mine hanging in his place. Look at it when you're in London,drop in to —— Street,you'll find the place,anyone will tell you where it is. This fellow would do anything for me. And now I'll tell you what I'll do: you fellows give me whatever you want to spend and I'll get you the best whiskey you ever tasted. It's his own private stock,you understand. I'll send it on to you—God knows you need it in this place. I wouldn't do this for anyone else,you understand" and he smiled kindly,"but we've been prisoners together,and we understand each other,and that's enough for gentlemen. I won't forget you." He drew himself up. "I shall write" he said slowly and distinctly,"to Vanderbilt about you. I shall tell him it's a dirty bloody shame that two young Americans,gentlemen born,should be in this foul place. He's a man who's quick to act. He'll not tolerate a thing like this—an outrage,a bloody outrage,upon two of his own countrymen. We shall see what happens then."

It was during this period that Count Bragard lent us for our personal use his greatest treasure,a water-glass. "I don't need it" he said simply and pathetically.

Now,as I have said,a change in our relations came.

It came at the close of one soggy damp raining afternoon. For this entire hopeless grey afternoon Count Bragard and B promenaded The Enormous Room. Bragard wanted the money—for the whiskey and the paints. The marmalade and the letter to Vanderbilt were, of course, gratis. Bragard was leaving us. Now was the time to give him money for what we wanted him to buy in Paris and London. I spent my time rushing about, falling over things, upsetting people, making curious and secret signs to B— which signs, being interpreted, meant Be careful!—But there was no need of telling B this particular thing. When the planton announced la soupe a fiercely weary face strode by me en route to his paillasse and his spoon. I knew that B had been careful. A minute later he joined me, and told me as much...

On the way downstairs we ran into the Surveillant. Bragard stepped from the ranks and poured upon the Surveillant a torrent of French, of which the substance was: you told them not to give me anything. The Surveillant smiled and bowed and wound and unwound his hands behind his back and denied anything of the sort.

It seems that B had heard that the kindly nobleman wasn't going to Paris at all.

Moreover,Monsieur Pet-airs had said to B something about Count Bragard being a suspicious personage—Monsieur Pet-airs,the R.A.'s best friend.

Moreover,as I have said,Count Bragard had been playing up to the poor Spanish Whoremaster to beat the band. Every day had he sat on a little stool beside the roly-poly millionaire,and written from dictation letter after letter in French—with which language the roly-poly was sadly unfamiliar....And when next day Count Bragard took back his treasure of treasures,his personal water-glass,remarking briefly that he needed it once again,I was not surprised. And when,a week or so later,he left—I was not surprised to have Mexique come up to us and placidly remark

"I give dat feller five francs. Tell me he send me overcoat,very good overcoat. But say:Please no tell anybody come from me. Please tell everybody your family send it." And with a smile "I t'ink dat feller fake."

Nor was I surprised to see,some weeks later,the poor Spanish Whoremaster rending his scarce hair as he lay in bed of a morning. And Mexique said with a smile

"Dat feller give dat English feller one hundred franc. Now he sorry."

All of which meant merely that Count Bragard should have spelt his name,not Bra-,but with an l.

And I wonder to this day that the only letter of mine which ever reached America and my doting family should have been posted by this highly entertaining personage en ville,whither he went as a trusted inhabitant of La Ferté to do a few necessary errands for himself;whither he returned with a good deal of colour in his cheeks and a good deal of vin rouge in his guts;going and returning with Tommy,the planton who brought him The Daily Mail every day until Bragard couldn't afford it, after which either B and I or Jean Le Nègre took it off Tommy's hands—Tommy for whom we had a delightful name which I sincerely regret being unable to tell, Tommy who was an Englishman for all his French planton's uniform and worshipped the ground on which the Count stood, Tommy who looked like a boiled lobster and had tears in his eyes when he escorted his idol back to captivity....Mirabile dictu, so it was.

Well, such was the departure of a great man from among us.

And now, just to restore the reader's faith in human nature, let me mention an entertaining incident which occurred during the latter part of my stay at La Ferté-Macé. Our society had been gladdened—or at any rate galvanized—by the biggest single contribution in its history; the arrival simultaneously of six purely extraordinary persons, whose names alone should be of more than general interest: The Magnifying Glass, The Trick Raincoat Sheeney, The Messenger Boy, The Hat, The Alsatian, The White-bearded Raper and His Son. In order to give the aforesaid reader an idea of the situation created by these arrivés, which situation gives the entrance of the Washing-Machine Man—the entertaining incident, in other words—its full and unique flavor, I must perforce sketch briefly each member of a truly imposing group. Let me say at once that, so terrible an impression did the members make, each inhabitant of The Enormous Room rushed at break-neck speed to his paillasse; where he stood at bay, assuming as frightening an attitude as possible. The Enormous Room was full enough already in all conscience. Between sixty and seventy paillasses, with their inhabitants and in nearly every case baggage, occupied it so completely as scarcely to leave room for le poêle at the further end and the card-table in the centre. No wonder we were struck with terror upon seeing the six nouveaux. Judas immediately protested to the planton who brought them up that there were no places,getting a roar in response and the door slammed in his face to boot. But the reader is not to imagine that it was the number alone of the arrivals which inspired fear and distrust—their appearance was enough to shake anyone's sanity. I do protest that never have I experienced a feeling of more profound distrust than upon this occasion;distrust of humanity in general and in particular of the following individuals:

First,an old man shabbily dressed in a shiny frock coat,upon whose peering and otherwise very aged face a pair of dirty spectacles rested. The first thing he did,upon securing a place,was to sit upon his paillasse in a professorial manner,tremulously extract a journal from his left coat pocket,tremblingly produce a large magnifying-glass from his upper right vest pocket,and forget everything. Subsequently,I discovered him promenading the room with an enormous expenditure of feeble energy,taking tiny steps flat-footedly and leaning in when he rounded a corner as if he were travelling at a terrific speed. He suffered horribly from rheumatism,could scarcely move after a night on the floor,and must have been at least sixty-seven years old.

Second,a palish foppish undersized prominent-nosed creature who affected a deep musical voice and the cut of whose belted raincoat gave away his profession—he was a pimp,and proud of it,and immediately upon his arrival boasted thereof,and manifested altogether as disagreeable a species of bullying vanity as I ever(save in the case of The Fighting Sheeney)encountered. He got his from Jean Le Nègre,as the reader will learn later.

Third,a super-Western-Union-Messenger type of ancient-youth,extraordinarily unhandsome if not positively ugly. He had a weak pimply grey face,was clad in a brownish uniform,puttees(on pipe-stem calves),and a Messenger Boy cap. Upon securing a place he instantly went to the card-table,seated himself hurriedly,pulled out a batch of blanks,and wrote a telegram to(I suppose)himself. Then he returned to his paillasse,lay down with apparently supreme contentment,and fell asleep.

Fourth,a tiny old man who looked like a caricature of an East-Side second-hand clothes dealer—having a long beard,a long worn and dirty coat reaching just to his ankles,and a small hat on his head. The very first night his immediate neighbor complained that "Le Chapeau"(as he was christened by The Zulu)was guilty of fleas. A great tempest ensued immediately. A planton was hastily summoned. He arrived,heard the case,inspected The Hat(who lay on his paillasse with his derby on,his hand far down the neck of his shirt,scratching busily and protesting occasionally his entire innocence),uttered(being the Black Holster)an oath of disgust,and ordered The Frog to "couper les cheveux de suite et la barbe aussi;après il va au bain,le vieux." The Frog approached and gently requested The Hat to seat himself upon a chair—the better of two chairs boasted by The Enormous Room. The Frog,successor to The Barber,brandished his scissors. The Hat lay and scratched. "Allez,Nom de Dieu" the planton roared. The poor Hat arose trembling,assumed a praying attitude;and began to talk in a thick and sudden manner. "Asseyez-vous là,tête de cochon." The pitiful Hat obeyed,clutching his derby to his head in both withered hands. Take off your hat,you son of a bitch,the planton yelled. I don't want to,the tragic Hat whimpered. BANG! The derby hit the floor,bounded upward and lay still. Proceed,the planton thundered to The Frog;who regarded him with a perfectly inscrutable expression on his extremely keen face,then turned to his subject,snickered with the scissors,and fell to. Locks ear-long fell in crisp succession. Pete The Shadow,standing beside the barber,nudged me;and I looked;and I beheld upon the floor the shorn locks rising and curling with movement of their own...."Now for the beard" said the Black Holster.—"No,no,Monsieur,s'il vous plaît,pas ma barbe,monsieur" The Hat wept, trying to kneel.—"Ta gueule or I'll cut your throat" the planton replied amiably; and The Frog, after another look, obeyed. And lo, the beard squirmed gently upon the floor, alive with a rhythm of its own; squirmed and curled crisply as it lay... When The Hat was utterly shorn, he was bathed and became comparatively unremarkable, save for the worn long coat which he clutched about him, shivering. And he borrowed five francs of me twice, and paid me punctually each time when his own money arrived, and presented me with chocolate into the bargain, tipping his hat quickly and bowing (as he always did whenever he addressed anyone). Poor Old Hat, B and I and The Zulu were the only men at La Ferté who liked you.

Fifth, a fat jolly decently dressed man.—He had been to a camp where everyone danced, because an entire ship's crew was interned there, and the crew were enormously musical, and the captain(having sold his ship)was rich and tipped the Director regularly;so everyone danced night and day,and the crew played,for the crew had brought their music with them.—He had a way of borrowing the paper(Le Matin)which we bought from one of the lesser plantons who went to the town and got the Matin there;borrowing it before we had read it—by the sunset. And his favorite observations were

"C'est un mauvais pays. Sale temps."

Fifth and sixth,a vacillating staggering decrepit creature with wildish white beard and eyes,who had been arrested—incredibly enough—for "rape". With him his son,a pleasant youth quiet of demeanor,inquisitive of nature,with whom we sometimes conversed on the subject of the English army.

Such were the individuals whose concerted arrival taxed to its utmost the capacity of The Enormous Room. And now for my incident—

Which incident is not peculiarly remarkable,but may(as I hope)serve to revive the reader's trust in humanity—

In the doorway,one day shortly after the arrival of the gentlemen mentioned,quietly stood a well-dressed handsomely middle-aged man,with a sensitive face culminating in a groomed Van Dyck beard. I thought for a moment that the Mayor of Orne,or whatever his title is had dropped in for an informal inspection of The Enormous Room. Thank God,I said to myself,it has never looked so chaotically filthy since I have had the joy of inhabiting it. And sans blague,The Enormous Room *was* in a state of really supreme disorder;shirts were thrown everywhere,a few twine clothes-lines supported various pants handkerchiefs and stockings,the poêle was surrounded by a gesticulating group of nearly undressed prisoners,the stink was actually sublime.

As the door closed behind him,the handsome man moved slowly and vigorously up The Enormous Room. His eyes were as big as turnips. His neat felt hat rose with the rising of his hair. His mouth opened in a gesture of unutterable astonishment. His knees trembled with surprise and terror, the creases of his trousers quivering. His hands lifted themselves slowly outward and upward till they reached the level of his head; moved inward till they grasped his head : and were motionless. In a deep awe-struck resonant voice he exclaimed simply and sincerely

"Nom de nom de nom de nom de nom de DIEU!"

Which introduces the reader to The Washing-Machine Man, a Hollander, owner of a store at Brest where he sold the highly utile contrivances which gave him his name. He, as I remember, had been charged with aiding and abetting in the case of escaping Holland deserters—but I know a better reason for his arrest : undoubtedly le gouvernement français caught him one day in the act of inventing a super-washing-machine, in fact a White-washing-machine, for the private use of the Kaiser and His Family...

Which brings us, if you please, to the first Delectable Mountain.

CHAPTER EIGHT

The Wanderer

One day somebody and I were "catching water" for Monsieur the Chef.

"Catching water" was ordinarily a mixed pleasure. It consisted, as I have mentioned, in the combined pushing and pulling of a curiously primitive two-wheeled cart over a distance of perhaps three hundred yards to a kind of hydrant situated in a species of square upon which the mediaeval structure known as Porte(or Camp)de Triage faced stupidly and threateningly. A planton always escorted the catchers through a big door, between the stone wall, which backed the men's cour, and the end of the building itself or in other words the canteen. The ten-foot stone wall was, like every other stone wall connected with La Ferté, topped with three feet of barbed-wire. The door by which we exited with the water-wagon to the street outside was at least eight feet high, adorned with several large locks. One pushing behind, one pulling in the shafts, we rushed the wagon over a sort of threshold or sill and into the street; and were immediately yelled at by the planton, who commanded us to stop until he had locked the door aforesaid. We waited until

told to proceed;then yanked and shoved the reeling vehicle up
the street to our right,that is to say along the wall of the build-
ing,but on the outside. All this was pleasant and astonishing.
To feel oneself,however temporarily,outside the eternal walls in
a street connected with a rather selfish and placid looking little
town(whereof not more than a dozen houses were visible)gave
the prisoner an at once silly and uncanny sensation,much
like the sensation one must get when he starts to skate for the
first time in a dozen years or so. The street met two others in
a moment,and here was a very flourishing sumach bush(as I
guess)whose berries shocked the stunned eye with a savage
splash of vermilion. Under this colour one discovered the Mecca
of water-catchers in the form of an iron contrivance operating
by means of a stubby lever which,when pressed down,yielded
grudgingly a spout of whiteness. The contrivance was placed
in sufficiently close proximity to a low wall so that one of the
catchers might conveniently sit on the wall and keep the water
spouting with a continuous pressure of his foot,while the other
catcher manipulated a tin pail with telling effect. Having filled
the barrel which rode on the two wagon-wheels,we turned it
with some difficulty and started it down the street with the tin
pail on top;the man in the shafts leaning back with all his might
to offset a certain velocity promoted by the down-grade,while
the man behind tugged helpingly at the barrel itself. On reach-
ing the door we skewed the machine skillfully to the left,thereby
bringing it to a complete standstill,and waited for the planton
to unlock the locks;which done,we rushed it violently over the
threshold,turned left,still running,and came to a final stop in
front of the cuisine. Here stood three enormous wooden tubs.
We backed the wagon around;then one man opened a spigot in
the rear of the barrel,and at the same time the other elevated
the shafts in a clever manner,inducing the jet d'eau to hit one

of the tubs. One tub filled,we switched the stream wittily to the next. To fill the three tubs(they were not always all of them empty)required as many as six or eight delightful trips. After which one entered the cuisine and got his well-earned reward—coffee with sugar.

I have remarked that catching water was a mixed pleasure. The mixedness of the pleasure came from certain highly respectable citizens,and more often citizenesses,of la ville de La Ferté-Macé;who had a habit of endowing the poor water-catchers with looks which I should not like to remember too well,at the same moment clutching whatever infants they carried or wore or had on leash spasmodically to them. Honestly,I never ceased to be surprised by the scorn,contempt,disgust,and frequently sheer ferocity manifested in the male and particularly in the female faces. All the ladies wore,of course,black;they were wholly unbeautiful of face or form,some of them actually repellent;not one should I,even under more favorable circumstances,have enjoyed meeting. The first time I caught water everybody in the town was returning from church,and a terrific sight it was. Vive la bourgeoisie I said to myself,ducking the shafts of censure by the simple means of hiding my face behind the moving water-barrel.

La vielle

But one day—as I started to inform the reader—somebody and I were catching water, and in fact had caught our last load, and were returning with it down the street; when I, who was striding rapidly behind (trying to lessen with both hands the impetus of the machine) suddenly tripped and almost fell with surprise—

On the curb of the little unbeautiful street a figure was sitting, a female figure dressed in utterly barbaric pinks and vermilions, having a dark shawl thrown about her shoulders; a positively Arabian face delimited by a bright coif of some tenuous stuff, slender golden hands holding with extraordinary delicacy what appeared to be a baby of not more than three months old, and beside her a black-haired child of perhaps three years and beside this child a girl of fourteen, dressed like the woman in crashing hues, with the most exquisite face I had ever known.

Nom de dieu, I thought vaguely. Am I or am I not completely asleep? And the man in the shafts craned his neck in stupid amazement, and the planton twirled his mustache and assumed that intrepid look which only a planton (or a gendarme) perfectly knows how to assume in the presence of female beauty.

That night The Wanderer was absent from la soupe, having been called by Apollyon to the latter's office upon a matter of superior import. Everyone was abuzz with the news. The gypsy's wife and three children, one a baby at the breast, were outside demanding to be made prisoners. Would the Directeur allow it? They had been told a number of times by plantons to go away, as they sat patiently waiting to be admitted to captivity. No threats pleas nor arguments had availed. The wife said she was tired of living without her husband—roars of laughter from all the Belgians and most of the Hollanders, I regret to say Pete included—and wanted merely and simply to share his confinement. Moreover, she said, without him she was unable to support his children; and it was better that they should grow up with their

The Wanderer sweeping

father as prisoners than starve to death without him. She would not be moved. The Black Holster told her he would use force—she answered nothing. Finally she had been admitted pending judgment. Also sprach, highly excited, the balayeur.

"Looks like a fucking hoor" was the Belgian-Dutch verdict, a verdict which was obviously due to the costume of the lady in question almost as much as to the untemperamental natures sojourning at La Ferté. B and I agreed that she and her children were the most beautiful people we had ever seen, or would ever be likely to see. So la soupe ended, and everybody belched and gasped and trumpeted up to The Enormous Room as usual.

That evening, about six o'clock, I heard a man crying as if his heart were broken. I crossed The Enormous Room. Half-lying on his paillasse, his great beard pouring upon his breast, his face lowered,his entire body shuddering with sobs,lay The Wanderer. Several of les hommes were about him,standing in attitudes ranging from semi-amusement to stupid sympathy,listening to the anguish which—as from time to time he lifted his majestic head—poured slowly and brokenly from his lips. I sat down beside him. And he told me "Je l'ai acheté pour six cent francs et je l'ai vendu pour quatre cent cinquante—it was not a horse of this race but of the race"(I could not catch the word)"as long as from here to that post—j'ai pleuré un quart d'heure comme si j'avais une gosse morte—and it is seldom I weep over horses—je dis:Bijou,quittes,au r'oir et bon jour"...

The vain little dancer interrupted about "réformé horses"... "Excuses donc—this was no réformé horse,such as goes to the front—these are some horses—pardon,whom you give eat,this,it is colique,that,the other,it's colique—this never—he could go forty kilometres a day..."

One of the strongest men I have seen in my life is crying because he has had to sell his favourite horse. No wonder les hommes in general are not interested. Someone said:Be of good cheer,Demestre,your wife and kids are well enough.

"Yes—they are not cold;they have a bed like that"(a high gesture toward the quilt of many colours on which we were sitting,such a quilt as I have not seen since;a feathery deepness soft to the touch as air in Spring)"qui vaut trois fois this of mine—but tu comprends,le matin il ne fait pas chaud"—then he dropped his head,and lifted it again crying

"Et mes outils,I had many—and my garments—where are they put,où—où? Kis! And I had chemises...this is poor"(looking at himself as a prince might look at his disguise)—"and like this,that—where?

"Si la voiture is not sold...I never will stay here for la durée de la guerre. No—bahsht! To resume,that is why I need..."

(more than upright in the priceless bed—the twicestreaming darkness of his beard, his hoarse sweetness of voice—his immense perfect face and deeply softnesses eyes—pouring voice)

"my wife sat over there, she spoke to No one and bothered Nobody—why was my wife taken here and shut up? Had she done anything? There is a wife who fait la putain and turns, to everyone and another, whom I bring another tomorrow...but a woman qui n'aime que son mari, qui n'attend que son mari"

(the tone bulged, and the eyes together)

"—Ces cigarettes ne fument pas!" I added an apology, having presented him with the package. "Why do you dépense pour these? They cost fifteen sous, you may spend for them if you like, you understand what I'm saying? But some time when you have nothing" (extraordinarily gently) "what then? Better to save for that day...better to buy du tabac and faire yourself; these sont fait de la poussière du tabac."

And there was someone to the right who was saying "Demain, c'est Dimanche alors"—wearily. The King lying upon his huge quilt, sobbing now only a little, heard:

"So—ah—il est tombé un dimanche—ma femme est en nourrice, elle donne la petite à téter" (the gesture charmed) "she said to them she would not eat if they gave her that—ça ne vaut rien du tout—il faut de la viande, tous les jours..." he mused. I tried to go.

"Assieds là" (graciousness of complete gesture. The sheer kingliness of poverty. He creased the indescribably soft couverture for me and I sat and looked into his forehead bounded by the cube of square sliced hair. Blacker than Africa. Than imagination.)

After this evening I felt that possibly I knew a little of The Wanderer, or he of me.

The Wanderer's wife and his two daughters and his baby lived in the women's quarters. I have not described and cannot describe these four. The little son of whom he was tremendously proud slept with his father in the great quilts in The Enormous Room. Of The Wanderer's little son I may say that he had lolling buttons of eyes sewed on gold flesh, that he had a habit of turning cartwheels in one third of his father's trousers, that we called him The Imp. He ran, he teased, he turned handsprings, he got in the way, and he even climbed the largest of the scraggly trees in the cour one day. "You will fall" Monsieur Peters (whose old eyes had a fondness for this irrepressible creature) remarked with conviction.—"Let him climb" his father said quietly. "I have climbed trees. I have fallen out of trees. I am alive." The Imp shinnied like a monkey, shouting and crowing, up a lean gnarled limb—to the amazement of the very planton who later tried to rape Celina and was caught. This planton put his gun in readiness and assumed an eager attitude of immutable heroism. "Will you shoot?" the father inquired politely. "Indeed it would be a big thing of which you might boast all your life; I, a planton, shot and killed a six year old child in a tree."—"C'est emmerdant" the planton countered, in some confusion—"he may be trying to escape. How do I know?"—"Indeed, how do you know anything?" the father murmured quietly, "It's a mystère." The Imp, all at once, fell. He hit the muddy ground with a disagreeable thud. The breath was utterly knocked out of him. The Wanderer picked him up kindly. His son began, with the catching of his breath, to howl uproariously. "Serves him right, the —— jackanapes" a Belgian growled.—"I told you so, didn't I?" Monsieur Pet-airs worryingly cried: "I said he would fall out of that tree!"—"Pardon, you were right I think" the father smiled pleasantly. "Don't be sad my little son, everybody falls out of trees, they're made for that by God" and he patted The Imp, squatting in the mud and smiling. In five minutes The Imp was trying to scale the shed. "Come down or I fire" the planton cried nervously...and so it was with The Wanderer's son

from morning till night. "Never" said Monsieur Pet-airs with sol-
emn desperation, "have I seen such an incorrigible child, a per-
fectly incorrigible child" and he shook his head and immediately
dodged a missile which had suddenly appeared from nowhere.

The Wanderer's Boy

Night after night The Imp would play around our beds, where
we held court with our chocolat and our bougie; teasing us, cajoling
us, flattering us, pretending tears, feigning insult, getting lectures
from Monsieur Peters on the evil of cigarette smoking, keeping us
in a state of perpetual inquietude. When he couldn't think of any-
thing else to do he sang at the top of his clear bright voice:

> "C'est la guerre
> faut pas t'en faire"

and turned a handspring or two for emphasis...Mexique once
cuffed him for doing something peculiarly mischievous, and he

set up a great crying—instantly The Wanderer was standing over Mexique,his hands clenched,his eyes sparkling—it took a good deal of persuasion to convince the parent that the son was in error,meanwhile Mexique placidly awaited his end...and neither B nor I,despite The Imp's tormentings,could keep from laughing when he all at once with a sort of crowing cry rushed for the nearest post,jumped up on his hands,arched his back,and poised head-downward;his feet just touching the pillar. Bare-footed,in a bright chemise and one-third of his father's trousers...

Being now in a class with "less hommes mariés" The Wanderer spent most of the day downstairs,coming up with his little son every night to sleep in The Enormous Room. But we saw him occasionally in the cour;and every other day when the dreadful cry was raised

"Allez,tout-le-monde,'plucher les pommes!"
and we descended to,in fair weather,the lane between the building and the cour,and in foul(very foul I should say)the dinosaur-coloured sweating walls of the dining-room—The Wanderer would quietly and slowly appear,along with other hommes mariés,and take up the peeling of the amazingly cold potatoes which formed the pièce de résistance(in guise of Soupe)for both women and men at La Ferté. And if the wedded males did not all of them show up for this unagreeable task,a dreadful hullabaloo was instantly raised—

"LES HOMMES MARIES!"
and forth would more or less sheepishly issue the delinquents.

And I think The Wanderer,with his wife and children whom he loved as never have I seen a man love anything in this world,was partly happy;walking in the sun when there was any,sleeping with his little boy in a great gulp of softness. And I remember him pulling his fine beard into two darknesses—huge-sleeved,pink-checked chemise—walking kindly like a bear—corduroy bigness of trousers,waistline always amorous of knees—finger-ends just catching tops of enormous pockets. When he feels,as I think,partly happy,he corrects our pronunciation of the ineffable Word—saying

"O,May-errr-DE!"

and smiles. And once Jean Le Nègre said to him,as he squatted in the cour with his little son beside him,his broad strong back as nearly always against one of the gruesome and minute pommiers—

"Barbu! j'vais couper ta barbe,barbu!" Whereat the father answered,slowly and seriously

"Quand vous arrachez ma barbe,il faut couper ma tête" regarding Jean Le Nègre with unspeakably sensitive tremendously deep peculiarly soft eyes. "My beard is finer than that;you have made it too coarse" he gently remarked one day,looking attentively at a piece of photographie which I had been caught in the act of perpetrating;whereat I bowed my head in silent shame.

"Demestre,Josef(femme,née Feliska)" I read another day in the Gestionnaire's book of judgment. O Monsieur le Gestionnaire,I should not have liked to have seen those names in my book of sinners,in my album of filth and blood and incontinence,had I been you...O little,very little,gouvernement français,and you the great and comfortable messieurs of the world,tell me why you have put a gypsy who dresses like Tomorrow among the squabbling pimps and thieves of yesterday...

He had been in New York one day.

One child died at sea.

"Les landes" he cried,towering over The Enormous Room suddenly one night in autumn,"je les connais commes ma poche—Bordeaux? Je sais où que c'est. Madrid? Je sais où que c'est. Tolède? Séville? Naples? Je sais où que c'est. Je les connais comme ma poche."

He could not read. "Tell me what it tells" he said briefly and without annoyance,when once I offered him the journal. And I took pleasure in trying to do so.

One fine day,perhaps the finest day,I looked from a window of The Enormous Room and saw(in the same spot that Lena had enjoyed her half-hour promenade during confinement in the cabinot,as related)the wife of The Wanderer,"née Feliska",giving his baby a bath in a pail,while The Wanderer sat in the sun smoking. About the pail an absorbed group of putains stood. Several plantons(abandoning for one instant their plantonic demeanor)leaned upon their guns and watched. Some even smiled a little. And the mother,holding the brownish naked crowing child tenderly,was swimming it quietly to and fro,to the delight of Celina in particular. To Celina it waved its arms greetingly. She stooped and spoke to it. The mother smiled. The Wanderer,looking from time to time at his wife,smoked and pondered by himself in the sunlight.

Le Bain

This baby was the delight of the putains at all times. They used to take turns carrying it when on promenade. The Wan-

derer's wife,at such moments,regarded them with a gentle and
jealous weariness.

There were two girls,as I said. One,the littlest girl I ever saw
walk and act by herself,looked exactly like a gollywog. This was
because of the huge mop of black hair. She was very pretty. She
used to sit with her mother and move her toes quietly for her
own private amusement. The older sister was as divine a crea-
ture as God in his skillful and infinite wisdom ever created. Her
intensely sexual face greeted us nearly always as we descended
pour la soupe. She would come up to B and me slenderly and
ask,with the brightest and darkest eyes in the world,

"Chocolat,M'sieu"

and we would present her with a big or small,as the case might
be,morceau de chocolat. We even called her Chocolat. Her skin
was nearly sheer gold;her fingers and feet delicately formed;her
teeth wonderfully white;her hair incomparably black and abun-
dant. Her lips would have seduced,I think,le gouvernement
français itself. Or any saint.

Le gouvernement français decided in its infinite but
unskillful wisdom that The Wanderer,being an inexpressibly
bad man(guilty of who knows what gentleness strength and
beauty)should suffer as much as he was capable of suffering. In
other words,it decided(through its Three Wise Men,who formed
the visiting Commission whereof I speak anon)that the wife,her
baby,her two girls,and her little son should be separated from
the husband by miles and by stone-walls and by barbed-wire and
by Law. Or perhaps(there was a rumour to this effect)the Three
Wise Men discovered that the father of these incredibly exquisite
children was not her lawful husband. And of course,this being
the case,the utterly and incomparably moral French govern-
ment saw its duty plainly;which duty was to inflict the ultimate
anguish of separation upon the sinners concerned. I know that

The Wanderer came from la commission with tears of anger in his great eyes. I know that some days later he,along with that deadly and poisonous criminal Monsieur Auguste,and that aged arch-traitor Monsieur Pet-airs,and that incomparably wicked person Surplice,and a ragged gentle being who one day presented us with a broken spoon which he had found somewhere—the gift being a purely spontaneous mark of approval and affection— who for this reason was known to us as The Spoonman,had the vast and immeasurable honour of departing for Précigné pour la durée de la guerre. If ever I can create by some occult process of imagining a deed so perfectly cruel as the deed perpetrated in the case of Josef Demestre,I shall consider myself a genius. Then let us admit that the Three Wise Men were geniuses. And let us,also and softly,admit that it takes a good and great government per- fectly to negate mercy. And let us,bowing our minds smoothly and darkly,repeat with Monsieur le Curé—"toujours l'enfer..."

The Wanderer was almost insane when he heard the judg- ment of la commission. And hereupon I must pay my respects to Monsieur Pet-airs;whom I had ever liked,but whose spirit I had not,up to the night preceding The Wanderer's departure,fully appreciated. Monsieur Pet-airs sat for hours at the card-table,his glasses continually fogging,censuring The Wanderer in tones of apparent annoyance for his frightful weeping(and now and then himself sniffing faintly with his big red nose);sat for hours pre- tending to take dictation from Josef Demestre,in reality com- posing a great letter or series of great letters to the civil and I guess military authorities of Orne on the subject of the injustice done to the father of four children,one a baby at the breast,now about to be separated from all he held dear and good in this world. "I appeal"(Monsieur Pet-airs wrote,in his boisterously careful,not to say elegant,script)"to your sense of mercy and of fair play and of honour. It is not merely an unjust thing which is being done,not merely an unreasonable thing,it is an unnatural thing..." As he wrote I found it hard to believe that this was the aged and decrepit and fussing biped whom I had known,whom I had caricatured,with whom I had talked upon ponderous subjects(a comparison between Belgian and French cities with respect to their location as favoring progress and prosperity,for example);who had with a certain comic shyness revealed to me a secret scheme for reclaiming inundated territories by means of an extraordinary pump "of my invention". Yet this was he,this was Monsieur Pet-airs Lui-Même:and I enjoyed peculiarly making his complete acquaintance for the first and only time.

May the Heavens prosper him.

The next day The Wanderer appeared in the cour walking proudly in a shirt of solid vermilion.

He kissed his wife—excuse me,Monsieur Malvy,I should say the mother of his children—crying very bitterly and suddenly.

The plantons yelled for him to line up with the rest,who were waiting outside the gate,bag and baggage. He covered his great king's eyes with his long golden hands and went.

With him disappeared unspeakable sunlight,and the dark keen bright strength of the earth.

CHAPTER NINE

Zoo-loo

This is the name of the second Delectable Mountain.

Zulu is he called, partly because he looks like what I have never seen, partly because the sounds somehow relate to his personality and partly because they seemed to please him.

He is, of all the indescribables whom I have known, definitely the most completely or entirely indescribable. Then (quoth my reader)you will not attempt to describe him, I trust.—Alas, in the medium which I am now using a certain amount or at least quality of description is disgustingly necessary. Were I free with a canvas and some colours...but I am not free. And so I will buck the impossible to the best of my ability. Which, after all, is one way of wasting your time.

He did not come and he did not go. He drifted.

His angular anatomy expended and collected itself with an effortless spontaneity which is the prerogative of perhaps fairies, or at any rate of those things in which we no longer believe. But he was more. There are certain things in which one is unable to believe for the simple reason that he never ceases to feel them. Things of this sort—things which are always inside of us and in fact are us and which consequently will not be pushed off or away where we can begin thinking about them—are no longer things;they,and the us which they are,equals A Verb;an IS. The Zulu,then,I must perforce call an IS.

In this chapter I shall pretend briefly to describe certain aspects and attributes of an IS. Which IS we have called The Zulu,who Himself intrinsically and indubitably escapes analysis. Allons!

Let me first describe a Sunday morning when we lifted our heads to the fight of the stove-pipes.

I was awakened by a roar,a human roar,a roar such as only a Hollander can make when a Hollander is honestly angry. As I rose from the domain of the subconscious,the idea that the roar belonged to Bill The Hollander became conviction. Bill The Hollander,alias America Lakes,slept next to The Young Pole(by whom I refer to that young stupid-looking farmer with that peaches-and-cream complexion and those black puttees who had formed the rear rank,with the aid of The Zulu Himself,upon the arrival of Babysnatcher,Bill,Box,Zulu,and Young Pole aforesaid). Now this same Young Pole was a case. Insufferably vain and self-confident was he. Monsieur Auguste palliated most of his conceited offensiveness on the ground that he was un garçon;we,on the ground that he was obviously and unmistakably The Zulu's friend. This Pole,I remember,had me design upon the wall over his paillasse(shortly after his arrival)a virile soldat clutching a somewhat dubious flag—I made the latter from descriptions furnished by Monsieur Auguste and The Young Pole himself—intended,I may add,to be the flag of Poland. Underneath which beautiful picture I was instructed to perpetrate the flourishing inscription

"VIVE LA POLOGNE"

which I did to the best of my limited ability and for Monsieur Auguste's sake. No sooner was the photographie complete than

The Young Pole, patriotically elated, set out to demonstrate the superiority of his race and nation by making himself obnoxious. I will give him this credit: he was pas méchant, he was in fact a stupid boy. The Fighting Sheeney took him down a peg by flooring him in the nightly "Boxe" which The Fighting Sheeney instituted immediately upon the arrival of The Trick Raincoat—a previous acquaintance of The Sheeney's at La Santé; the similarity of occupations (or non-occupation; I refer to the profession of pimp) having cemented a friendship between these two. But, for all that The Young Pole's Sunday-best clothes were covered with filth, and for all that his polished puttees were soiled and scratched by the splintery floor of The Enormous Room (he having rolled well off the blanket upon which the wrestling was supposed to occur), his spirit was dashed but for the moment. He set about cleaning and polishing himself, combing his hair, smoothing his cap— and was as cocky as ever next morning. In fact I think he was cockier; for he took to guying Bill The Hollander in French, with which tongue Bill was only faintly familiar and of which, consequently, he was doubly suspicious. As The Young Pole lay in bed of an evening after lumières éteintes, he would guy his somewhat massive neighbor in a childish almost girlish voice, shouting with laughter when The Triangle rose on one arm and volleyed Dutch at him, pausing whenever The Triangle's good-nature threatened to approach the breaking-point, resuming after a minute or two when The Triangle appeared to be on the point of falling into the arms of Morpheus. This sort of blaguing had gone on for several nights without dangerous results. It was, however, inevitable that sooner or later something would happen—and as we lifted our heads on this particular Sunday morn we were not surprised to see The Hollander himself standing over The Young Pole, with clenched paws, wringing shoulders, and an apocalyptic face whiter than Death's horse.

The Young Pole seemed incapable of realizing that the climax

Zulu

had come. He lay on his back, cringing a little and laughing fool-
ishly. The Zulu(who slept next to him on our side)had, appar-
ently, just lighted a cigarette which projected upward from a slender
holder. The Zulu's face was as always absolutely expressionless. His
chin, with a goodly growth of beard, protruded tranquilly from the
blanket which concealed the rest of him with the exception of his
feet—feet which were ensconced in large somewhat clumsy leather
boots. As The Zulu wore no socks, the X's of the rawhide lacings
on his bare flesh(blue, of course, with cold)presented a rather fas-
cinating kinesis. The Zulu was, to all intents and purposes, gazing
at the ceiling...

Bill The Hollander, clad only in his shirt, his long lean muscled
legs planted far apart, shook one fist after another at the recum-
bent Young Pole, thundering(curiously enough in English)

"Come on you Gottverdummer son of a bitch of a Polak and fight! Get up out o'there you Polak hoor and I'll kill you, you Gottverdummer bastard you! I stood enough o' your Gottverdummer nonsense you Gottverdummer" etc.

As Bill The Hollander's thunder crescendoed steadily, cramming the utmost corners of The Enormous Room with Gottverdummers which echoingly telescoped one another producing a dim huge shaggy mass of vocal anger, The Young Pole began to laugh less and less; began to plead and excuse and palliate and demonstrate—and all the while the triangular tower in its naked legs and its palpitating chemise brandished its vast fists nearer and nearer, its ghastly yellow lips hurling cumulative volumes of rhythmic profanity, its blue eyes snapping like fire-crackers, its enormous hairy chest heaving and tumbling like a monstrous hunk of sea-weed, its flat soiled feet curling and uncurling their ten sour mutilated toes.

The Zulu puffed gently as he lay.

Bill The Hollander's jaw, sticking into the direction of The Young Pole's helpless gestures, looked (with the pitiless scorching face behind it) like some square house carried in the fore of a white cyclone. The Zulu depressed his chin; his eyes (poking slowly from beneath the visor of the cap which he always wore, in bed or out of it) regarded the vomiting tower with an abstracted interest. He allowed one hand delicately to escape from the blanket and quietly to remove from his lips the holder with its gently-burning cigarette.

"You won't eh? You bloody Polak coward!"

and with a speed in comparison to which lightning is snail-like the tower reached twice for the peaches-and-cream cheeks of the prone victim; who set up a tragic bellowing of his own, writhed upon his somewhat dislocated paillasse, raised his elbows shieldingly, and started to get to his feet by way of his trembling knees—

to be promptly knocked flat. Such a howling as The Young Pole set up I have rarely heard:he crawled sideways;he got on one knee;he made a dart forward—and was caught cleanly by an uppercut,lifted through the air a yard,and spread-eagled against the stove which collapsed with an unearthly crash yielding an inky shower of soot upon the combatants and almost crowning The Hollander simultaneously with three four-foot sections of pipe. The Young Pole hit the floor shouting on his head at the apogee of a neatly executed back-somersault,collapsed;rose yelling,and with flashing eyes picked up a length of the ruined tuyau which he lifted high in air—at which The Hollander seized in both fists a similar piece,brought it instantly forward and sideways with incognizable velocity and delivered such an immense wallop as smoothed The Young Pole horizontally to a distance of six feet;where he suddenly landed stove-pipe and all in a crash

America Lakes, Bathhouse John and The Young Skipper's Mate

of entire collapse,having passed clear over The Zulu's bed. The
Zulu,remarking

"Muh"

floated hingingly to a sitting position and was saluted by

"Lie down you Gottverdummer Polaker,I'll get you next"—
in spite of which he gathered himself to rise upward,catching
as he did so a swish of The Hollander's pipe-length which made
his cigarette leap neatly,holder and all,upward and outward. The
Young Pole had by this time recovered sufficiently to get upon his
hands and knees behind The Zulu;who was hurriedly but calmly
propelling himself in the direction of the cherished cigarette-
holder,which had rolled under the remains of the stove. Bill The
Hollander made for his enemy,raising perpendicularly ten feet
in air the unrecognizably dented summit of the pipe which his
colossal fists easily encompassed,the muscles in his treelike arms
rolling beneath the chemise like balloons. The Young Pole with a
shriek of fear climbed The Zulu—receiving just as he had com-
passed this human hurdle a crack on the seat of his black pants
that stood him directly upon his head. Pivoting slightly for an
instant he fell loosely at full length on his own paillasse,and lay sob-
bing and roaring,one elbow protectingly raised,interspersing the
inarticulations of woe with a number of sincerely uttered "Assez!"s.
Meanwhile The Zulu had discovered the whereabouts of his trea-
sure,had driftingly resumed his original position;and was quietly
inserting the also-captured cigarette which appeared somewhat
confused by its violent aerial journey. Over The Young Pole stood
toweringly Bill The Hollander,his shirt almost in ribbons about
his thick bulging neck,thundering as only Hollanders thunder

"Have you got enough you Gottverdummer Polak?"
and The Young Pole,alternating nursing the mutilated pulp
where his face had been and guarding it with futile and helpless
and almost infantile gestures of his quivering hands,was sobbing

"Oui,Oui,Oui,Assez!"

And Bill The Hollander hugely turned to The Zulu,stepping accurately to the paillasse of that individual,and demanded

"And you,you Gottverdummer Polaker,do you want t'fight?" at which The Zulu gently waved in recognition of the compliment and delicately and hastily replied,between slow puffs,

"Mog."

Whereat Bill The Hollander registered a disgusted kick in The Young Pole's direction and swearingly resumed his paillasse.

All this,the reader understands,having taken place in the terribly cold darkness of the half-dawn.

That very day,after a great deal of examination(on the part of the Surveillant)of the participants in this Homeric struggle— said examination failing to reveal the particular guilt or the particular innocence of either—Judas,immaculately attired in a white coat,arrived from downstairs with a step-ladder and proceeded with everyone's assistance to reconstruct the original tuyau. And a pretty picture Judas made. And a pretty bum job he made. But anyway the stove-pipe drew;and everyone thanked God and fought for places about le poêle. And Monsieur Pet-airs hoped there would be no more fights for a while.

One might think that The Young Pole had learned a lesson. But no. He had learned(it is true)to leave his immediate neighbor America Lakes to himself;but that is all he had learned. In a few days he was up and about,as full de la blague as ever. The Zulu seemed at times almost worried about him. They spoke together in Polish frequently and—on The Zulu's part—earnestly. As subsequent events proved,whatever counsel The Zulu imparted was wasted upon his youthful friend. But let us turn for a moment to The Zulu himself.

He could not,of course,write any language whatever. Two words of French he knew:they were fromage and chapeau. The

former he pronounced "grumidge". In English his vocabulary was
even more simple, consisting of the single word "po-lees-man".
Neither B nor myself understood a syllable of Polish (tho' we sub-
sequently learned Jin-dobri, nima-Zatz, zampni-pisk and shimay
pisk, and used to delight The Zulu hugely by giving him

"Jin-dobri, pan"

every morning, also by asking him if he had a "papierosa"); con-
sequently in that direction the path of communication was to all
intents shut. And withal—I say this not to astonish my reader but
merely in the interests of truth—I have never in my life so per-
fectly understood (even to the most exquisite nuances) whatever
idea another human being desired at any moment to communi-
cate to me, as I have in the case of The Zulu. And if I had one-
third the command over the written word that he had over the
unwritten and the unspoken—not merely that; over the unspeak-
able and the unwritable—God knows this history would rank
with the deep art of all time.

It may be supposed that he was master of an intricate and del-
icate system whereby ideas were conveyed through signs of var-
ious sorts. On the contrary. He employed signs more or less, but
they were in every case extraordinarily simple. The secret of his
means of complete and unutterable communication lay in that
very essence which I have only defined as an IS; ended and began
with an innate and unlearnable control over all which one can
only describe as the homogeneously tactile. The Zulu, for exam-
ple, communicated the following facts in a very few minutes, with
unspeakable ease, one day shortly after his arrival:

He had been formerly a Polish farmer, with a wife and four
children. He had left Poland to come to France, where one
earned more money. His friend (The Young Pole) accompa-
nied him. They were enjoying life placidly in it may have been
Brest—I forget—when one night the gendarmes suddenly broke

into their room,raided it,turned it bottomside up,handcuffed
the two arch-criminals wrist to wrist,and said "Come with us."
Neither The Zulu nor The Young Pole had the ghost of an idea
what all this meant or where they were going. They had no choice
but to obey,and obey they did. Everyone boarded a train. Every-
one got out. Bill The Hollander and The Babysnatcher appeared
under escort,handcuffed to each other. They were immediately
re-handcuffed to the Polish delegation. The four culprits were
hustled,by rapid stages,through several small prisons to La Ferté-
Macé. During this journey(which consumed several nights and
days)the handcuffs were not once removed. The prisoners slept
sitting up or falling over one another. They urinated and def-
ecated with the handcuffs on,all of them hitched together. At
various times they complained to their captors that the agony
caused by the swelling of their wrists was unbearable—this
agony,being the result of over-tightness of the handcuffs,might
easily have been relieved by one of the plantons without loss of
time or prestige. Their complaints were greeted by commands
to keep their mouths shut or they'd get it worse than they had
it. Finally they hove in sight of La Ferté and the handcuffs were
removed in order to enable two of the prisoners to escort The
Zulu's box upon their shoulders,which said prisoners were only
too happy to do under the circumstances. This box,containing
not only The Zulu's personal effects but also a great array of car-
tridges knives and heaven knows what extraordinary souvenirs
which he had gathered from God knows where,was a strong
point in the disfavor of The Zulu from the beginning;and was
consequently brought along as evidence. Upon arriving all had
been searched,the box included,and sent to The Enormous
Room. The Zulu(at the conclusion of this dumb and eloquent
recital)slipped his sleeve gently above his wrist and exhibited a
bluish ring,at whose persistence upon the flesh he evinced great

surprise and pleasure,winking happily to us. Several days later I got the same story from The Young Pole in French;but after some little difficulty due to linguistic misunderstandings,and only after a half-hour's intensive conversation. So far as direct-ness accuracy and speed are concerned,between the method of language and the method of The Zulu there was not the slightest comparison.

Not long after The Zulu arrived I witnessed a mystery:it was toward the second Soupe,and B and I were proceeding(our spoons in our hands)in the direction of the door,when beside us suddenly appeared The Zulu—who took us by the shoulders gently and(after carefully looking about him)produced from,as nearly as one could see,his right ear a twenty franc note;asking us in a few well-chosen silences to purchase with it confiture,fromage,and chocolat at the canteen. He silently apologized for encumbering

us with these errands, averring that he had been found when he arrived to have no money upon him and consequently wished to keep intact this little tradition. We were too delighted to assist so remarkable a prestidigitator—we scarcely knew him at that time—and après la soupe we bought as requested, conveying the treasures to our bunks and keeping guard over them. About fifteen minutes after the planton had locked everyone in, The Zulu driftingly arrived before us; whereupon we attempted to give him his purchases—but he winked and told us wordlessly that we should (if we would be so kind) keep them for him, immediately following this suggestion by a request that we open the marmalade or jam or whatever it might be called—preserve is perhaps the best word. We complied with alacrity. Now (he said soundlessly), you may if you like offer me a little. We did. Now have some yourselves, The Zulu commanded. So we attacked the confiture with a will, spreading it on pieces or rather chunks of the brownish bread whose faintly rotten odour is one element of the life at La Ferté which I, for one, find it easier to remember than to forget. And next, in similar fashion, we opened the cheese and offered some to our visitor; and finally the chocolate. Whereupon The Zulu rose up, thanked us tremendously for our gifts, and—winking solemnly—floated off.

Next day he told us that he wanted us to eat all we could of the delicacies we had purchased, whether or no he happened to be in the vicinity. He also informed us that when they were gone we should buy more until the 20 francs gave out. And, so generous were our appetites, it was not more than two or three weeks later that The Zulu, having discovered that our supplies were exhausted, produced from his back hair a neatly folded twenty franc note; wherewith we invaded the canteen with renewed violence. About this time the Spy got busy and The Zulu, with The Young Pole for interpreter, was summoned to Monsieur le Directeur, who stripped The Zulu and searched every wrinkle and crevice of his tranquil anatomy for money(so The Zulu vividly informed us)—finding not a sou. The Zulu,who vastly enjoyed the discomfiture of Monsieur,cautiously extracted(shortly after this)a twenty franc note from the back of his neck,and presented it to us with extreme care. I may say that most of his money went for cheese,of which The Zulu was almost abnormally fond. Nothing more suddenly delightful has happened to me than happened,one day,when I was leaning from the next to the last window—the last being the property of users of the cabinet— of The Enormous Room,contemplating the muddy expanse below,and wondering how the Hollanders had ever allowed the last two windows to be opened. Margherite passed from the door of the building proper to the little washing-shed. As the sentinel's back was turned I saluted her,and she looked up and smiled pleasantly. And then—a hand leapt quietly outward from the wall,just to my right;the fingers clenched gently upon one-half a newly broken cheese;the hand moved silently in my direction cheese and all,pausing when perhaps six inches from my nose. I took the cheese from the hand,which departed as if by magic;and a little later had the pleasure of being joined at my window by The Zulu,who was brushing cheese crumbs from his long slender Mandarin mustaches,and who expressed profound astonishment and equally profound satisfaction upon noting that I too had been enjoying the pleasures of cheese. Not once,but several times,this Excalibur appearance startled myself and B:in fact the extreme modesty and incomparable shyness of The Zulu found only in this procedure a satisfactory method of bestowing presents upon his two friends...I would I could see that long hand once more,the sensitive fingers poised upon a half-Camembert;the bodiless arm swinging gently and surely with a derricklike grace and certainly in my direction....

Not very long after The Zulu's arrival occurred an incident which I give with pleasure because it shows the dauntless and indomitable, not to say intrepid, stuff of which plantons are made. The single seau which supplied the(at this time)sixty-odd inhabitants of The Enormous Room with drinking water had done its duty, shortly after our arrival from the first Soupe, with such thoroughness as to leave a number of unfortunates(among whom I was one)waterless. The interval between soupe and promenade loomed darkly and thirstily before said unfortunates. As the minutes passed, it loomed with greater and greater distinctness. At the end of twenty minutes our thirst—stimulated by an especially salty dose of luke-warm water for lunch—attained truly desperate proportions. Several of the bolder thirsters leaned from the various windows of the room and cried

"De l'eau, planton; de l'eau, s'il vous plaît"
upon which the guardian of the law looked up suspiciously; pausing a moment as if to identify the scoundrels whose temerity had so far got the better of their understanding as to lead them to address him, a planton, in familiar terms—and then grimly resumed his walk, gun on shoulder, revolver on hip, the picture of simple and unaffected majesty. Whereat, seeing that entreaties were of no avail, we put our seditious and dangerous heads together and formulated a very great scheme: to wit, the lowering of an empty tin-pail about eight inches high, which tin-pail had formerly contained confiture, which confiture had long since passed into the guts of Monsieur Auguste, The Zulu, B, myself, and—as The Zulu's friend—The Young Pole. Now this fiendish imitation of The Old Oaken Bucket That Hung In The Well was to be lowered to the good-hearted Margherite(who went to and fro from the door of the building to the washing-shed); who was to fill it for us at the pump situated directly under us in a cavernous chilly cave on the ground floor, then rehitch it to the rope, and guide its upward beginning. The rest was in the hands of Fate.

Bold might the planton be;we were no fainéants. We made a little speech to everyone in general desiring them to lend us their belts. The Zulu,the immensity of whose pleasure in this venture cannot be even indicated,stripped off his belt with unearthly agility—Monsieur Auguste gave his,which we tongue-holed to The Zulu's—somebody else contributed a necktie—another a shoe-string—The Young Pole his scarf,of which he was impossibly proud—etc. The extraordinary rope so constructed was now tried out in The Enormous Room,and found to be about thirty-eight feet long;or in other words of ample length,considering that the window itself was only three stories above terra firma. Margherite was put on her guard by signs,executed when the planton's back was turned(which it was exactly half the time,as the planton's patrol stretched at right angles to the wing of the building whose troisième étage we occupied). Having attached the minute bucket to one end(the stronger looking end,the end which had more belts and less neckties and handkerchiefs)of our improvised

rope,B Harree myself and The Zulu bided our time at la fenêtre—
then seizing a favorable opportunity,in enormous haste began
paying out the infernal contrivance. Down went the sinful tin-
pail,safely past the window-ledge just below us,straight and true
into the waiting hands of the faithful Margherite—who had just
received it and was on the point of undoing the bucket from the
first belt when,lo! who should come in sight around the corner
but the pimply-faced brilliantly-uniformed glitteringly-putteed
sergent de plantons lui-même. Such amazement as dominated
his puny features I have rarely seen equaled. He stopped dead in
his tracks;for one second stupidly contemplated the window,our-
selves,the wall,seven neckties,five belts,three handkerchiefs,a
scarf,two shoe-strings,the jam-pail,and Margherite—then,wheel-
ing,noticed the planton(who peacefully and with dignity was pur-
suing a course which carried him further and further from the
zone of operations)and finally,spinning around again,cried shrilly

"Qu'est-ce que vous avez foutu avec cette machin-là?"
At which cry the planton staggered,rotated,brought his gun
clumsily off his shoulder,and stared,trembling all over with emo-
tion,at his superior.

"Là-bas!" screamed the pimply sergent de plantons,pointing
fiercely in our direction.

Margherite,at his first command,had let go the jam-pail and
sought shelter in the building. Simultaneously with her flight
we all began pulling on the rope for dear life,making the bucket
bound against the wall.

Upon hearing the dreadful exclamation "Là-bas!" the planton
almost fell down. With a supreme effort he turned toward the
wing of the building. The sight which greeted his eyes caused
him to excrete a single mouthful of vivid profanity,made him
grip his gun like a hero,set every nerve in his noble and faithful
body tingling. Apparently however he had forgotten completely

his gun,which lay faithfully and expectingly in his two noble hands.

"Attention!" screamed the sergeant.

The planton did something to his gun very aimlessly and rapidly.

"FIRE!" shrieked the sergeant,scarlet with rage and mortification.

The planton,cool as steel,raised his gun.

"NOM DE DIEU TIREZ!"

The bucket,in big merry sounding jumps,was approaching the window below us.

The planton took aim,falling fearlessly on one knee,and closing both eyes. I confess that my blood stood on tip-toe;but what was death to the loss of that jam-bucket,let alone every-one's apparel which everyone had so generously lent? We kept on hauling silently. Out of the corner of my eye I beheld the planton—now on both knees,musket held to his shoulder by his left arm and pointing unflinchingly at us one and all—hunting with his right arm and hand in his belt for cartridges! A few seconds after this fleeting glimpse of heroic devotion had penetrated my considerably heightened sensitivity—UP suddenly came the bucket and over backwards we all went together on the floor of The Enormous Room. And as we fell I heard a cry like the cry of a boiler announcing noon—

"Too late!"

I recollect that I lay on the floor for some minutes,half on top of The Zulu and three-quarters smothered by Monsieur Auguste,shaking with laughter...

Then we all took to our hands and knees,and made for our bunks.

I believe no one(curiously enough)got punished for this atrocious misdemeanor—except the planton;who was punished for not shooting us,although God knows he had done his very best.

And now I must chronicle the famous duel which took place between The Zulu's compatriot,The Young Pole,and that here-before introduced pimp,The Fighting Sheeney;a duel which came as a climax to a vast deal of teasing on the part of The Young Pole—who,as previously remarked,had not learned his lesson from Bill The Hollander with the thoroughness which one might have expected of him.

In addition to a bit of French and considerable Spanish,Rocky-feller's valet spoke Russian very(I did not have to be told)badly. The Young Pole,perhaps sore at being rolled on the floor of The Enormous Room by the worthy Sheeney,set about nagging him just as he had done in the case of neighbor Bill. His favorite epithet for the conqueror was "moshki" or "moski",I never was sure which. Whatever it meant(The Young Pole and Monsieur Auguste informed me that it meant "Jew" in a highly derogatory sense)its effect upon the noble Sheeney was definitely unpleas-ant. But when coupled with the word "moskosi",accent on the second syllable or long o,its effect was more than unpleasant— it was really disagreeable. At intervals throughout the day,on promenade,of an evening,the ugly phrase

"MOS-ki mosKOsi"

resounded through The Enormous Room. The Fighting Sheeney, then rapidly convalescing from syphilis,bided his time. The Young Pole moreover had a way of jesting upon the subject of The Sheeney's infirmity. He would,particularly during the afternoon promenade,shout various none too subtle allusions to Moshki's physical condition for the benefit of les femmes. And in response would come peals of laughter from the girls' windows,shrill peals and deep guttural peals intersecting and breaking joints like overlapping shingles on the roof of Craziness. So hearty did these responses become one afternoon that,in answer to loud pleas from the injured Moshki,the pimply sergent de plantons himself came to the gate in the barbed-wire fence and delivered a lecture upon the seriousness of venereal ailments(heart-felt,I should judge by the looks of him)as follows:

"Il ne faut pas rigoler de ça. Savez-vous? C'est une maladie,ça" which little sermon contrasted agreeably with his usual remarks concerning and in the presence of les femmes,whereof the essence lay in a single phrase of prepositional significance—

"bonne pour coucher avec"

he would say shrilly,his puny eyes assuming an expression of amorous wisdom which was most becoming...The Sheeney looked sheepish,and waited.

One day we were all upon afternoon promenade,it being beau temps(for that part of the world),under the auspices of by all odds one of the littlest and mildest and most delicate specimens of mankind that ever donned the high and dangerous duties of a planton. As B says:"He always looked like a June bride." This mannikin could not have been five feet high,was perfectly proportioned(unless we except the musket upon his shoulder and the bayonet at his belt),and minced to and fro with a feminine grace which suggested—at least to les deux citoyens of These United States—the extremely authentic epithet "fairy". He had such a pretty face! and so cute a mustache! and such darling legs! and such a wonderful smile! For plantonic purposes the smile— which brought two little dimples into his pink cheeks—was for the most part suppressed. However it was impossible for this little thing to look stern:the best he could do was to look poignantly sad. Which he did with great success,standing like a tragic last piece of uneaten candy in his big box at the end of the cour,and eyeing the sinful hommes with sad pretty eyes. Won't anyone eat me?—he seemed to ask.—I'm really delicious,you know,perfectly delicious,really I am.

To resume:everyone being in the cour the cour was well

filled,not only from the point of view of space but of sound. A barn-yard crammed with pigs cows horses ducks geese hens cats and dogs could not possibly have produced one-fifth of the racket that emanated,spontaneously and inevitably,from the cour. Above which racket I heard tout à coup a roar of pain and surprise;and looking up with some interest and also in some alarm,beheld The Young Pole backing and filling and slipping in the deep ooze under the strenuous jolts jabs and even haymakers of The Fighting Sheeney;who,with his coat off and his cap off and his shirt open at the neck,was swatting luxuriously and for all he was worth that round helpless face and that peaches-and-cream complexion. From where I stood,at a distance of six or eight yards,the impact of The Sheeney's fist on The Young Pole's jaw and cheeks was disconcertingly audible. The latter made not the slightest attempt to defend himself,let alone retaliate;he merely skidded about,roaring,and clutching desperately out of harm's way his long white scarf,of which(as I have mentioned)he was extremely proud. But for the sheer brutality of the scene it would have been highly ludicrous. The Sheeney was swinging like a windmill and hammering like a blacksmith. His ugly head lowered,the chin protruding,lips drawn back in a snarl,teeth sticking forth like a gorilla's,he banged and smote that moon-shaped physiognomy as if his life depended upon utterly annihilating it. And annihilate it he doubtless would have,but for the prompt(not to say punctual)heroism of The June Bride—who,lowering his huge gun,made a rush for the fight;stopped at a safe distance;and began squeaking at the very top and even summit of his faint girlish voice

"Aux armes! Aux armes!"

which plaintive and intrepid utterance by virtue of its very fragility penetrated the building and released the Black Holster—who bounded through the gate,roaring a salutation as he bounded,and in a jiffy had cuffed the participants apart. "All right, whose fault is this!" he roared. And a number of highly reputable spectators such as Judas and The Fighting Sheeney himself said it was The Young Pole's fault. "Allez! Au cabinot! De suite!"—and off trickled the sobbing Young Pole, winding his great scarf comfortingly about him, to the dungeon.

Some few minutes later we encountered The Zulu speaking with Monsieur Auguste. Monsieur Auguste was very sorry. He admitted that The Young Pole had brought his punishment upon himself. But he was only a boy. The Zulu's reaction to the affair was absolutely profound: he indicated les femmes with one eye, his trousers with another, and converted his utterly plastic personality into an amorous machine for several seconds, thereby vividly indicating the root of the difficulty—then drifting softly off began playing hide-and-seek with the much delighted Little Man In The Orange Cap. That the stupidity of his friend The

Young Pole hurt The Zulu deeply I discovered by looking at him as he lay in bed the next morning,limply and sorrowfully prone;beside him the empty paillasse which meant cabinot... his perfectly extraordinary face(a face perfectly at once fluent and angular,expressionless and sensitive)told me many things whereof even The Zulu might not speak,things which in order entirely to suffer he kept carefully and thoroughly ensconced behind his rigid and mobile eyes.

From the day that The Young Pole emerged from cabinot he was our friend. The blague had been at last knocked out of him,thanks to Un Mangeur de Blanc,as the little Machine-Fixer expressly called The Fighting Sheeney. Which mangeur,by the way(having been exonerated from all blame by the more enlightened spectators of the unequal battle)strode immediately and ferociously over to B and me,a hideous grin crackling upon the coarse surface of his mug,and demanded—hiking at the front of his trousers—

"Bon,eh? Bien fait,eh?"
and a few days later asked us for money,even hinting that he would be pleased to become our special protector. I think,as a matter of fact,we "lent" him one-eighth of what he wanted(perhaps we lent him five cents)in order to avoid trouble and get rid of him. At any rate he didn't bother us particularly afterwards;and if a nickel could accomplish that a nickel should be proud of itself.

And always,through the falling greyness of the desolate autumn,The Zulu was beside us,or wrapped around a tree in the cour,or melting in a post after tapping Mexique,or suffering from toothache—or losing his shoes and finding them under Garibaldi's bed(with a huge perpendicular wink which told tomes about Garibaldi's fatal propensities for ownership),or marveling silently at the power of les femmes à propos his young friend—who,occasionally resuming his former bravado,would stand in the black evil rain with his white scarf twined about him, singing as of old

"Je suis content
pour mettre dedans
suis pas pressé
pour tirer
ah-la-la-la ..."

...And The Zulu came out of la commission with identically the expressionless expression which he had carried into it; and God knows what the Three Wise Men found out about him, but (whatever it was) they never found and never will find that Something whose discovery was worth to me more than all the round and powerless money of the world—

limbs' tin grace, wooden wink, shoulderless unhurried body, velocity of a grasshopper, soul up under his arm-pits, mysteriously falling over the ownness of two feet, floating fish of his slimness half a bird...

Gentlemen, I am inexorably grateful for the gift of these ignorant and indivisible things.

CHAPTER TEN

Surplice

L et us ascend the third Delectable Mountain, which is called Surplice.

I will admit, in the beginning, that I never knew Surplice. This for the simple reason that I am unwilling to know except as a last resort. And it is by contrast with Harree The Hollander, whom I knew, and Judas, whom I knew, that I shall be able to give you (perhaps) a little of Surplice, whom I did not know. For that matter I think Monsieur Auguste was the only person who might possibly have known him; and I doubt whether Monsieur Auguste was capable of descending to such depths in the case of so fine a person as Surplice.

Take a sheer animal of a man. Take the incredible Hollander with cobalt-blue breeches, shock of orange hair pasted over forehead, pink long face, twenty-six years old, had been in all the countries of all the world: "Australia girl fine girl—Japanese girl cleanest of the world—Spanish girl all right—English girl no good, no face—everywhere these things: Norway sailors German girls Swedisher matches Holland candles"...had been to Philadelphia, worked on a yacht for a millionaire; knew and had worked in the Krupp factories;was on two boats torpedoed and one which struck a mine when in sight of shore through the "looking-glass":"Holland almost no soldier—India"(the Dutch Indies)"nice place,always warm there,I was in cavalry;if you kill a man or steal one hundred franc or anything,in prison twenty-four hours;every week black girl sleep with you because government want white children,black girl fine girl,always doing something,your fingernails or clean your ears or make wind because it's hot...No one can beat German people;if Kaiser tell man to kill his father and mother he do it quick!"—the tall,strong,course,vital youth who remarked

"I sleep with black girl who smoke a pipe in the night."

Take this animal. You hear him,you are afraid of him,you smell and you see him and you know him—but you do not touch him.

Or a man who makes us thank God for animals,Judas as we called him: who keeps his mustaches in press during the night(by means of a kind of transparent frame which is held in place by a band over his head);who grows the nails of his two little fingers with infinite care;has two girls with both of whom he flirts carefully and wisely,without ever once getting into trouble;talks in French;converses in Belgian;can speak eight languages and is therefore always useful to Monsieur le Surveillant—Judas with his shining horrible forehead,pecked with little indentures;with his Reynard full-face—Judas with his pale almost putrescent fatty body in the douche—Judas with whom I talked one night about Russia,he wearing my pelisse—the frightful and impeccable Judas:take this man. You see him,you smell the hot stale odour of Judas's body;you are not afraid of him,in fact you hate him;you hear him and you know him. But you do not touch him.

And now take Surplice,whom I see and hear and smell and touch and even taste,and whom I do not know.

Take him in dawn's soft squareness,gently stooping to pick

chewed cigarette-ends from the spitty floor...hear him,all
night;retchings which light into the dark...see him all day and
all days,collecting his soaked ends and stuffing them gently into
his round pipe(when he can find none he smokes tranquilly little
splinters of wood)...watch him scratching his back(exactly like a
bear)on the wall...or in the cour,speaking to no one,sunning his
soul...

He is,we think,Polish. Monsieur Auguste is very kind to
him,Monsieur Auguste can understand a few words of his lan-
guage and thinks they mean to be Polish. That they are trying
hard to be and never can be Polish.

Everyone else roars at him,Judas refers to him before his face
as a dirty pig,Monsieur Peters cries angrily

"Il ne faut pas cracher par terre"
eliciting a humble not to say abject apology;the Belgians spit
on him;the Hollanders chaff him and bulldoze him now and
then,crying "Syph'lis"—at which he corrects them with offended
majesty

"pas syph'lis,Surplice"
causing shouts of laughter from everyone—of nobody can he
say My Friend,of no one has he ever said or will he ever say My
Enemy.

When there is labour to do he works like a dog...the day we
had nettoyage de chamber,for instance,and Surplice and The Hat
did most of the work;and B and I were caught by the planton try-
ing to stroll out into the cour...every morning he takes the pail
of solid excrement down,without anyone's suggesting that he take
it;takes it as if it were his,empties it in the sewer just beyond the
cour des femmes,or pours a little(just a little)very delicately on
the garden where Monsieur le Directeur is growing a flower for
his daughter—he has,in fact,an unobstreperous affinity for excre-

ment;he lives in it;he is shaggy and spotted and blotched with it;he sleeps in it;he puts it in his pipe and says it is delicious...

And he is intensely religious,religious with a terrible and exceedingly beautiful and absurd intensity...every Friday he will be found sitting on a little kind of stool by his paillasse,reading his prayer-book upside down;turning with enormous delicacy the thin difficult leaves,smiling to himself as he sees and does not read. Surplice is actually religious,and so are Garibaldi and I think The Woodchuck(a little dark sad man who spits blood with regularity);by which I mean they go to la messe for la messe,whereas everyone else goes pour voir les femmes. And I don't know for certain why The Woodchuck goes,but I think it's because he feels entirely sure he will die. And Garibaldi is afraid,immensely afraid. And Surplice goes in order to be surprised,surprised by the amazing gentleness and delicacy of God—Who put him,Surplice,upon his knees in La Ferté-Macé,knowing that Surplice would appreciate His so doing.

He is utterly ignorant. He thinks America is out a particular window on your left as you enter The Enormous Room. He cannot understand the submarine. He does now know that there is a war. On being informed upon these subjects he is unutterably surprised,he is inexpressibly astonished. He derives huge pleasure from this astonishment. His filthy rather proudly noble face radiates the pleasure he receives upon being informed that people are killing people for nobody knows what reason,that boats go under water and fire six-foot long bullets at ships, that America is not really just outside this window close to which we are talking,that America is in fact over the sea. The sea:is that water?—"c'est de l'eau,monsieur?" Ah:a great quantity of water;enormous amounts of water,water and then water;water and water and water and water and water. "Ah! You cannot see the other side of this water,monsieur? Wonderful,monsieur!"— He meditates it,smiling quietly;its wonder,how wonderful it is,no other side,and yet—the sea. In which fish swim. Wonderful.

He is utterly curious. He is utterly hungry. We have bought cheese with The Zulu's money. Surplice comes up,bows timidly and ingratiatingly with the demeanor of a million-times whipped but somewhat proud dog. He smiles. He says nothing,being terribly embarrassed. To help his embarrassment,we pretend we do not see him. That makes things better—

"Fromage,monsieur?"

"Oui,c'est du fromage."

"Ah-h-h-h-h-h-h..."

his astonishment is supreme. C'est du fromage. He ponders this. After a little

"monsieur,c'est bon,monsieur?"

asking the question as if his very life depended on the answer—

"Yes,it is good" we tell him reassuringly.

"Ah-h-h. Ah-h."

He is once more superlatively happy. It is good,le fromage. Could anything be more superbly amazing? After perhaps a minute

"monsieur—monsieur—c'est cher le fromage?"

"Very" we tell him truthfully. He smiles,blissfully astonished. Then,with extreme delicacy and the utmost timidity conceivable

"monsieur,combien ça coûte,monsieur?"

We tell him. He totters with astonishment and happiness. Only now,as if we had just conceived the idea,we say carelessly

"en voulez-vous?"

He straightens,thrilled from the top of his rather beautiful filthy head to the soleless slippers with which he promenades in rain and frost—

"Merci,Monsieur!"

We cut him a piece. He takes it quiveringly,holds it a second as a king might hold and contemplate the best and biggest jewel of his realm,turns with profuse thanks to us—and disappears...

He is perhaps most curious of this pleasantly sounding thing which everyone around him,everyone who curses and spits upon and bullies him,desires with a terrible desire—Liberté. Whenever anyone departs Surplice is in an ecstasy of quiet excitement. The lucky man may be Fritz;for whom Bathhouse John is taking up a collection as if he,Fritz,were a Hollander and not a Dane— for whom Bathhouse John is striding hither and thither,shaking a hat into which we drop coins for Fritz;Bathhouse John, chipmunk-cheeked,who talks Belgian French English and Dutch in his dreams,who has been two years in La Ferté(and they say he declined to leave,once,when given the chance),who cries "baigneur de femmes moi",and every night hoists himself into his wooden bunk crying "goo-dni-te";whose favorite joke is "une section pour les femmes",which he shouts occasionally in the cour as he lifts his paper-soled slippers and stamps in the freezing mud,chuckling and blowing his nose on the Union Jack...and

now Fritz,beaming with joy,shakes hands and thanks us all and
says to me "Good-bye,Johnny" and waves and is gone forever—
and behind me I hear a timid voice

"monsieur,Liberté?"

and I say Yes,feeling that Yes in my belly and in my head at the
same instant;and Surplice stands beside me,quietly marvel-
ling,extremely happy,uncaring that le parti did not think to say
good-bye to him. Or it may be Harree and Pompom who are run-
ning to and fro shaking hands with everybody in the wildest state
of excitement,and I hear a voice behind me

"liberté,monsieur? Liberté?"

and I say No,Précigné,feeling weirdly depressed,and Surplice is
standing to my left,contemplating the departure of the incor-
rigibles with interested disappointment—Surplice of whom no
man takes any notice when that man leaves,be it for Hell or
Paradise....

And once a week the maître de chamber throws soap on the
paillasses,and I hear a voice

"monsieur,voulez pas?"

and Surplice is asking that we give him our soap to wash with.

Sometimes,when he has made quelques sous by washing for
others,he stalks quietly to The Butcher's chair(everyone else
who wants a shave having been served)and receives with shut
eyes and a patient expression the blade of The Butcher's dullest
razor—for The Butcher is not the man to waste a good razor on
Surplice;he,The Butcher as we call him,the successor of The
Frog(who one day somehow managed to disappear like his pre-
decessor The Barber),being a thug and a burglar fond of telling
us pleasantly about German towns and prisons,prisons where
men are not allowed to smoke,clean prisons where there is a daily
medical inspection,where anyone who thinks he had a grievance
of any sort has the right of immediate and direct appeal;he,The

Butcher,being perhaps happiest when he can spend an evening showing us little parlor-tricks fit for children of four and three years old;quite at his best when he remarks

"sickness doesn't exist in France"

meaning that one is either well or dead;or

"if they(the French)get an inventor they put him in prison."

—So The Butcher is stooping heavily upon Surplice and slicing and gashing busily and carelessly,his thick lips stuck a little pursewise,his buried pig's eyes glistening—and in a moment he cries "Fini!" and poor Surplice rises unsteadily,horribly slashed,bleeding from at least three two-inch cuts and a dozen large scratches;totters over to his couch holding on to his face as if he were afraid it would fall off any moment;and lies down gently at full length,sighing with pleasurable surprise,cogitating the inestimable delights of cleanness...

It struck me at the time as intensely interesting that,in the case of a certain type of human being,the more cruel are the miseries inflicted upon him the more cruel does he become

toward any one who is so unfortunate as to be weaker or more miserable than himself. Or perhaps I should say that nearly every human being, given sufficiently miserable circumstances, will from time to time react to those very circumstances (whereby his own personality is mutilated) through a deliberate mutilation on his own part of a weaker or already more mutilated personality. I daresay that this is perfectly obvious. I do not pretend to have made a discovery. On the contrary, I merely state what interested me peculiarly in the course of my sojourn at La Ferté: I mention that I was extremely moved to find that, however busy sixty men may be kept suffering in common, there is always one man or two or three who can always find time to make certain of their comrades enjoying a little extra suffering. In the case of Surplice, to be the butt of everyone's ridicule could not be called precisely suffering; inasmuch as Surplice, being unspeakably lonely, enjoyed any and all insults for the simple reason that they constituted or at least implied a recognition of his existence. To be made a fool of was, to this otherwise completely neglected individual, a mark of distinction; something to take pleasure in; to be proud of. The inhabitants of The Enormous Room had given to Surplice a small but essential part in the drama of La Misère: he would play that part to the utmost of his ability; the cap-and-bells should not grace a head unworthy of their high significance. He would be a great fool, since that was his function; a supreme entertainer, since his duty was to amuse. After all, men in La Misère as well as anywhere else rightly demand a certain amount of amusement; amusement is, indeed, peculiarly essential to suffering; in proportion as we are able to be amused we are able to suffer; I, Surplice, am a very necessary creature after all.

I recall one day when Surplice beautifully demonstrated his ability to play the fool. Someone had crept up behind him as he was stalking to and fro, head in air proudly, hands in pockets, pipe in teeth, and had (after several heart-breaking failures) succeeded in attaching to the back of his jacket by means of a pin a huge placard carefully prepared beforehand, bearing the numerical inscription

606

in vast writing. The attacher, having accomplished his difficult feat, crept away. So soon as he reached his paillasse a volley of shouts went up from all directions, shouts in which all nationalities joined, shouts or rather jeers which made the pillars tremble and the windows rattle—

"SIX CENT SIX! SYPH'LIS!"

Surplice started from his reverie, removed his pipe from his lips, drew himself up proudly, and—facing one after another the sides of The Enormous Room—blustered in his bad and rapid French accent

"Pas syph'lis! Pas syph'lis!"

at which, rocking with mirth, everyone responded at the top of his voice

"SIX CENT SIX!"

Whereat, enraged, Surplice made a dash at Pete The Shadow and was greeted by

"Get away you bloody Polak or I'll give you something you'll be sorry for"—this from the lips of America Lakes. Cowed, but as majestic as ever, Surplice attempted to resume his promenade and his composure together. The din bulged

"Six cent six! Syph'lis! Six cent six!"

—increasing in volume with every instant. Surplice, beside himself with rage, rushed another of his fellow-captives (a little old man, who fled, under the table) and elicited threats of

"Come on now you Polak hoor and quit that business or I'll

kill you" upon which he dug his hands into the pockets of his almost transparent pantaloon and marched away in a fury, literally frothing at the mouth.—

"Six Cent Six!"

everyone cried. Surplice stamped with wrath and mortification. "C'est dommage" Monsieur Auguste said gently beside me. "C'est un bon-homme, le pauvre, il ne faut pas l'em-merd-er."

"Look behind you!"

somebody yelled. Surplice wheeled, exactly like a kitten trying to catch its own tail, and provoked thunders of laughter. Nor could anything at once more pitiful and ridiculous, more ludicrous and horrible, be imagined.

"On your coat! Look on your jacket!"

Surplice bent backward, staring over his left then his right shoulder, pulled at his jacket first one way then the other—thereby making his improvised tail to wag which sent The Enormous Room into spasms of merriment—finally caught sight of the incriminating appendage, pulled his coat to the left, seized the paper, tore it off, threw it fiercely down, and stamped madly on the crumpled 606; spluttering and blustering and waving his arms; slavering like a mad dog. Then he faced the most prominently vociferous corner and muttered thickly and crazily

"Wuhwuhwuhwuhwuh..."

Then he strode rapidly to his paillasse and lay down; in which position I caught him, a few minutes later, smiling and even chuckling...very happy...as only an actor is happy whose efforts have been greeted with universal applause...

In addition to being called "Syph'lis" he was popularly known as "Chaude Pisse, the Pole". If there is anything particularly terrifying about prisons, or at least imitations of prisons such as La Ferté, it is possibly the utter obviousness with which (quite unknown to themselves) the prisoners demonstrate willy-nilly certain fundamental psychological laws. The case of Surplice is

a very exquisite example: everyone, of course, is afraid of les mal-
adies vénériennes—accordingly all pick an individual(of whose
inner life they know and desire to know nothing, whose external
appearance satisfies the mind à propos what is foul and disgust-
ing)and, having tacitly agreed upon this individual as a Symbol
of all that is evil, proceed to heap insults upon him and enjoy his
very natural discomfiture...but I shall remember Surplice on his
both knees sweeping sacredly together the spilled sawdust from
a spittoon-box knocked over by the heel of the omnipotent plan-
ton; and smiling as he smiled at la messe when Monsieur le Curé
told him that there was always Hell...

He told us one day a great and huge story of an important
incident in his life, as follows:

"monsieur, réformé moi—oui monsieur—réformé—travaille,
beaucoup de monde, maison, très haute, troisième étage, tout le
monde, planches, en haut—planches pas bonnes—chancelle,
tout"—(here he began to stagger and rotate before us)"commence
à tomber, tombe, tombe, tout, tous, vingt-sept hommes-briques-
planches-brouettes-tous—dixmètres—zuhzuhzuhzuhzuhPOOM!
—tout le monde blessé, tout le monde tué, pas moi, réformé—oui
monsieur"—and he smiled, rubbing his head foolishly. Twenty-
seven men, bricks, planks and wheelbarrows. Ten metres. Bricks
and planks. Men and wheelbarrows...

Also he told us, one night, in his gentle, crazy, shrugging
voice, that once upon a time he played the fiddle with a big woman
in Alsace-Lorraine for fifty francs a night;"c'est la misère"—add-
ing quietly, I can play well, I can play anything, I can play n'im-
porte quoi.

Which I suppose and guess I scarcely believed—until one
afternoon a man brought up a harmonica which he had pur-
chased en ville; and the man tried it; and everyone tried it; and
it was perhaps the cheapest instrument and the poorest that

money can buy,even in the fair country of France;and everyone was disgusted—but,about six o'clock in the evening,a voice came from behind the last experimenter;a timid hasty voice

"monsieur,monsieur,permettez?"
the last experimenter turned and to his amazement saw Chaude Pisse the Pole,whom everyone had(of course)forgotten—

The man tossed the harmonica on the table with a scornful look(a menacingly scornful look)at the object of universal exe-cration;and turned his back. Surplice,trembling from the sum-mit of his filthy and beautiful head to the naked soles of his filthy and beautiful feet,covered the harmonica delicately and surely with one shaking paw;seated himself with a surprisingly deliber-ate and graceful gesture;closed his eyes,upon whose lashes there were big filthy tears...

...and suddenly

He put the harmonica softly upon the table. He rose. He went quickly to his paillasse. He neither moved nor spoke nor responded to the calls for more music,to the cries of "Bis!"—"Bien joué!"—"Allez!"—"Vas-y!" He was crying,quietly and carefully,to himself...quietly and carefully crying,not wishing to annoy any-one...hoping that people could not see that Their Fool had tem-porarily failed in his part.

The following day he was up as usual before anyone else,hunt-ing for chewed cigarette-ends on the spitty slippery floor of The Enormous Room;ready for insult,ready for ridicule,for buf-fets,for curses.

Alors—

one evening,some days after everyone who was fit for la com-mission had enjoyed the privilege of examination by that inex-orable and delightful body—one evening very late,in fact just before lumières éteintes,a strange planton arrived in The Enor-mous Room and hurriedly read a list of five names,adding "demain partir de bonne heure"

and shut the door behind him. Surplice was, as usual, very interested, enormously interested. So were we: for the names respectively belonged to Monsieur Auguste, Monsieur Pet-airs, The Wanderer, Surplice and The Spoonman. These men had been judged. These men were going to Précigné. These men would be prisonniers pour la durée de la guerre.

I have already told how Monsieur Pet-airs sat with the frantically weeping Wanderer writing letters, and sniffing with his big red nose, and saying from time to time: "Be a man, Demestre, don't cry, crying does no good."—Monsieur Auguste was broken-hearted. We did our best to cheer him; we gave him a sort of Last Supper at our bedside, we heated some red wine in the tincup and he drank with us. We presented him with certain tokens of our love and friendship, including—I remember—a huge cheese...and then, before us, trembling with excitement, stood Surplice—

We asked him to sit down. The onlookers (there were always onlookers at every function, however personal, which involved Food or Drink) scowled and laughed. Le con, Surplice, chaude pisse—how could he sit with men and gentlemen? Surplice sat down gracefully and lightly on one of our beds, taking extreme care not to strain the somewhat capricious mechanism thereof; sat very proudly; erect; modest but unfearful. We offered him a cup of wine. A kind of huge convulsion gripped, for an instant, fiercely his entire face: then he said in a whisper of sheer and unspeakable wonderment, leaning a little toward us without in any way suggesting that the question might have an affirmative answer,

"pour moi, monsieur?"

We smiled at him and said "Prenez, monsieur." His eyes opened. I have never seen eyes since. He remarked quietly, extending one hand with majestic delicacy

"Merci, monsieur."

...Before he left B gave him some socks and I presented him with a flannel shirt, which he took softly and slowly and simply and otherwise not as an American would take a million dollars.

"I will not forget you" he said to us, as if in his own country he were a more than great king...and I think I know where that country is, I think I know this; I, who never knew Surplice, know.

For he has the territory of harmonicas, the acres of flutes, the meadows of clarinets, the domain of violins. And God says: Why did they put you in prison? What did you do to the people? "I made them dance and they put me in prison. The soot-people hopped; and to twinkle like sparks on a chimney-back and I made 80 francs every dimanche, and beer and wine, and to eat well. Maintenant...c'est fini...Et tout de suite" (gesture of cutting himself in two) "la tête." And He says: O you who put the jerk into joys, come up hither. There's a man up here called Christ who like violins.

CHAPTER ELEVEN

Jean Le Nègre

On a certain day, the ringing of the bell and accompanying rush of men to the window facing the entrance gate was supplemented by an unparalleled volley of enthusiastic exclamations in all the languages of La Ferté-Macé—provoking in me a certainty that the queen of fair women had arrived. This certainty thrillingly withered when I heard the cry: "Il y a un noir!" Fritz was at the best peep-hole, resisting successfully the onslaughts of a dozen fellow-prisoners, and of him I demanded in English, "Who's come?"—"Oh a lot of girls" he yelled, "and there's a NIGGER too"—hereupon writhing with laughter.

I attempted to get a look, but in vain; for by this at least two dozen men were at the peep-hole, fighting and gesticulating and slapping each other's backs with joy. However, my curiosity was not long in being answered. I heard on the stairs the sound of mounting feet, and knew that a couple of plantons would before many minutes arrive at the door with their new prey. So did everyone else—and from the farthest beds uncouth figures sprang and rushed to the door, eager for the first glimpse of the nouveau: which was very significant, as the ordinary procedure on arrival of prisoners was for everybody to rush to his own bed and stand guard over it.

Even as the plantons fumbled with the locks I heard the inimitable unmistakable divine laugh of a negro. The door opened at last. Entered a beautiful pillar of black strutting muscle topped with a tremendous display of the whitest teeth on earth. The muscle bowed politely in our direction, the grin remarked musically;"Bo'jour,tou'l'monde";then came a cascade of laughter. Its effect on the spectators was instantaneous:they roared and danced with joy. "Comment vous appelez-vous?" was fired from the hubbub.—"J'm'appelle Jean,moi" the muscle rapidly answered with sudden solemnity,proudly gazing to left and right as if expecting a challenge to this statement:but when none appeared,it relapsed as suddenly into laughter—as if hugely amused at itself and everyone else including a little and tough boy,whom I had not previously noted although his entrance had coincided with the muscle's.

Thus into the misère of La Ferté-Macé stepped lightly and proudly Jean Le Nègre.

Of all the fine people in La Ferté,Monsieur Jean("le noir" as

Jean Le Nègre

he was entitled by his enemies)swaggers in my memory as the finest.

Jean's first act was to complete the distribution(begun,he announced,among the plantons who had escorted him upstairs) of two pockets full of Cubebs. Right and left he gave them up to the last,remarking carelessly "J'ne veux,moi."

Après la soupe(which occurred a few minutes after le noir's entry)B and I and the greater number of prisoners descended to the cour for our afternoon promenade. The Cook spotted us immediately and desired us to "catch water";which we did,three cartfuls of it,earning our usual café sucré. On quitting the cuisine after this delicious repast(which as usual mitigated somewhat the effects of the swill that was our official nutriment)we entered the cour. And we noticed at once a well-made figure standing conspicuously by itself,and poring with extraordinary intentness over the pages of a London Daily Mail which it was holding upside-down. The reader was culling choice bits of news of a highly sensational nature,and exclaiming from time to time—"Est-ce vrai! V'là,le roi d'Angleterre est malade. Quelque chose!—Comment? La reine aussi? Bon Dieu! Qu'est-ce que c'est?—Mon père est mort! Merde!—Eh,b'en! La guerre est finie. Bon."—It was Jean Le Nègre,playing a little game with Himself to beguile the time.

When we had mounted à la chamber,two or three tried to talk with this extraordinary personage in French;at which he became very superior and announced:"J'suis anglais,moi. Parlez anglais. Comprends pas français,moi." At this a crowd escorted him over to B and me—anticipating great deeds in the English language. Jean looked at us critically and said "Vous parlez anglais? Moi parlez anglais."—"We are Americans,and speak English" I answered.—"Moi anglais" Jean said. "Mon père,capitaine de gendarmerie,Londres. Comprends pas français,moi. SPEE-King-liss"—he laughed all over himself.

At this display of English on Jean's part the English-speaking Hollanders began laughing. "The son of a bitch is crazy" one said.

And from that moment B and I got on famously with Jean.

His mind was a child's. His use of language was sometimes exalted fibbing,sometimes the purely picturesque. He courted above all the sound of words,more or less disdaining their meaning. He told us immediately(in pidgin French)that he was born without a mother because his mother died when he was born,that his father was(first)sixteen(then)sixty years old,that his father gagnait cinq cent francs par jour(later,par année),that he was born in London and not in England,that he was in the French army and had never been in any army.

He did not,however,contradict himself in one statement:"Les français sont des cochons"—to which we heartily agreed,and which won him the approval of the Hollanders.

The next day I had my hands full acting as interpreter for "le noir qui comprend pas français". I was summoned from the cour to elucidate a great grief which Jean had been unable to explain to the Gestionnaire. I mounted with a planton to find Jean in hysterics;speechless;his eyes starting out of his head. As nearly as I could make out,Jean had had sixty francs when he arrived,which money he had given to a planton upon his arrival,the planton having told Jean that he would deposit the money with the Gestionnaire in Jean's name(Jean could not write). The planton in question who looked particularly innocent denied this charge upon my explaining Jean's version;while the Gestionnaire puffed and grumbled,disclaiming any connection with the alleged theft and protesting sonorously that he was hearing about Jean's sixty francs for the first time. The Gestionnaire shook his thick piggish finger at the book wherein all financial transactions were to be found—from the year one to the present year,month,day hour and minute(or words to that effect). "Mais c'est pas là" he kept repeating stupidly. The Surveillant was uh-ahing at a great rate and attempting to pacify Jean in French. I myself was somewhat fearful for Jean's sanity and highly indignant at the planton. The matter ended with the planton's being sent about his business;simultaneously with Jean's dismissal to the cour,whither I accompanied him. My best efforts to comfort Jean in this matter were quite futile. Like a child who had been unjustly punished he was inconsolable. Great tears welled in his eyes. He kept repeating "sees-tee franc—planton voleur",and—absolutely like a child who in anguish calls itself by the name which has been given itself by grown-ups—"steel Jean munee." To no avail I called the planton a menteur,a voleur,a fils de chienne and various other names. Jean felt the wrong itself too keenly to be interested in my denunciation of the mere agent through whom injustice had(as it happened)been consummated.

But—again like an inconsolable child who weeps his heart out when no human comfort avails and wakes the next day without an apparent trace of the recent grief—Jean Le Nègre,in the course of the next twenty-four hours,had completely recovered his normal buoyancy of spirit. The sees-tee franc were gone. A wrong had been done. But that was yesterday. Today—
and he wandered up and down,joking,laughing,singing

"après la guerre finit"...

In the cour Jean was the mecca of all female eyes. Handkerchiefs were waved to him;phrases of the most amorous nature greeted his every appearance. To all these demonstrations he by no means turned a deaf ear;on the contrary. Jean was irrevocably vain. He boasted of having been enormously popular with the girls wherever he went and of having never disdained their admiration. In Paris one day—(and thus it happened that we discovered why le gouvernement français had arrested Jean)—

One afternoon, having rien à faire, and being flush (owing to his success as a thief, of which vocation he made a great deal, adding as many ciphers to the amounts as fancy dictated) Jean happened to cast his eyes in a store window where were displayed all possible appurtenances for the militaire. Vanity was rooted deeply in Jean's soul. The uniform of an English captain met his eyes. Without a moment's hesitation he entered the store, bought the entire uniform including leather puttees and belt (of the latter purchase he was especially proud), and departed. The next store contained a display of medals of all descriptions. It struck Jean at once that a uniform would be incomplete without medals. He entered this store, bought one of every decoration—not forgetting the Colonial, nor yet the Belgian Cross (which on account of its size and colour particularly appealed to him)—and went to his room. There he adjusted the decorations on the chest of his blouse, donned the uniform, and sallied importantly forth to capture Paris.

Everywhere he met with success. He was frantically pursued by women of all stations from les putains to les princesses. The police salaamed to him. His arm was wearied with the returning of innumerable salutes. So far did his medals carry him that, although on one occasion a gendarme dared to arrest him for beating-in the head of a fellow English officer (who being a mere lieutenant, should not have objected to Captain Jean's stealing the affections of his lady), the sergent de gendarmerie before whom Jean was arraigned on a charge of attempting to kill refused to even hear the evidence, and dismissed the case with profuse apologies to the heroic Captain. " 'Le gouvernement français, Monsieur, extends to you through me its profound apology for the insult which your honour has received.' Ils sont des cochons, les français" said Jean, and laughed throughout his entire body.

Having had the most blue-blooded ladies of the capital cooing upon his heroic chest,having completely beaten up with the full support of the law whosoever of lesser rank attempted to cross his path or refused him the salute—having had "great fun" saluting generals on les grands boulevards and being in turn saluted("tous les généraux,tous,salute me,Jean have more medel"),and this state of affairs having lasted for about three months—Jean began to be very bored("me très ennuyé"). A fit of temper("me très fâché")arising from this ennui led to a rixe with the police,in consequence of which(Jean,though outnumbered three to one,having almost killed one of his assailants)our hero was a second time arrested. This time the authorities went so far as to ask the heroic captain to what branch of the English army he was at present attached;to which Jean first replied "parle pas français,moi" and immediately after announced that he was a Lord of the Admiralty,that he had committed robberies in Paris to the tune of sees meel-i-own franc,that he was a son of the Lord Mayor of London by the Queen,that he had lost a leg in Algeria,and that the French were cochons. All of which assertions being duly disproved,Jean was remanded to La Ferté for psychopathic observation and safe keeping on the technical charge of wearing an English officer's uniform.

Jean's particular girl at La Ferté was "LOO-Loo". With Lulu it was the same as with les princesses in Paris—"me no travaille,ja-MAIS. Les femmes travaillent,geev Jean mun-ee,sees,sees-tee,see-cent francs. Jamais travaille,moi." Lulu smuggled Jean money;and not for some time did the woman who slept next Lulu miss it. Lulu also sent Jean a lace embroidered handkerchief,which Jean would squeeze and press to his lips with a beatific smile of perfect contentment. The affair with Lulu kept Mexique and Pete The Hollander busy writing letters;which Jean dictated,rolling his eyes and scratching his head for words.

At this time Jean was immensely happy. He was continually

Jean and Pete: a love letter

playing practical jokes on one of the Hollanders, or Mexique, or
The Wanderer, or in fact anyone of whom he was particularly
fond. At intervals between these demonstrations of irrepressibil-
ity(which kept everyone in a state of laughter)he would stride up
and down the filth-sprinkled floor with his hands in the pockets
of his stylish jacket, singing at the top of his lungs his own version
of the famous song of songs—

après la guerre finit,
soldat angalis parti,
mademoiselle que je laissais en France
avec des pickaninee. PLENTY!

and laughing till he shook and had to lean against a wall.

B and Mexique made some dominoes. Jean had not the least
idea of how to play, but when we three had gathered for a game
he was always to be found leaning over our shoulders, completely

absorbed,once in a while offering us sage advice,laughing utterly when someone made a cinque or a multiple thereof.

One afternoon,in the interval between la soupe and promenade,Jean was in especially high spirits. I was lying down on my collapsible bed when he came up to my end of the room and began showing off exactly like a child. This time it was the game of l'armée française which Jean was playing.—"Jamais soldat,moi. Connais toute,l'armée française." John The Bathhouse,stretched comfortably in his bunk near me,grunted. "Toute" Jean repeated.—And he stood in front of us;stiff as a stick in imitation of a French lieutenant with an imaginary company in front of him. First he would be the lieutenant giving commands,then he would be the Army executing them. He began with the manual of arms.

"Com-pag-nie ..." then,as he went through the manual holding his imaginary gun—"htt,htt,htt."—Then as the officer commending his troops:"Bon. Très bon. Très bien fait"—laughing with head thrown back and teeth aglitter at his own success. Jean Le Baigneur was so tremendously amused that he gave up sleeping to watch. L'armée drew a crowd of admirers from every side. For at least three quarters of an hour this game went on...

Another day Jean,being angry at the weather and having eaten a huge amount of soupe,began yelling at the top of his voice "MERDE à la France" and laughing heartily. No one paying especial attention to him,he continued(happy in this new game with himself)for about fifteen minutes. Then The Sheeney With The Trick Raincoat(that undersized specimen,clad in femininefitting raiment with flashy shoes,who was by trade a pimp)being about half Jean's height and a tenth of his physique,strolled up to Jean—who had by this time got as far as my bed—and,sticking his sallow face as near Jean's as the neck could reach,said in a solemn voice:"Il ne faut pas dire ça." Jean,astounded,gazed at the intruder for a moment;then demanded "Qui dit ça? Moi? Jean? Jamais,ja-MAIS. MERDE à la France!" nor would he yield a point,backed up as he was by the moral support of everyone present except The Sheeney—who found discretion the better part of valor and retired with a few dark threats;leaving Jean master of the situation and yelling for The Sheeney's particular delectation:"MAY-RRR-DE à la France!" more loudly than ever.

A little after the epic battle with stovepipes between The Young Pole and Bill The Hollander,the wrecked poêle(which was patiently waiting to be repaired)furnished Jean with perhaps his most brilliant inspiration. The final section of pipe(which conducted the smoke through a hole in the wall to the outer air)remained in place all by itself,projecting about six feet into the room at a height of seven or eight feet from the floor. Jean noticed this;got a chair;mounted on it,and by applying alternately his ear and his mouth to the end of the pipe created for himself a telephone,with the aid of which he carried on a conversation with The Wanderer(at that moment visiting his family on the floor below)to this effect:

—Jean,grasping the pipe and speaking angrily into it,being evidently nettled at the poor connection—"Heh-loh, hello,hello,hello"—surveying the pipe in consternation—"Merde. Ça marche pas"—trying again with a deep frown—"heh-LOH!"— tremendously agitated—"HEHLOH!"—a beatific smile supplanting the frown—"hello Barbu. Est-ce que tu es là? Oui? Bon!"—evincing tremendous pleasure at having succeeded in establishing the connection satisfactorily—"Barbu? Est-ce que tu m'écoutes? Oui? Qu'est-ce que c'est Barbu? Comment? Moi? Qui,MOI? JEAN? jaMAIS! jamais,jaMAIS,Barbu. J'ai jamais dit que vous avez des puces. C'était pas moi,tu sais. JaMAIS,c'était un autre. Peut-être c'était Mexique"—turning his head in Mexique's direction and roaring with laughter—"Hello,HEH-LOH.

Barbu? Tu sais, Barbu, j'ai jamais dit ça. Au contraire, Barbu. J'ai dit que vous avez des totos"—another roar of laughter—"Comment? C'est pas vrai? Bon. Alors. Qu'est-ce que vous avez, Barbu? Des poux—OHHHHHHHHH. Je comprends. C'est mieux"—shaking with laughter, then suddenly tremendously serious—"Hellohellohellohello HEHLOH!"—addressing the stovepipe—"C'est une mauvaise machin, ça"—speaking into it with the greatest distinctness—"HEL-L-LOH. Barbu? Liberté, Barbu. Oui. Comment? C'est ça. Liberté pour tou'l'monde. Quand? Après la soupe. Oui. Liberté pour tou'l'monde après la soupe!"—to which jest astonishingly reacted a certain old man known as The West Indian Negro (a stocky credulous creature with whom Jean would have nothing to do, and whose tales of Brooklyn were indeed outclassed by Jean's histoires d'amour) who leaped rheumatically from his paillasse at the word "Liberté" and rushed limpingly hither and thither inquiring Was it true?—to the enormous and excruciating amusement of The Enormous Room in general.

After which Jean, exhausted with laughter, descended from the chair and lay down on his bed to read a letter from Lulu (not knowing a syllable of it). A little later he came rushing up to my bed in the most terrific state of excitement, the whites of his eyes gleaming, his teeth bared, his kinky hair fairly standing on end, and cried:

"You fuck me, me fuck you? Pas bon. You fuck you, me fuck me:—bon. Me fuck me, you fuck you!" and went away capering and shouting with laughter, dancing with great grace and as great agility and with an imaginary partner the entire length of the room.

There was another game—a pure child's game—which Jean played. It was the name game. He amused himself for hours together by lying on his paillasse, tilting his head back, rolling up his eyes, and crying in a high quavering voice—"JAW-neeeeeee."

After a repetition or two of his own name in English,he would demand sharply "Qui m'appelle? Mexique? Est-ce que tu m'appelles,Mexique?" and if Mexique happened to be asleep,Jean would rush over and cry in his ear,shaking him thoroughly— "Est-ce tu m'appelles,toi?" Or it might be Barbu,or Pete The Hollander,or B or myself,of whom he sternly asked the question— which was always followed by quantities of laughter on Jean's part. He was never perfectly happy unless exercising his inexhaustible imagination...

The West Indian Negro

Of all Jean's extraordinary selves,the moral one was at once the most rare and most unreasonable. In the matter of les femmes he could hardly have been accused by his bitterest enemy of being a Puritan. Yet the Puritan streak came out one day,in a discussion which lasted for several hours. Jean,as in the case of France,spoke in dogma. His contention was very simple:"La femme qui fume n'est pas une femme." He defended it hotly against the attacks of all the nations represented;in vain did Belgian and Hollander,Russian and Pole,Spaniard and Alsatian,charge and counter-charge—Jean remained unshaken. A woman could do anything but smoke—if she smoked she ceased automatically to be a woman and became something unspeakable. As Jean was at this time sitting alternately on B's bed and mine,and as the alternations became increasingly frequent as the discussion waxed hotter,we were not sorry when the planton's shout "A la promenade les hommes!" scattered the opposing warriors. Then up leaped Jean(who had almost come to blows innumerable times)and rushed laughing to the door,having already forgotten the whole thing.

Now we come to the story of Jean's undoing,and may the gods which made Jean Le Nègre give me grace to tell it as it was.

The trouble started with Lulu. One afternoon,shortly after the telephoning,Jean was sick at heart and couldn't be induced either to leave his couch or to utter a word. Everyone guessed the reason—Lulu had left for another camp that morning. The planton told Jean to come down with the rest and get soupe. No answer. Was Jean sick? "Oui,me seek." And steadfastly he refused to eat,till the disgusted planton gave it up and locked Jean in alone. When we ascended after la soupe we found Jean as we had left him,stretched on his couch,big tears on his cheeks. I asked him if I could do anything for him;he shook his head. We offered him cigarettes—no,he did not wish to smoke. As B and I went away we heard him moaning to himself "Jawnee no see LooLoo no more." With the exception of ourselves,the inhabitants of La Ferté-Macé took Jean's desolation as a great joke. Shouts of Lulu! rent the welkin on all sides. Jean stood it for an hour;then he leaped up,furious,and demanded(confronting the man from whose lips the cry had last issued)— "Feeneesh LooLoo?" The latter coolly referred him to the man next to him;he in turn to someone else;and round and round the room Jean stalked,seeking the offender,followed by louder and louder shouts of Lulu! and Jawnee! the authors of which(so soon as he challenged them)denied with innocent faces their guilt and recommended that Jean look closer next time. At last

Jean took to his couch in utter misery and disgust. The rest of les hommes descended as usual for the promenade—not so Jean. He ate nothing for supper. That evening not a sound issued from his bed.

Next morning he awoke with a broad grin,and to the salutations of Lulu! replied,laughing heartily at himself "FEENEESH Loo Loo." Upon which the tormentors(finding in him no longer a victim)desisted;and things resumed their normal course. If an occasional Lulu! upraised itself,Jean merely laughed,and repeated(with a wave of his arm)"FEENEESH." Finished Lulu seemed to be.

But un jour I had remained upstairs during the promenade,both because I wanted to write and because the weather was worse than usual. Ordinarily,no matter how deep the mud in the cour,Jean and I would trot back and forth,resting from time to time under the little shelter out of the drizzle,talking of all things under the sun. I remember on one occasion we were the only ones to brave the rain and slough—Jean in paper-thin soled slippers(which he had recently succeeded in drawing from the Gestionnaire)and I in my huge sabots—hurrying back and forth with the rain pouring on us,and he very proud. On this day,however,I refused the challenge of the boue.

The promenaders had been singularly noisy,I thought. Now they were mounting to the room making a truly tremendous racket. No sooner were the doors opened than in rushed half a dozen frenzied friends,who began telling me all at once about a terrific thing which my friend the noir had just done. It seems that The Sheeney With The Trick Raincoat had pulled at Jean's handkerchief(Lulu's gift in other days)which Jean wore always conspicuously in his outside breast pocket;that Jean had taken The Sheeney's head in his two hands,held it steady,abased his own head,and rammed the helpless Sheeney as a bull would do—the impact of Jean's head upon The Sheeney's nose causing that well-known feature to occupy a new position in the neighborhood of the right ear. B corroborated this description, adding The Sheeney's nose was broken and that everyone was down on Jean for fighting in an unsportsmanlike way. I found Jean still very angry, and moreover very hurt because everyone was now shunning him. I told him that I personally was glad of what he'd done; but nothing would cheer him up. The Sheeney now entered, very terrible to see, having been patched up by Monsieur Richard with copious plasters. His nose was not broken, he said thickly, but only bent. He hinted darkly of trouble in store for le noir; and received the commiserations of everyone present except Mexique, The Zulu, B and me. The Zulu, I remember, pointed to his own nose (which was not unimportant), then to Jean, then made a moue of excruciating anguish, and winked audibly.

Jean's spirit was broken. The well-nigh unanimous verdict against him had convinced his minutely sensitive soul that it had done wrong. He lay quietly, and would say nothing to anyone.

Some time after the soup, about eight o'clock, The Fighting Sheeney and The Trick Raincoat suddenly set upon Jean Le Nègre à propos nothing; and began pommelling him cruelly. The conscience-stricken pillar of beautiful muscle—who could have easily killed both his assailants at one blow—not only offered no reciprocatory violence but refused even to defend himself. Unresistingly, wincing with pain, his arms mechanically raised and his head bent, he was battered frightfully to the window by his bed, thence into the corner (upsetting the stool in the pissoir), then along the wall to the door. As the punishment increased he cried out like a child: "Laissez-moi tranquille!"—again and again; and in his voice the insane element gained rapidly. Finally, shrieking in agony, he rushed to the nearest window; and while the Sheeneys together pommelled him yelled for help to the planton beneath.—

The unparalleled consternation and applause produced by this one-sided battle had long since alarmed the authorities. I was still trying to break through the five-deep ring of spectators(among whom was The Messenger Boy,who advised me to desist and got a piece of advice in return)—when with a tremendous crash open burst the door;and in stepped four plantons with drawn revolvers,looking frightened to death,followed by the Surveillant who carried a sort of baton and was crying faintly:"Qu'est-ce que c'est!"

At the first sound of the door the two Sheeneys had fled,and were now playing the part of innocent spectators. Jean alone occupied the stage. His lips were parted. His eyes were enormous. He was panting as if his heart would break. He still kept his arms raised as if seeing everywhere before him fresh enemies. Blood spotted here and there the wonderful chocolate carpet of his skin,and his whole body glistened with sweat. His shirt was in ribbons over his beautiful muscles.

Seven or eight persons at once began explaining the fight to the Surveillant,who could make nothing out of their accounts and therefore called aside a trusted older man in order to get his version. The two retired from the room. The plantons,finding the expected wolf a lamb,flourished their revolvers about Jean and threatened him in the insignificant and vile language which plantons use to anyone whom they can bully. Jean kept repeating dully "laissez-moi tranquille. Ils voulaient me tuer." His chest shook terribly with vast sobs.

Now the Surveillant returned and made a speech,to the effect that he had received independently of each other the stories of four men,that by all counts le nègre was absolutely to blame,that le nègre had caused an inexcusable trouble to the authorities and to his fellow-prisoners by this wholly unjustified conflict,and that as a punishment the nègre would now suffer the consequences of his guilt in the cabinot.—Jean had dropped his arms to his sides.

His face was twisted with anguish. He made a child's gesture, a pitiful hopeless movement with his slender hands. Sobbing he protested: "C'est pas ma faute, monsieur le surveillant! Ils m'attaquaient! J'ai rien fait! Ils voulaient me tuer! Demandez à lui"— he pointed to me desperately. Before I could utter a syllable the Surveillant raised his hand for silence: le nègre had done wrong. He should be placed in the cabinot.

—Like a flash, with a horrible tearing sob, Jean leaped from the surrounding plantons and rushed for the coat which lay on his bed screaming—"AHHHHH—mon couteau!"—"Look out or he'll get his knife and kill himself!" someone yelled; and the four plantons seized Jean by both arms just as he made a grab for his jacket. Thwarted in this hope and burning with the ignominy of his situation, Jean cast his enormous eyes up at the nearest pillar, crying hysterically: "Tout le monde me fout au cabinot parce que je suis noir."—In a second, by a single movement of his arms, he sent the four plantons reeling to a distance of ten feet: leaped at the pillar: seized it in both hands like a Samson, and (gazing for another second with a smile of absolute beatitude at its length) dashed his head against it. Once, twice, thrice he smote himself, before the plantons seized him—and suddenly his whole strength wilted; he allowed himself to be overpowered by them and stood with bowed head, tears streaming from his eyes—while the smallest pointed a revolver at his heart.

This was a little more than the Surveillant had counted on. Now that Jean's might was no more, the bearer of the croix de guerre stepped forward and in a mild placating voice endeavored to soothe the victim of his injustice. It was also slightly more than I could stand, and slamming aside the spectators I shoved myself under his honour's nose. "Do you know" I asked, "whom you are dealing with in this man? A child. There are a lot of Jeans where I come from. You heard what he said? He is black, is he not,and gets no justice from you. You heard that. I saw the whole affair. He was attacked,he put up no resistance whatever,he was beaten by two cowards. He is no more to blame than I am."—The Surveillant was waving his wand and cooing "Je comprends,je comprends,c'est malheureux."—"You're god damn right it's malheureux" I said,forgetting my French.—"Quand même,he has resisted authority" the Surveillant gently continued:"Now Jean,be quiet,you will be taken to the cabinot. You may as well go quietly and behave yourself like a good boy."

At this I am sure my eyes started out of my head. All I could think of to say was:"Attends,un petit moment." To reach my own bed took but a second. In another second I was back,bearing my great and sacred pelisse I marched up to Jean. "Jean" I remarked with a smile,"Tu vas au cabinot,mais tu vas revenir tout de suite. Je sais bien que tu as parfaitement raison. Mets cela"—and I pushed him gently into my coat. "Voici mes cigarettes,Jean;tu peux fumer comme tu veux"—I pulled out all I had,one full paquet jaune of Marylands and half a dozen loose ones,and deposited them carefully in the right hand pocket of the pelisse. Then I patted him on the shoulder and gave him the immortal salutation—"Bonne chance,mon ami!" He straightened proudly. He stalked like a king through the doorway. The astounded plantons and the embarrassed Surveillant followed,the latter closing the doors behind him. I was left with a cloud of angry witnesses.

An hour later the doors opened,Jean entered quietly,and the doors shut. As I lay on my bed I could see him perfectly. He was almost naked. He laid my pelisse on his mattress,then walked calmly up to a neighboring bed and skillfully and unerringly extracted a brush from under it. Back to his own bed he tip-toed,sat down on it,and began brushing my coat. He brushed it for a half hour,speaking to no one,spoken to by no one. Finally he put the brush back,disposed the pelisse carefully on his arm,came to my bed,and as carefully laid it down. Then he took from the right hand outside pocket a full pacquet jaune and six loose ciga-rettes,showed them for my approval,and returned them to their place. "Merci" was his sole remark. B got Jean to sit down beside him on his bed and we talked for a few minutes,avoiding the sub-ject of the recent struggle. Then Jean went back to his own bed and lay down.

It was not till later that we learned the climax—not till le petit belge avec le bras cassé,le petit balayeur,came hurrying to our end of the room and sat down with us. He was bursting with excitement,his well arm jerked and his sick one stumped about and he seemed incapable of speech. At length words came.

"M'sieu'Jean"(now that I think of it,I believe someone had told him that all male children in America are named Jean at their birth)"j'ai vu QUELQUE CHOSE! le nègre,vous savez?—il est FORT! M'sieu'Jean,c'est un GEANT,croyez moi! C'est pas un homme,tu sais? Je l'ai vu,moi"—and he indicated his eyes.

We pricked our ears.

The balayeur,stuffing a pipe nervously with his tiny thumb said:"You saw the fight up here? So did I. The whole of it. Le noir avait raison. Well,when they took him downstairs,I slipped out too—Je suis le balayeur,savez-vous? and the balayeur can go where other people can't."

—I gave him a match,and he thanked me. He struck it on his trousers with a quick pompous gesture,drew heavily on his squeaky pipe,and at last shot a minute puff of smoke into the air;then another,and another. Satisfied,he went on;his good hand grasping the pipe between its index and second fingers and resting on one little knee,his legs crossed,his small body hunched forward,wee unshaven face close to mine—went on in the confidential tone of one who relates an unbelievable miracle to a couple of intimate friends:

"M'sieu'Jean,I followed. They got him to the cabinot. The door stood open. At this moment les femmes descendaient,it was their corvée d'eau,vous savez. He saw them,le noir. One of them cried from the stairs,Is a Frenchman stronger than you,Jean? The plantons were standing around him,the Surveillant was behind. He took the nearest planton,and tossed him down the corridor so that he struck against the door at the end of it. He picked up two more,one in each arm,and threw them away. They fell on top of the first. The last tried to take hold of Jean,and so Jean took him by the neck"—(the balayeur strangled himself for our benefit)—"and that planton knocked down the other three,who had got on their feet by this time. You should have seen the Surveillant. He had run away and was saying 'Capture him,capture him.' The plantons rushed Jean,all four of them. He caught them as they came and threw them about. One knocked down the Surveillant. The femmes cried 'Vive Jean',and clapped their hands. The Surveillant called to the plantons to take Jean,but they wouldn't go near Jean,they said he was a black devil. The women kidded them. They were so sore. And they could do nothing. Jean was laughing. His shirt was almost off him. He asked the plantons to come and take him,please. He asked the Surveillant,too. The women had set down their pails and were dancing up and down and yelling. The Directeur came down and sent them flying. The Surveillant and his plantons were as helpless as if they had been children. M'sieu'Jean—quelque chose."

I gave him another match. "Merci,M'sieu'Jean." He struck it,drew on his pipe,lowered it,and went on:

"They were helpless,and men. I am little. I have only one arm,tu sais. I walked up to Jean and said,Jean,you know me,I am your friend. He said,Yes. I said to the plantons,Give me that rope. They gave me the rope that they would have bound him

with. He put out his wrists to me. I tied his hands behind his back. He was like a lamb. The plantons rushed up and tied his feet together. Then they tied his hands and feet together. They took the lacings out of his shoes for fear he would use them to strangle himself. They stood him up in an angle between two walls in the cabinot. They left him there for an hour. He was supposed to have been in there all night;but the Surveillant knew that he would have died,for he was almost naked,and vous savez,M'sieu'Jean,it was cold in there. And damp. A fully clothed man would have been dead in the morning. And he was naked...M'sieu'Jean—un géant!"

—This same petit belge had frequently protested to me that Il est fou,le noir. He is always playing when sensible men try to sleep. The last few hours(which had made of the fou a géant)made of the scoffer a worshipper. Nor did le bras cassé ever from that time forth desert his divinity. If as balayeur he could lay hands on a morceau de pain or de viande,he bore it as before to our beds;but Jean was always called over to partake of the forbidden pleasure.

As for Jean, one would hardly have recognized him. It was as if the child had fled into the deeps of his soul, never to reappear. Day after day went by, and Jean(instead of courting excitement as before)cloistered himself in solitude; or at most sought the company of B and me and Le Petit Belge for a quiet chat or a cigarette. The morning after the three fights he did not appear in the cour for early promenade along with the rest of us(including The Sheeneys). In vain did les femmes strain their necks and eyes to find the noir qui était plus fort que six français. And B and I noticed our bed-clothing airing upon the window-sills. When we mounted, Jean was patting and straightening our blankets, looking for the first time in his life guilty of some enormous crime. Nothing however had disappeared. Jean said "Me feeks lits tous les jours." And every morning he aired and made our beds for us, and we mounted to find him smoothing affectionately some final ruffle, obliterating with enormous solemnity some microscopic crease. We gave him cigarettes when he asked for them(which was almost never)and offered them when we knew he had none or when we saw him borrowing from someone else whom his spirit held in less esteem. Of us he asked no favors. He liked us too well.

When B went away, Jean was almost as desolate as I.

After a fortnight later, when the grey dirty snow-slush hid the black filthy world which we saw from our windows, and when people lived in their ill-smelling beds, it came to pass that my particular amis—The Zulu, Jean, Mexique—and I had all the remaining misérables of La Ferté descended at the decree of Caesar Augustus to endure our bi-weekly bain. I remember gazing stupidly at Jean's chocolate-coloured nakedness as it strode to the tub, a rippling texture of muscular miracle. Tout le monde had baigné(including The Zulu, who tried to escape at the last minute and was nabbed by the planton whose business it was to count heads and see that none escaped the ordeal)and now tout le monde was shivering all together in the anteroom,begging to be allowed to go upstairs and get into bed—when Le Baigneur,Monsieur Richard's strenuous successor that is,set up a hue and cry that one serviette was lacking. The Fencer was sent for. He entered;heard the case;and made a speech. If the guilty party would immediately return the stolen towel,he,the Fencer,would guarantee that party pardon;if not,everyone present should be searched,and the man on whose person the serviette was found va attraper quinze jours de cabinot. This eloquence yielding no results,the Fencer exorted the culprit to act like a man and render to Caesar what is Caesar's. Nothing happened. Everyone was told to get in single file and make ready to pass out the door. One after one we were searched;but so general was the curiosity that as fast as they were inspected the erstwhile bed-enthusiasts,myself included,gathered on the sidelines to watch their fellows instead of availing themselves of the opportunity to go upstairs. One after one we came opposite the Fencer,held up our arms,had our pockets run through and our clothing felt over from head to heel,and were exonerated. When Caesar came to Jean,Caesar's eyes lighted,and Caesar's hitherto perfunctory proddings and pokings became inspired and methodical. Twice he went over Jean's entire body,while Jean,his arms raised in a bored gesture,his face completely expressionless,suffered loftily the examination of his person. A third time the desperate Fencer tried;his hands,starting at Jean's neck,reached the calf of his leg—and stopped. The hands rolled up Jean's right trouser-leg to the knee. They rolled up the underwear on his leg—and there,placed perfectly flat to the skin,appeared the missing serviette. As the Fencer seized it,Jean laughed—the utter laughter of old days—and the onlookers cackled uproariously,while with a broad smile the Fencer proclaimed:"I thought I knew where I should find it." And he added,more pleased with himself than anyone had ever seen him—"Maintenant,vous pouvez tous monter à la chambre." We mounted,happy to get back to bed;but none so happy as Jean Le Nègre. It was not that the cabinot threat had failed to materialize—at any minute a planton might call Jean to his punishment:indeed this was what everyone expected. It was that the incident had absolutely removed that inhibition which(from the day when Jean le noir became Jean le géant)had held the child,which was Jean's soul and destiny,prisoner. From that instant till the day I left him he was the old Jean—joking, fibbing,laughing,and always playing—Jean L'Enfant.

Pete and Jean

And I think of Jean Le Nègre....you are something to dream over,Jean;summer and winter(birds and darkness)you go walking into my head;you are a sudden and chocolate-coloured thing,in your hands you have a habit of holding six or eight plantons(which you are about to throw away)and the flesh of your body is like the flesh of a very deep cigar. Which I am still and always quietly smoking:always and still I am inhaling its very fragrant and remarkable muscles. But I doubt if ever I am quite through with you,if ever I will toss you out of my heart into the sawdust of forgetfulness. Kid,Boy,I'd like to tell you:la guerre est finie.

O yes,Jean:I do not forget,I remember Plenty;the snow's

coming,the snow will throw again a very big and gentle shadow into The Enormous Room and into the eyes of you and me walking always and wonderfully up and down....

—Boy,Kid,Nigger with the strutting muscles—take me up into your mind once or twice before I die(you know why:just because the eyes of me and you will be full of dirt some day). Quickly take me up into the bright child of your mind,before we both go suddenly all loose and silly(you know how it will feel). Take me up(carefully;as if I were a toy)and play carefully with me,once or twice,before I and you go suddenly all limp and foolish. Once or twice before you go into great Jack roses and ivory— (once or twice Boy before we together go wonderfully down into the Big Dirt laughing,bumped with the last darkness).

CHAPTER TWELVE

Three Wise Men

It must have been late in November when la commission arrived. La commission, as I have said, visited La Ferté tous les trois mois. That is to say B and I(by arriving when we did)had just escaped its clutches. I consider this one of the luckiest things in my life.

La commission arrived one morning, and began working immediately.

A list was made of les hommes who were to pass la commission, another of les femmes. These lists were given to the planton with the Wooden Hand. In order to avert any delay, those of les hommes whose names fell in the first half of the list were allowed to enjoy the usual stimulating activities afforded by La Ferté's supreme environment: they were, in fact, confined to The Enormous Room, subject to instant call—moreover they were not called one by one, or as their respective turns came, but in groups of three or four; the idea being that la commission should suffer no smallest annoyance which might be occasioned by loss of time. There were always, in other words, eight or ten men waiting in the upper corridor opposite a disagreeably crisp door, which door belonged to that mysterious room wherein la commission transacted its inestimable affairs. Not more than a couple of yards away ten or eight women waited their turns. Conversation between les hommes and les femmes had been forbidden in the fiercest terms by Monsieur le Directeur: nevertheless conversation spasmodically occurred, thanks to the indulgent nature of the Wooden Hand. The Wooden Hand must have been cuckoo— he looked it. If he wasn't I am totally at a loss to account for his indulgence.

B and I spent a morning in The Enormous Room without results, an astonishing acquisition of nervousness excepted. Après la soupe (noon) we were conducted en haut, told to leave our spoons and bread (which we did) and—in company with several others whose names were within a furlong of the last man called—were descended to the corridor. All that afternoon we waited. Also we waited all next morning. We spent our time talking quietly with a buxom pink-cheeked Belgian girl who was in attendance as translator for one of les femmes. This Belgian told us that she was a permanent inhabitant of La Ferté, that she and another femme honnête occupied a room by themselves, that her brothers were at the front in Belgium, that her ability to speak fluently several languages (including English and German) made her invaluable to Messieurs la commission, that she had committed no crime, that she was held as a suspecte, that she was not entirely unhappy. She struck me immediately as being not only intelligent but alive. She questioned us in excellent English as to our offences, and seemed much pleased to discover that we were—to all appearances—innocent of wrong-doing.

From time to time our subdued conversation was interrupted by admonitions from the amiable Wooden Hand. Twice the door SLAMMED open, and Monsieur le Directeur bounced out frothing at the mouth and threatening everyone with infinite cab-

inot,on the ground that everyone's deportment or lack of it was
menacing the aplomb of the commissioners. Each time the Black
Holster appeared in the background and carried on his master's
bullying until everyone was completely terrified—after which we
were left to ourselves and the Wooden Hand once again.

B and I were allowed by the latter individual—he was that
day,at least,an individual and not merely a planton—to peek over
his shoulder at the men's list. The Wooden Hand even went so far
as to escort our seditious minds to the nearness of their exam-
ination by the simple yet efficient method of placing one of his
human fingers opposite the name of him who was(even at that
moment)within,submitting to the inexorable justice of le gou-
vernement français. I cannot honestly say that the discovery of
this proximity of ourselves to our respective fates wholly pleased
us;yet we were so weary of waiting that it certainly did not wholly
terrify us. All in all,I think I have never been so utterly un-at-ease
as while waiting for the axe to fall,metaphorically speaking,upon
our squawking heads.

We were still conversing with the Belgian girl when a man
came out of the door unsteadily,looking as if he had submitted to
several strenuous fittings of a wooden leg upon a stump not quite
healed. The Wooden Hand,nodding at B,remarked hurriedly in
a low voice:

"Allez!"

And B(smiling at La Belge and at me)entered. He was followed
by the Wooden Hand,as I suppose for greater security.

The next twenty minutes or whatever it was were by far the
most nerve-wracking which I had as yet experienced. La Belge
said to me

"Il est gentil,votre ami"

and I agreed. And my blood was bombarding the roots of my toes
and the summits of my hair.

After(I need not say)two or three million aeons,B emerged. I had not time to exchange a look with him—let alone a word—for the Wooden Hand said from the doorway

"Allez,l'autre américain"

and I entered in more confusion than can easily be imagined;entered the torture chamber,entered the inquisition,entered the tentacles of that sly and beaming polyp,le gouvernement français...

As I entered I said,half-aloud:The thing is this,to look 'em in the eyes and keep cool whatever happens,not for the fraction of a moment forgetting that they are made of merde,that they are all of them composed entirely of merde—I don't know how many inquisitors I expected to see;but I guess I was ready for at least fifteen,among them President Poincaré Lui-même. I hummed noiselessly

"si vous passez par ma vil-le
n'oubliez pas ma maison:
on y mang-e de bonne sou-pe Ton Ton Tay-ne;
faite de merde et les onions,Ton Ton Tayne Ton Ton Ton"

remembering the fine forgeron of Chevincourt who used to sing this, or something very like it, upon a table.—Entirely for the benefit of les deux américains, who would subsequently render Eats uh lonje wae to Tee-pear-raer-ee, wholly for the gratification of a room-full of what Mr. A. liked to call "them bastards", alias "dirty" Frenchmen, alias les poilus, les poilus divins...

A little room. The Directeur's office? Or the Surveillant's? Comfort. O yes, very very comfortable. On my right a table. At the table three persons. Reminds me of Noyon a bit, not unpleasantly of course. Three persons: reading from left to right as I face them—a soggy sleepy slumpy lump in a gendarme's cape and cap, quite old, captain of gendarmes, not at all interested, wrinkled coarse face, only semi-méchant, large hard clumsy hands floppingly disposed on table; wily tidy man in civilian clothes, pen in hand, obviously lawyer, avocat type, little bald on top, sneaky civility, smells of bad perfume or at any rate sweetish soap; tiny red-headed person, also civilian, creased worrying excited face, amusing little body and hands, brief and jumpy, must be a Dickens character, ought to spend his time sailing kites of his own construction over other people's houses in gusty weather. Behind the Three, all tied up with deference and inferiority, mild and spineless, Apollyon.

Would the reader like to know what I was asked?

Ah, would I could say! Only dimly do I remember those moments—only dimly do I remember looking through the lawyer at Apollyon's clean collar—only dimly do I remember the gradual collapse of the capitaine de gendarmerie, his slow but sure assumption of sleepfulness, the drooping of his soggy tête de cochon lower and lower till it encountered one hand whose elbow, braced firmly upon the table, sustained its insensate limpness—only dimly do I remember the enthusiastic antics of the little red-head when I spoke with patriotic fervor

of the wrongs which La France was doing mon ami et moi—
only dimly do I remember,to my right,the immobility of the
Wooden Hand,reminding one of a clothing-dummy,or a life-
size doll which might be made to move only by him who knew
the proper combination...At the outset I was asked: Did I want
a translator? I looked and saw the secrétaire,weak-eyed and
lemon-pale,and I said "Non." I was questioned mostly by the
the avocat,somewhat by the Dickens,never by either the cap-
tain(who was asleep)or the Directeur(who was timid in the
presence of these great and good delegates of hope faith and
charity per the French government). I recall that,for some rea-
son,I was perfectly cool. I put over six or eight hot shots without
losing in the least this composure,which surprised myself and
pleased myself and altogether increased myself. As the questions
came for me I met them half-way,spouting my best or worst
French in a manner which positively astonished the tiny red-
headed demigod. I challenged with my eyes and with my voice
and with my manner Apollyon Himself,and Apollyon Himself
merely cuddled together,depressing his hairy body between its
limbs as a spider sometimes does in the presence of danger. I
expressed immense gratitude to my captors and to le gouver-
nement français for allowing me to see and hear and smell and
touch the things which inhabited La Ferté-Macé,Orne,France.
I do not think that la commission enjoyed me much. It told
me,through its sweetish-soap-leader,that my friend was a
criminal—this immediately upon my entering—and I told it
with a great deal of well-chosen politeness that I disagreed. In
telling how and why I disagreed I think I managed to shove my
shovel-shaped imagination under the refuse of their intellects.
At least once or twice.

Rather fatiguing—to stand up and be told: Your friend is no
good;have you anything to say for yourself?—And to say a great

deal for yourself and for your friend and for les hommes—or try your best to—and be contradicted,and be told "Never mind that,what we wish to know is" and instructed to keep to the subject;et cetera,ad infinitum. At last they asked each other if each other wanted to ask the man before each other anything more,and each other not wanting to do so,they said

"C'est fini."

As at Noyon,I had made an indisputably favorable impression upon exactly one of my three examiners. I refer,in the present case,to the red-headed little gentleman who was rather decent to me. I do not exactly salute him in recognition of this decency;I bow to him,as I might bow to somebody who said he was sorry he couldn't give me a match but there was a cigar-store just around the corner you know.

At "C'est fini" the Directeur leaped into the lime-light with a savage admonition to the Wooden Hand—who saluted,opened the door suddenly,and looked at me with(dare I say it?)admiration. Instead of availing myself of this means of escape I turned to the little kite-flying gentleman and said

"If you please,sir,will you be so good as to tell me what will become of my friend?"

The little kite-flying gentleman did not have time to reply,for the perfumed presence stated drily and distinctly

"We cannot say anything to you upon that point."

I gave him a pleasant smile which said,If I could see your intestines very slowly embracing a large wooden drum rotated by means of a small iron crank turned gently and softly by myself,I should be extraordinarily happy—and I bowed softly and gently to Monsieur le Directeur and I went through the door using all the perpendicular inches which God had given me.

Once outside I began to tremble like a peuplier in l'automne... "L'automne humide et monotone"

—"Allez en bas, pour la soupe" the Wooden Hand said not unkindly. I looked about me. "There will be no more men before the commission until tomorrow" the Wooden Hand said. "Go get your dinner in the kitchen."

I descended.

Afrique was all curiosity—what did they say? what did I say?—as he placed before me a huge, a perfectly huge, an inexcusably huge plate of something more than luke-warm grease...B and I ate at a very little table in la cuisine, excitedly comparing notes as we swallowed the red-hot stuff..."Du pain; prenez, mes amis" Afrique said. "Mangez comme vous voulez" the Cook quoth benignantly, with a glance at us over his placid shoulder...Eat we most surely did. We could have eaten the French government.

The morning of the following day we went on promenade once more. It was neither pleasant nor unpleasant to promenade in the cour while somebody else was suffering in the Room of Sorrow. It was, in fact, rather thrilling.

The afternoon of this day we were all up in The Enormous Room when la commission suddenly entered with Apollyon strutting and lisping behind it, explaining, and poopoohing, and graciously waving his thick wicked arms.

Everyone in The Enormous Room leaped to his feet, removing as he did so his hat—with the exception of les deux américains, who kept theirs on, and The Zulu, who couldn't find his hat and had been trying for some time to stalk it to its lair. La commission reacted interestingly to The Enormous Room: the captain of gendarmes looked soggily around and saw nothing with a good deal of contempt; the scented soap squinted up his face and said "Faugh" or whatever a French bourgeois avocat says in the presence of a bad smell(la commission was standing by the door and consequently close to the cabinet); but the little red-head kite-flying gentleman looked actually horrified.

"Is there in the room anyone of Austrian nationality?"

The Silent Man stepped forward quietly.

"Why are you here?"

"I don't know" The Silent Man said, with tears in his eyes.

"NONSENSE! You're here for a very good reason and you know what it is and you could tell it if you wished you imbecile, you incorrigible, you criminal" Apollyon shouted; then, turning to the avocat and the red-headed little gentleman, "He is a dangerous alien, he admits it, he has admitted it—DON'T YOU ADMIT IT, EH? EH?" He roared at The Silent Man, who fingered his black cap without raising his eyes or changing in the least the simple and supreme dignity of his poise. "He is incorrigible" said (in a low snarl) the Directeur. "Let us go, gentlemen, when you have seen enough." But the red-headed man, as I recollect, was contemplating the floor by the door, where six pails of urine solemnly stood, three of them having overflowed slightly from time to time upon the reeking planks...And the Directeur was told that les hommes should have a tin trough to urinate into, for the sake of sanitation; and that this trough should be immediately installed, installed without delay—"O yes indeed sirs" Apollyon simpered "a very good suggestion; it shall be done immediately: yes indeed. Do let me show you the—it's just outside—" and he bowed them out with no little skill. And the door SLAMMED behind Apollyon and the Three Wise Men.

This, as I say, must have occurred toward the last of November. For a week we waited.

Jan had already left us. Fritz, having waited months for a letter from the Danish consul in reply to the letters which he, Fritz, wrote every so often and sent through le bureau— meaning the secrétaire—had managed to get news of his whereabouts to said consul by unlawful means; and was immediately, upon reception of this news by the consul, set free and invited to join a ship at the nearest port. His departure(than which a more joyous I have never witnessed)has been already mentioned in connection with the third Delectable Mountain,as has been the departure for Précigné of Pompom and Harree ensemble. Bill The Hollander,Monsieur Pet-airs,Mexique,The Wanderer,the little Machine-Fixer,Pete,Jean Le Nègre,The Zulu and Monsieur Auguste(second time)were some of our remaining friends who passed the commission with us. Along with ourselves and these fine people were judged gentlemen like The Trick Raincoat and The Fighting Sheeney. One would think,possibly,that Justice—in the guise of the Three Wise Men—would have decreed different fates,to(say)The Wanderer and The Fighting Sheeney. Au contraire. As I have previously remarked,the ways of God and of the good and great French government are alike inscrutable.

Bill The Hollander,whom we had grown to like whereas at first we were inclined to fear him,Bill The Hollander who washed some towels and handkerchiefs and what-nots for us and turned them a bright pink,Bill The Hollander who had tried so hard to teach The Young Pole the lesson which he could only learn from The Fighting Sheeney,left us about a week after la commission. As I understand it,they decided to send him back to Holland under guard in order that he might be jailed in his native land as a deserter. It is beautiful to consider the unselfishness of le gouvernement français in this case. Much as le gouvernement français would have liked to have punished Bill on its own account and for its own enjoyment,it gave him up—with a Christian smile—to the punishing clutches of a sister or brother government:without a murmur denying itself the incense of his sufferings and the music of his sorrows. Then too it is really inspiring to note the perfect collaboration of la justice français and la justice hollandaise in a critical moment of the world's history. Bill certainly should feel that it was a great honour to be allowed to exemplify this wonderful accord,this exquisite mutual understanding,between the punitive departments of two nations superficially somewhat unrelated—that is,as regards customs and language. I fear Bill didn't appreciate the intrinsic usefulness of his destiny. I seem to remember that he left in a rather Gottverdummerish condition. Such is ignorance.

Poor Monsieur Pet-airs came out of the commission looking extraordinarily épaté. Questioned,he averred that his penchant for inventing force-pumps had prejudiced ces messieurs in his disfavor;and shook his poor old head and sniffed hopelessly. Mexique exited in a placidly cheerful condition,shrugging his shoulders and remarking

The Young Skipper's Mate

"I no do nut'ing. Dese fellers tell me wait few days,after you go free",whereas Pete looked white and determined and said little—except in Dutch to The Young Skipper and his mate;which pair took la commission more or less as a healthy bull-calf takes nourishment:there was little doubt that they would refind la liberté in a short while,judging from the inability of the Three Wise

Men to prove them even suspicious characters. The Zulu uttered a few inscrutable gestures made entirely of silence and said he would like us to celebrate the accomplishment of this ordeal by buying ourselves and himself a good fat cheese apiece—his friend The Young Pole looked as if said ordeal had scared the life out of him temporarily;he was unable to say whether or no he and "mon ami" would leave us:la commission had adopted,in the case of these twain,an awe-inspiring taciturnity. Jean Le Nègre,who was one of the last to pass,had had a tremendously exciting time,due to the fact that le gouvernement française's polished tools had failed to scratch his mystery either in French or English—he came dancing and singing toward us;then,suddenly suppressing every vestige of emotion,solemnly extended for our approval a small scrap of paper on which was written

CALAIS

remarking:"Qu'est-ce que ça veut dire?"—and when we read the word for him,"m'en vais à Calais,moi,travailler à Calais,très bon!"—with a jump and a shout of laughter pocketing the scrap and beginning the Song of Songs

"après la guerre finit…"

A trio which had been hit and hard hit by the Three Wise Men were or was The Wanderer and the Machine-Fixer and Monsieur Auguste—the former having been insulted in respect to Choc-olat's mother(who also occupied the witness-stand)and having retaliated,as nearly as we could discover,with a few remarks straight from the shoulder à propos Justice(O Wanderer,did you expect honour among the honourable?);the Machine-Fixer having been told to shut up in the midst of a passionate plea for

mercy,or at least fair-play,if not in his own case in the case of
the wife who was crazed by his absence;Monsieur Auguste hav-
ing been asked(as he had been asked three months before by the
honourable commissioners)Why did you not return to Russia
with your wife and your child at the outbreak of the war?—and
having replied,with tears in his eyes and that gentle ferocity of
which he was occasionally capable,

"Par-ce-que je n'en a-vais pas les moy-ens. Je ne suis pas un
million-naire,mes-sieurs."

The Babysnatcher,The Trick Raincoat,The Messenger Boy,
The Fighting Sheeney and similar gentry passed the commis-
sion without the slightest apparent effect upon their disagreeable
personalities.

It was not long after Bill The Hollander's departure that we
lost two Delectable Mountains in The Wanderer and Surplice.
Remained The Zulu and Jean Le Nègre...B and I spent most
of our time when on promenade collecting rather beautifully
hued leaves in la cour. These leaves we inserted in one of my
note-books,along with all the colours which we could find on
cigarette-boxes chocolate-wrappers labels of various sorts and
even postage-stamps.(We got a very brilliant red from a cer-
tain piece of cloth.)Our efforts puzzled everyone(including
the plantons)more than considerably;which was natural,con-
sidering that everyone did not know that by this exceedingly
simple means we were effecting a study of colour itself,in
relation to what is popularly called "abstract" and sometimes
"non-representative" painting. Despite their natural puzzle-
ment everyone(plantons excepted)was extraordinarily kind
and brought us often valuable additions to our chromatic col-
lection. Had I,at this moment and in the city of New York,the
complete confidence of one twentieth as many human beings I
should not be so inclined to consider The Great American Pub-

lic as the most aesthetically incapable organization ever created for the purpose of perpetuating defunct ideals and ideas. But of course The Great American Public has a handicap which my friends at La Ferté did not as a rule have—education. Let no one sound his indignant yawp at this. I refer to the fact that,for an educated gent or lady,to create is first of all to destroy—that there is and can be no such thing as authentic art until the bons trucs(whereby we are taught to see and imitate on canvas and in stone and by words this so-called world)are entirely and thoroughly and perfectly annihilated by that vast and painful process of Unthinking which may result in a minute bit of purely personal Feeling. Which minute bit is Art.

Ah well,the revolution—I refer of course to the intelligent revolution—is on the way;is perhaps nearer than some think is possibly knocking at the front doors of The Great Mister Harold Bell Wright and The Great Little Miss Polyanna. In the course of the next ten thousand years it may be possible to find Delectable Mountains without going to prison—captivity I mean,Monsieur le Surveillant—it may be possible,I dare say,to encounter Delectable Mountains who are not in prison...

The autumn wore on.

Rain did,from time to time,not fall:from time to time a sort of unhealthy almost-light leaked from the large uncrisp corpse of the sky,returning for a moment to our view the ruined landscape. From time to time the eye,traveling carefully with a certain disagreeable suddenly fear no longer distances of air coldish and sweet,stopped upon the incredible nearness of the desolate without motion autumn. Awkward and solemn clearness,making louder the unnecessary cries,the hoarse laughter,of the invisible harlots in their muddy yard,pointing a cool actual finger at the silly and ferocious group of manshaped beings huddled in the mud under four or five little trees,came strangely in my own

mind pleasantly to suggest the ludicrous and hideous and beau-
tiful antics of the insane. Frequently I would discover so perfect
a command over myself as to easily reduce la promenade to a
recently invented mechanism; or to the demonstration of a collec-
tion of vivid and unlovely toys around and around which, guard-
ing them with impossible heroism, funnily moved purely unreal
plantons, always absurdly marching, the maimed and stupid dolls
of my imagination. Once I was sitting alone on the long beam of
silent iron and suddenly had the gradual complete unique expe-
rience of death...

It became amazingly cold.

One evening B and myself and I think it was the Machine-
Fixer were partaking of the warmth of a bougie hard by and in fact
between our ambulance beds, when the door opened, a planton
entered, and a list of names(none of which we recognized)was
hurriedly read off with(as in the case of the last partis including
The Wanderer and Surplice)the admonition

"Soyez prêts partir demain matin de bonne heure"
—and the door shut loudly and quickly. Now one of the names
which had been called sounded somewhat like "Broom", and a

strange inquietude seized us on this account. Could it possibly have been "Brown"? We made inquiries of certain of our friends who had been nearer the planton than ourselves. We were told that Pete and The Trick Raincoat and The Fighting Sheeney and Rockyfeller were leaving—about "Brown" nobody was able to enlighten us. Not that opinions in this matter were lacking. There were plenty of opinions—but they contradicted each other to a painful extent. Les hommes were in fact about equally divided;half considering that the occult sound had been intended for "Brown",half that the somewhat asthmatic planton had unwittingly uttered a spontaneous grunt or sigh,which sigh or grunt we had mistaken for a proper noun. Our uncertainty was augmented by the confusion emanating from a particular corner of The Enormous Room,in which corner The Fighting Sheeney was haranguing a group of spectators on the pregnant topic:What I won't do to Précigné when I get there. In deep converse with Bathhouse John we beheld the very same youth who,some time since,had drifted to a place beside me at la soupe—Pete The Ghost,white and determined,blond and fragile:Pete The Shadow...

I forget who,but someone—I think it was the little Machine-Fixer—established the truth that an American was to leave the next morning. That,moreover,said American's name was Brun.

Whereupon B and I became extraordinarily busy.

The Zulu and Jean Le Nègre,upon learning that B was among the partis,came over to our beds and sat down without uttering a word. The former,through a certain shy orchestration of silence,conveyed effortlessly and perfectly his sorrow at the departure;the latter,by his bowed head and a certain very delicate restraint manifested in the wholly exquisite poise of his firm alert body,uttered at least a universe of grief.

The little Machine-Fixer was extremely indignant;not only that his friend was going to a den of thieves and ruffians,but that

his friend was leaving in such company as that of cette crap-
ule(meaning Rockyfeller)and les deux mangeurs de blanc(to
wit, The Trick Raincoat and The Fighting Sheeney). "C'est mal-
heureux" he repeated over and over,wagging his poor little head
in rage and despair—"it's no place for a young man who has
done no wrong,to be shut up with pimps and cutthroats,pour
la durée de la guerre:le gouvernement français a bien fait!" and
he brushed a tear out of his eye with a desperate rapid brittle
gesture...But what angered the Machine-Fixer most was that B
and I were about to be separated—"M'sieu'Jean"(touching me
gently on the knee)"they have no hearts,la commission;they
are not simply unjust,they are cruel,savez-vous? Men are not
like these;they are not men,they are Name of God I don't know
what,they are worse than the animals;and they pretend to Jus-
tice"(shivering from top to toe with an indescribable sneer)"Jus-
tice! My God,Justice!"

All of which,somehow or other,did not exactly cheer us.

And,the packing completed,we drank together for The Last
Time. The Zulu and Jean Le Nègre and the Machine-Fixer and
B and I—and Pete The Shadow drifted over,whiter than I think I
ever saw him,and said simply to me

"I'll take care o'your friend,Johnny"
....and then at last it was lumières éteintes;and les deux améri-
cains lay in their beds in the cold rotten darkness,talking in low
voices of the past,of Pétrouchka,of Paris,of that brilliant and
extraordinary and impossible something:Life.

Morning. Whitish. Inevitable. Deathly cold.

There was a great deal of hurry and bustle in The Enormous
Room. People were rushing hither and thither in the heavy
half-darkness. People were saying good-bye to people. Say-

ing good-bye to friends. Saying good-bye to themselves. We lay and sipped the black evil dull certainly not coffee;lay on our beds,dressed,shuddering with cold,waiting. Waiting. Several of les hommes whom we scarcely knew came up to B and shook hands with him and said good-luck and good-bye. The darkness was going rapidly out of the dull black evil stinking air. B suddenly realized that he had no gift for The Zulu;he asked a fine Norwegian to whom he had given his leather belt if he,the Norwegian,would mind giving it back because there was a very dear friend who had been forgotten. The Norwegian,with a pleasant smile,took off the belt and said "Certainly"...he had been arrested at Bordeaux,where he came ashore from his ship,for stealing three cans of sardines when he was drunk...a very great and dangerous criminal...he said "Certainly" and gave B a pleasant smile,the pleasantest smile in the world. B wrote his own address and name in the inside of the belt,explained in French to The Young Pole that anytime The Zulu wanted to reach him all he had to do was to consult the belt;The Young Pole translated;The Zulu nodded;the Norwegian smiled appreciatively;The Zulu received the belt with a gesture to which words cannot do the faintest justice—

A planton was standing in The Enormous Room,a planton roaring and cursing and crying "Dépêchez-vous,ceux qui vont

partir."—B shook hands with Jean and Mexique and the Machine-Fixer and The Young Skipper,and Bathhouse John(to whom he had given his ambulance tunic,and who was crazy-proud in consequence)and the Norwegian and the Washing-Machine Man and The Hat and many of les hommes whom we scarcely knew.—The Black Holster was roaring

"Allez,nom de dieu,l'américain!"

I went down the room with B and Pete,and shook hands with both at the door. The other parties,alias The Trick Raincoat and The Fighting Sheeney,were already on the way downstairs. The Black Holster cursed us and me in particular and slammed the door angrily in my face—

through the little peephole I caught a glimpse of them,entering the street. I went to my bed and lay down quietly in my great pelisse. The clamor and filth of the room brightened and became distant and faded. I heard the voice of the jolly Alsatian saying

"Courage,mon ami,votre camarade n'est pas mort;vous le verrez plus tard"

and after that,nothing. In front of and on and within my eyes lived suddenly a violent and gentle and dark silence.

The Three Wise Men had done their work. But wisdom cannot rest...

Probably at that very moment they were holding their court in another La Ferté committing to incomparable anguish some few merely perfectly wretched criminals:little and tall,tremulous and brave—all of them white and speechless,all of them with tight bluish lips and large whispering eyes,all of them with fingers weary and mutilated and extraordinarily old...desperate fingers,closing,to feel the final luke-warm fragment of life glide neatly and softly into forgetfulness.

CHAPTER THIRTEEN

I Say Good-Bye to La Misère

To convince the reader that this history is mere fiction(and rather vulgarly violent fiction at that)nothing perhaps is needed save that ancient standby of sob-story writers and thrill-artists alike—the Happy Ending. As a matter of fact,it makes not the smallest difference to me whether anyone who has thus far participated in my travels does or does not believe that they and I are(as that mysterious animal "the public" would say)"real". I do however very strenuously object to the assumption,on the part of anyone,that the heading of this my final chapter stands for anything in the nature of happiness. In the course of recalling(in God knows a rather clumsy and perfectly inadequate way)what happened to me between the latter part of August 1917 and the first day of January 1918,I have proved to my own satisfaction(if not to anyone else's)that I was happier in La Ferté-Macé,with The Delectable Mountains about me,than the very keenest words can pretend to express. I dare say it all comes down to a definition of happiness. And a definition of happiness I most certainly do not intend to attempt;but I can and will say this:to leave La Misère with the knowledge,and worse than that the feeling,that some of the finest people in the world are doomed to remain prisoners thereof for no one knows how long—are doomed to continue,possibly for years and tens of years and all the years which terribly are between them and their deaths,the grey and indivisible Non-existence which without apology you are quitting for Reality—cannot by any stretch of the imagination be conceived as constituting a Happy Ending to a great and personal adventure. That I write this chapter at all is due,purely and simply,to the I dare say unjustified hope on my part that—by recording certain events—it may hurl a little additional light into a very tremendous darkness...

At the outset let me state that what occurred subsequent to the departure for Précigné of B and Pete and The Sheeneys and Rockyfeller is shrouded in a rather ridiculous indistinctness;due,I have to admit,to the depression which this departure inflicted upon my altogether too human nature. The judgment of the Three Wise Men had—to use a peculiarly vigorous(not to say vital)expression of my own day and time—knocked me for a loop. I spent the days intervening between the separation from "votre camarade" and my somewhat supernatural departure for freedom in attempting to partially straighten myself. When finally I made my exit,the part of me popularly referred to as "mind" was still in a slightly bent if not twisted condition. Not until some weeks of American diet had revolutionized my exterior did my interior completely resume the contours of normality. I am particularly neither ashamed nor proud of this(one might nearly say)mental catastrophe. No more ashamed or proud,in fact,than of the infection of three fingers which I carried to America as a little token of La Ferté's good-will. In the latter case I certainly have no right to boast,even should I find myself so inclined;for B took with him to Précigné a case of what his father,upon B's arrival in The Home of The Brave,diagnosed as scurvy—which scurvy made my mutilations look like thirty cents or even less. One of my vividest memories of La Ferté consists in a succession of crackling noises associated with the disrobing of my friend. I recall that we appealed to Monsieur Ree-shar together, B in behalf of his scurvy and I in behalf of my hand plus a queer little row of sores, the latter having proceeded to adorn that part of my face which was trying hard to be graced with a mustache. I recall that Monsieur Ree-shar decreed a bain for B, which bain meant immersion in a large tin tub partially filled with not quite luke-warm water. I, on the contrary, obtained a speck of zinc ointment on a minute piece of cotton, and considered myself peculiarly fortunate. Which details cannot possibly offend the reader's aesthetic sense to a greater degree than have already certain minutiae connected with the sanitary arrangements of the Directeur's little home for homeless boys and girls—therefore I will not trouble to beg the reader's pardon; but will proceed with my story proper or improper.

"Mais qu'est-ce que vous avez" Monsieur le Surveillant demanded, in a tone of profound if kindly astonishment, as I wended my lonely way to la soupe some days after the disappearance of les partis.

I stood and stared at him very stupidly without answering, having indeed nothing at all to say.

"But why are you so sad?" he asked.

"I suppose I miss my friend" I ventured.

"Mais—mais—" he puffed and panted like a very old and fat person trying to persuade a bicycle to climb a hill—"mais—vous avez de la chance!"

"I suppose I have" I said without enthusiasm.

"Mais-mais-parfaitement—vous avez de la chance—uh-ah—uh-ah—parce que—comprenez-vous—votre camarade—uh-ah—a attrapé prison!"

"Uh-ah" I said wearily.

"Whereas" continued Monsieur, "you haven't. You ought to be extraordinarily thankful and particularly happy!"

"I should rather have gone to prison with my friend" I stated briefly; and went into the dining-room, leaving the Surveillant uh-ahing in nothing short of complete amazement.

I really believe that my condition worried him, incredible as this may seem. At the time I gave neither an extraordinary nor a particular damn about Monsieur le Surveillant; nor indeed about "l'autre américain", alias myself. Dimly, through a fog of disinterested inapprehension, I realized that—with the exception of the plantons and of course Apollyon—everyone was trying very hard to help me; that The Zulu, Jean, the Machine-Fixer, Mexique, The Young Skipper, even the Washing-Machine Man (with whom I promenaded frequently when no one else felt like taking the completely unagreeable air) were kind, very kind, kinder than I can possibly say. As for Afrique and the Cook—there was nothing too good for me at this time. I asked the latter's permission to cut wood, and was not only accepted as a sawyer but encouraged with assurances of the best coffee there was, with real sugar dedans. In the little space outside the cuisine, between the building and la cour, I sawed away of a morning to my great satisfaction;from time to time clumping my saboted way into the Chef's domain in answer to a subdued signal from Afrique. Of an afternoon I sat with Jean or Mexique or The Zulu on the long beam of silent iron,pondering very carefully nothing at all,replying to their questions or responding to their observations in a highly mechanical manner. I felt myself to be,at last,a doll—taken out occasionally and played with and put back into its house and told to go to sleep...

One afternoon I was lying on my couch,thinking of the usual Nothing,when a sharp cry sung through The Enormous Room

"Il tombe de la neige—Noël! Noël!"

I sat up. The Garde Champêtre was at the nearest window,dancing a little horribly and crying

"Noël! Noël!"

I went to another window and looked out. Sure enough. Snow was falling,gradually and wonderfully falling,silently falling through the thick soundless autumn...It seemed to me supremely beautiful,the snow. There was about it something unspeakably crisp and exquisite,something perfect and minute and gentle and fatal...The Garde Champêtre's cry began a poem in the back of my head, a poem about the snow, a poem in French, beginning Il tombe de la neige, Noël, Noël. I watched the snow. After a long time I returned to my bunk and I lay down, closing my eyes; feeling the snow's minute and crisp touch falling gently and exquisitely, falling perfectly and suddenly, through the thick soundless autumn of my imagination...

"L'américain! L'américain!"

Someone is speaking to me.

"Le petit belge avec le bras cassé est là-bas, à la porte, il veut parler..."

I marched the length of the room. The Enormous Room is filled with a new and beautiful darkness, the darkness of the snow outside, falling and falling and falling with the silent and actual gesture which has touched the soundless country of my mind as a child touches a toy it loves...

Through the locked door I heard a nervous whisper: "Dis à l'américain que je veux parler avec lui"—"Me voici" I said.

"Put your ear to the key-hole, M'sieu'Jean" said the Machine-Fixer's voice. The voice of the little Machine-Fixer, tremendously excited. I obey—"Alors. Qu'est-ce que c'est, mon ami?"

"M'sieu'Jean! Le Directeur va vous appeler tout de suite! You must get ready instantly! Wash and shave, eh? He's going to call you right away. And don't forget! Oloron! You will ask to go to Oloron-Sainte-Marie, where you can paint! Oloron-Sainte-Marie, Basses-Pyrenées! N'oubliez pas, M'sieu'Jean! Et dépêchez-vous!"

"Merci bien, mon ami!"—I remember now. The little Machine-Fixer and I had talked. It seemed that la commission had decided that I was not a criminal, but only a suspect. As a suspect I would be sent to some place in France, any place I wanted to go provided it was not on or near the sea-coast. That was in order that I should not perhaps try to escape from France. The Machine-Fixer had advised me to ask to go to Oloron-Sainte-Marie. I should say that, as a painter, the Pyrenées particularly appealed to me. "Et qu'il fait beau, là-bas! The snow on the mountains! And it's not cold. And what mountains! You can live there very cheaply. As a suspect you will merely have to report once a month to the chief of police of Oloron-Sainte-Marie; he's an old friend of mine! He's a fine fat red-cheeked man, very kindly. He will make it easy for you, M'sieu' Jean, and will help you out in every way, when you tell him you are a friend of the little Belgian with the broken arm. Tell him I sent you. You will have a very fine time, and you can paint: such scenery to paint! My God—not like what you see from these windows. I advise you by all means to ask to go to Oloron."

So thinking I lathered my face, standing before Judas's mirror.

"You don't rub enough" the Alsatian advised, "il faut frotter bien!" A number of fellow-captives were regarding my toilet with surprise and satisfaction. I discovered in the mirror an astounding beard and a good layer of dirt. I worked busily, counseled by several voices, censured by the Alsatian, encouraged by Judas himself. The shave and the wash completed I felt considerably refreshed.

WHANG.

"L'américain en bas!" It was the Black Holster. I carefully adjusted my tunic and obeyed him.

The Directeur and the Surveillant were in consultation when I entered the latter's office. Apollyon, seated at a desk, surveyed me very fiercely. His subordinate swayed to and fro, clasping and unclasping his hands behind his back, and regarded me with an expression of almost benevolence. The Black Holster guarded the doorway.

Turning on me ferociously—"Votre ami est mauvais, très mauvais, SAVEZ-VOUS?" le Directeur shouted.

I answered quietly "Oui? Je ne le savais pas."

"He is a bad fellow, a criminal, a traitor, an insult to civilization" Apollyon roared into my face.

"Yes?" I said again.

"You'd better be careful!" the Directeur shouted. "Do you know what's happened to your friend?"

"Sais pas" I said.

"He's gone to prison where he belongs!" Apollyon roared. "Do you understand what that means?"

"Peut-être" I answered, somewhat insolently I fear.

"You're lucky not to be there with him! Do you understand?" Monsieur le Directeur thundered, "and next time pick your friends better, take more care I tell you, or you'll go where he is—TO PRISON FOR THE REST OF THE WAR!"

"With my friend I should be well content in prison" I said evenly, trying to keep looking through him and into the wall behind his black big spidery body.

"In God's Name what a fool!" the Directeur bellowed furiously—and the Surveillant remarked pacifying "Il aime trop son camarade, c'est tout."—"But his comrade is a traitor and a villain!" objected the Fiend, at the top of his harsh voice—"Comprenezvous: votre ami est UN SALAUD!" he snarled at me.

He seems afraid that I don't get his idea, I said to myself. "I understand what you say" I assured him.

"And you don't believe it?" he screamed, showing his fangs and otherwise looking like an exceedingly dangerous maniac.

"Je ne le crois pas, Monsieur."

"O God's name!" he shouted. "What a fool, quel idiot, what a beastly fool!" And he did something through his frothcovered lips, something remotely suggesting laughter.

Hereupon the Surveillant again intervened. I was mistaken. It was lamentable I could not be made to understand. Very true.

But I had been sent for—"do you know,you have been decided to be a suspect" Monsieur le Surveillant turned to me,"and now you may choose where you wish to be sent." Apollyon was blowing and wheezing and muttering...clenching his huge pinkish hands.

I addressed the Surveillant,ignoring Apollyon. "I should like,if I may,to go to Oloron-Sainte-Marie."

"What do you want to go there for?" the Directeur exploded threateningly.

I explained that I was by profession an artist,and had always wanted to view the Pyrenées. "The environment of Oloron would be most stimulating to an artist"—

"Do you know it's near Spain?" he snapped,looking straight at me.

I knew it was,and therefore replied with a carefully childish ignorance:"Spain? Indeed! Very interesting."

"You want to escape from France,that's it?" the Directeur snarled.

"Oh,I hardly should say that" the Surveillant interposed soothingly,"he is an artist,and Oloron is a very pleasant place for an artist. A very nice place. I hardly think his choice of Oloron a cause for suspicion. I should think it a very natural desire on his part."—His superior subsided snarling.

After a few more questions I signed some papers which lay on the desk,and was told by Apollyon to get out.

"When can I expect to leave?" I asked the Surveillant.

"Oh,it's only a matter of days,of weeks perhaps" he assured me benignantly.

"You'll leave when it's proper for you to leave!" Apollyon burst out,"do you understand?"

"Yes,indeed. Thank you very much" I replied with a bow,and exited. On the way to The Enormous Room the Black Holster said to me sharply

"Vous allez partir?"

"Oui."

He gave me such a look as would have turned a mahogany piano leg into a mound of smoking ashes, and slammed the key into the lock.

—Everyone gathered about me. "What news?"

"I have asked to go to Oloron as a suspect" I answered.

"You should have taken my advice and asked to go to Cannes" the fat Alsatian reproached me. He had indeed spent a great while advising me—but I trusted the little Machine-Fixer.

"Parti?" Jean Le Nègre said with huge eyes, touching me gently.

"Non, non. Plus tard, peut-être. Pas maintenant" I assured him. And he patted my shoulder and smiled, "Bon!" And we smoked a cigarette in honour of the snow, of which Jean—in contrast to the majority of les hommes—highly and unutterably approved. "C'est joli!" he would say, laughing wonderfully. And next morning he and I went on an exclusive promenade, I in my sabots, Jean in a pair of slippers which he had received (after many requests) from the bureau. And we strode to and fro in the muddy cour admiring la neige, not speaking.

One day, after the snow-fall, I received from Paris a complete set of Shakespeare in the Everyman edition. I had forgotten completely that B and I—after trying and failing to get William Blake—had ordered and paid for the better known William; the ordering and communicating in general being done with the collaboration of Monsieur Pet-airs. It was a curious and interesting feeling which I experienced upon first opening to As You Like It...the volumes had been carefully inspected, I learned, by the secrétaire, in order to eliminate the possibility of their concealing something valuable or dangerous. And in this connection let me add that the secrétaire, or (if not he) his superiors, were a good judge of what is valuable—if not what is dangerous. I know this because,whereas my family several times sent me socks in every case inclosing cigarettes,I received invariably the former sans the latter. Perhaps it is not fair to suspect the officials of La Ferté of this peculiarly mean theft;I should,possibly,doubt the honesty of that very same French censor whose intercepting of B's correspondence had motivated our removal from the Section Sanitaire. Heaven knows I wish(like the Three Wise Men)to give justice where justice is due.

Somehow or other,reading Shakespeare did not appeal to my disordered mind. I tried Hamlet and Julius Caesar once or twice and gave it up,after telling a man who asked "Shah-kay-spare,who is Shah-kay-spare?" that Mr. S. was the Homer of the English-speaking peoples—which remark,to my surprise,appeared to convey a very definite idea to the questioner and sent him away perfectly satisfied. Most of the timeless time I spent promenading in the rain and sleet with Jean Le Nègre,or talking with Mexique,or exchanging big gifts of silence with The Zulu. For Oloron—I did not believe in it,and I did not particularly care. If I went away,good;if I stayed,so long as Jean and The Zulu and Mexique were with me,good.

At least the Surveillant let me alone on the Soi-Même topic. After my brief visit to Satan I wallowed in a perfect luxury of dirt. And no one objected. On the contrary everyone(realizing that the enjoyment of dirt may be made the basis of a fine art)beheld with something like admiration my more and more uncouth appearance. Moreover,by being dirtier than usual I was protesting in a(to me)very satisfactory way against all that was neat and tidy and bigoted and solemn and founded upon the anguish of my fine friends. And my fine friends,being my fine friends,understood. Simultaneously with my arrival at the summit of dirtiness—by the calendar,as I guess,December the twenty-first—came the Black Holster into The Enormous Room and with an excited and angry mien proclaimed loudly

"L'américain! Allez chez le Directeur. De suite."

I protested mildly that I was dirty—

"N'importe. Allez avec moi" and down I went to the amazement of everyone and the great amusement of myself. "By Jove, wait till he sees me this time" I remarked half-audibly...

The Directeur said nothing when I entered.

The Directeur extended a piece of paper, which I read.

The Directeur said, with an attempt at amiability "Alors, vous allez sortir."

I looked at him in eleven-tenths of amazement. I was standing in the bureau de Monsieur le Directeur du Camp de Triage de La Ferté-Macé, Orne, France, and holding in my hand a slip of paper which said that if there was a man named Edward E. Cummings he should report immediately to the American Embassy, Paris, and I had just heard the words

"Alors, vous allez sortir."

Which words were pronounced in a voice so subdued, so constrained, so mild, so altogether ingratiating, that I could not imagine to whom it belonged. Surely not to the Fiend, to Apollyon, to the Prince of Hell, to Satan, to Monsieur le Directeur du Camp de Triage de La Ferté-Macé—

"Get ready. You will leave immediately."

Then I noticed the Surveillant. Upon his face I saw an almost smile. He returned my gaze and remarked

"uh-ah, uh-ah, Oui."

"That's all" the Directeur said. "You will call for your money at the bureau of the Gestionnaire before leaving."

"Go and get ready" the Fencer said, and I certainly saw a smile...

"I? Am? Going? To? Paris?" somebody who certainly wasn't myself remarked in a kind of whisper.

"Parfaitement."—Pettish. Apollyon. But how changed. Who the devil is myself? Where in Hell am I? What is Paris—a place,a somewhere,a city,life,to live:infinitive. Present first singular I live. Thou livest. The Directeur. The Surveillant. La Ferté-Macé,Orne,France. "Edward E. Cummings will report immediately." Edward E. Cummings. The Surveillant. A piece of yellow paper. The Directeur. A necktie. Paris. Life. Liberté. La liberté. "La Liberté"—I almost shouted in agony.

"Dépêchez-vous. Savez-vous,vous allez partir de suite. Cet après-midi. Pour Paris."

I turned,I turned so suddenly as almost to bowl over the Black Holster,Black Holster and all;I turned toward the door,I turned upon the Black Holster,I turned into Edward E. Cummings, I turned into what was dead and is now alive,I turned into a city,I turned into a dream—

I am standing in The Enormous Room for the last time. I am saying good-bye. No,it is not I who am saying good-bye. It is in fact somebody else,possibly myself. Perhaps myself has shaken hands with a little creature with a wizened arm,a little creature in whose eyes tears for some reason are;with a placid youth(Mexique?)who smiles and says shakily

"Good-bye Johnny,I no for-get you"
with a crazy old fellow who somehow or other has got inside B's tunic and is gesticulating and crying out and laughing;with a frank-eyed boy who claps me on the back and says

"Good-bye and good-luck t'you"
(is he The Young Skipper,by any chance?);with a lot of hungry wretched beautiful people—I have given my bed to The Zulu by Jove,and The Zulu is even now standing guard over it,and his friend The Young Pole has given me the address of "mon ami" and there are tears in The Young Pole's eyes,and I seem to be amazingly tall and altogether tearless—and this is the nice Norwegian,who got drunk at Bordeaux and stole three(or four was it?)cans of sardines...and now I feel before me someone who

also has tears in his eyes,someone who is in fact crying,someone
whom I feel to be very strong and young as he hugs me quietly in
his firm alert arms,kissing me on both cheeks and on the lips...

"Goo-bye boy"

—O good-bye,good-bye,I am going away Jean;have a good
time,laugh wonderfully when le neige comes...

And I am standing somewhere with arms lifted up. "Si vous
avez une lettre,sais-tu,il faut dire. For if I find a letter on you it
will go hard with the man that gave it to you to take out." Black.
The Black Holster even. Does not examine my baggage. Wonder
why? "Allez!" Jean's letter to his gonzesse in Paris still safe in my
little pocket under my belt. Ha ha,by God,that's a good one on
you,you Black Holster,you Very Black Holster. That's a good one.
Glad I said good-bye to the Cook. Why didn't I give Monsieur
Auguste's little friend,the cordonnier,more than six francs for
mending my shoes? He looked so injured. I am a fool,and I am
going into the street,and I am going by myself with no planton
into the little street of the little city of La Ferté-Macé which is a
little,a very little city in France,where once upon a time I used to
catch water for an old man...

I have already shaken hands with the Cook,and with the
cordonnier who has beautifully mended my shoes. I am saying
good-bye to les deux balayeurs. I am shaking hands with the lit-
tle(the very little)Machine-Fixer again. I have given him a franc
and I have given Garabaldi a franc. We had a drink a moment
ago on me. The tavern is just opposite the gare,where there will
soon be a train. I will get upon the soonness of the train and
ride into the now of Paris. No,I must change at a station called
Briouze did you say? Good-bye,mes amis,et bonne chance! They
disappear,pulling and pushing at a cart,les deux balayeurs...de
mes couilles...by Jove what a tin noise is coming,see the wooden
engineer,he makes a funny gesture utterly composed(composed

silently and entirely) of merde. Merde! Merde. A wee tiny absurd whistle coming from nowhere, from outside of me. Two men opposite. Jolt. A few houses a fence a wall a bit of neige float foolishly by and through a window. These gentlemen in my compartment do not seem to know that La Misère exists. They are talking politics. Thinking that I don't understand. By Jesus, that's a good one. "Pardon me, gentlemen, but does one change at the next station for Paris?" Surprised. I thought so. "Yes, Monsieur, the next station." By Hell I surprised somebody...

Who are a million, a trillion, a nonillion young men? All are standing. I am standing. We are wedged in and on and over and under each other. Sardines. Knew a man once who was arrested for stealing sardines. I, sardine, look at three sardines, at three million sardines, at a carful of sardines. How did I get here? O yes of course. Briouze. Horrible name "Briouze". Made a bluff at riding deuxième classe on a troisième classe ticket bought for me by les deux balayeurs. Gentlemen in the compartment talked French with me till conductor appeared. "Tickets, gentlemen?" I extended mine dumbly. He gave me a look "How? This is third class!" I look intelligently ignorant. "Il ne comprend pas français" says the gentleman. "Ah!" says the conductor, "tease ease eye-ee thoorde claz tea-keat. You air een tea say-coend claz. You weel go ean-too tea thoorde claz weal you yes pleace at once?" So I got stung after all. Third is more amusing certainly, though goddamn hot with these sardines, including myself of course. Oh yes of course. Poilus en permission. Very old some. Others mere kids. Once saw a planton who never saw a razor. Yet he was réformé. C'est la guerre. Several of us get off and stretch at a little tank-town-station. Engine thumping up front somewhere in the darkness. Wait. They get their bidons filled. Wish I had a bidon, a dis donc bidon n'est-ce pas. Faut pas t'en faire, who sang or said that?

PEE-p...

We're off.

I am almost asleep. Or myself. What's the matter here? Sardines writhing about,cut it out,no room for that sort of thing. Jolt.

"Paris"

Morning. Morning in Paris. I found my bed full of fleas this morning,and I couldn't catch the fleas,though I tried hard because I was ashamed that anyone should find fleas in my bed which is at the Hôtel des Saints-Pères whither I went in a fiacre and the driver didn't know where it was. Wonderful. This is the American Embassy. I must look funny in my pelisse. Thank God for the breakfast I ate somewhere...good-looking girl,Parisienne,at the switch-board upstairs. "Go right in,sir." A-1 English by God. So this is the person to whom Edward E. Cummings is immediately to report.

"Is this Mr. Cummings?"

"Yes." Rather a young man,very young in fact. Jove I must look queer.

"Sit down! We've been looking all over creation for you."

"Yes?"

"Have some cigarettes?"

By God he gives me a sac of Bull. Extravagant they are at the American Embassy. Can I roll one? I can. I do.

Conversation. Pleased to see me. Thought I was lost for good. Tried every means to locate me. Just discovered where I was. What was it like? No,really? You don't mean it! Well I'll be damned! Look here;this man B,what sort of a fellow is he? Well I'm interested to hear you say that. Look at this correspondence. It seems to me that a fellow who could write like that wasn't dangerous. Must be a little queer. Tell me,isn't he a trifle foolish? That's what I thought. Now I'd advise you to leave France as soon as you can. They're picking up ambulance men left and right,men who've got no business to be in Paris. Do you want to leave by the next boat? I'd advise it. Good. Got money? If you haven't we'll pay your fare. Or half of it. Plenty,eh? Norton-Harjes,I see. Mind going second class? Good. Not much difference on this line. Now you can take these papers and go to...No time to lose,as she sails tomorrow. That's it. Grab a taxi,and hustle. When you've got those signatures bring them to me and I'll fix you all up. Get your ticket first,here's a letter to the manager of the Compagnie Générale. Then go through the police department. You can do it if you hurry. See you later. Make it quick,eh? Good-bye!

The streets. Les rues de Paris. I walked past Notre-Dame. I bought tobacco. Jews are peddling things with American trademarks on them,because in a day or two it's Christmas I suppose. Jesus it is cold. Dirty snow. Huddling people. La guerre. Always la guerre. And chill. Goes through these big mittens. Tomorrow I shall be on the ocean. Pretty neat the way that passport was put through. Rode all day in a taxi,two cylinders,running on one. Everywhere waiting lines. I stepped to the head and was attended to by the officials of the great and good French government. Gad that's a good one. A good one on le gouvernement français. Pretty good. Les rues sont tristes. Perhaps there's no Christmas,perhaps the French government has forbidden Christmas. Clerk at Norton-Harjes seemed astonished to see me. O God it is cold in Paris. Everyone looks hard under lamplight,because it's winter I suppose. Everyone hurried. Everyone hard. Everyone cold. Everyone huddling. Everyone alive;alive:alive.

Shall I give this man five francs for dressing my hand? He said "anything you like,monsieur." Ship's doctor probably well-paid. Probably not. Better hurry before I put my lunch. Aweinspiring stink,because it's in the bow. Little member of the crew immersing his guess what in a can of some liquid or other,groaning from time to time,staggers when the boat tilts. "Merci bien,Monsieur!" That was the proper thing. Now for the—never can reach it—here's the première classe one—any port in a storm...Feel better now. Narrowly missed American officer but just managed to make it. Was it yesterday or day before saw the Vaterland,I mean the what deuce is it—that biggest in the world afloat boat. Damned rough. Snow falling. Almost slid through the railing that time. Snow. The snow is falling into the sea;which quietly receives it:into which it utterly and peacefully disappears. Man with a college degree returning from Spain,not disagreeable sort,talks Spanish with that fat man who's an Argentinian. -Tinian? -Tinish,perhaps. All the same. In other words Tin. Nobody at the table knows I speak English or am American. Hell,that's a good one on nobody. That's a pretty fat kind of a joke on nobody. Think I'm French. Talk mostly with those three or four Frenchmen going on permission to somewhere via New York. One has an accordion. Like second class. Wait till you see les gratte-ciel,I tell 'em. They say "Oui?" and don't believe. I'll show them. America. The land of the flea and the home of the dag' short for dago of course. My spirits are constantly improving. Funny Christmas,second day out. Wonder if we'll dock New Year's Day. My God what a list to starboard. They say a waiter broke his arm when it happened,ballast shifted. Don't believe it. Something wrong. I know I nearly fell downstairs...

My God what an ugly island. Hope we don't stay here long. All the red-bloods first-class much excited about land. Damned ugly,I think.

Hullo.

The tall,impossibly tall,incomparably tall,city shoulderingly upward into hard sunlight leaned a little through the octaves of its parallel edges,leaningly strode upward into firm hard snowy sunlight;the noises of America nearingly throbbed with smokes and hurrying dots which are men and which are women and which are things new and curious and hard and strange and vibrant and immense,lifting with a great undulous stride firmly into immortal sunlight...

Glossary of Foreign Terms

This glossary is intended primarily for readers who have little or no knowledge of French or the other languages spoken by the occupants of "The Enormous Room". Nevertheless, it is hoped that those who are familiar with the tongues of La Ferté-Macé will find some of the entries helpful, particularly those for slang and colloquial terms no longer in current use; idiomatic expressions and sentence structures that reflect the unusual speech patterns of specific individuals; and the author's own transliteration of foreign languages and dialects for which there are no standard equivalents in English or the languages themselves.

As a general rule, all words, phrases and sentences are listed alphabetically with phrases and sentences in their original word order (e.g., "à bon marché" is listed under "à", "Le Bon Dieu" under "Le", and "se promener" under "se"). However, individual nouns in French appear only in the singular, unless the plural is formed by means other than the addition of an "s" (e.g., "journal (journaux)" and "nouveau (x)"), and without their definite (l', le, la, les) or indefinite (un, une) articles, unless the meaning of a noun is altered by the omission of its article or, in one instance, its article and the accompanying verb in English (e.g., "gratte-ciel (les)" and "grève (made la)"). All exceptions are treated like the examples given above.

For the convenience of the reader, words, phrases and sentences in series within a single paragraph are listed under the entry for the first word, phrase or sentence in the sequence (e.g., "Bon. Très bon. Très bien fait" is listed under "Bon"; "L'américain. Allez chez le Directeur. De suite" under "L'américain", and "saucisse, fromage, pain, chocolat, pinard rouge" under "saucisse"). The presence of a descriptive or explanatory interpolation in English within a series is indicated by three asterisks (***).

The editor would like to take this opportunity to acknowledge, with thanks, his indebtedness to the author's daughter and D. Jon Grossman for their invaluable assistance with the translations from the French; to Dr. George Stachurko for his help with the Polish and Russian terms; and to Professor Richard Kennedy and the publishers for their many helpful suggestions. The responsibility for the final form and content of the glossary, however, is the editor's alone.

A

à bon marché   cheaply
à la chambre   to the room
A la douche les hommes   To the shower, men
A la promenade les hommes   Exercise time, men
A la santé de ma marraine charmante.   Your good health my charming godmother.
A la soupe   Soup time; Meal time
A la soupe les hommes   Meal time, men
adorée   loved one
affaires   belongings
algérien   Algerian
Allez!   Go on!

Allez! Au cabinot! De suite!   Go on! To solitary confinement!
At once!

Allez avec lui,chercher ses affaires,de suite.   Go with him,to
fetch his belongings,at once.

Allez,descendez.   Go on,go down.

Allez en bas,pour la soupe   Go downstairs,for soup

Allez,l'autre américain   Go on,the other American

Allez,Nom de Dieu   Go on,for God's sake

Allez,nom de dieu,l'américain!   Go on,for God's
sake,American!

Allez,tout-le-monde,'plucher les pommes!   Go on,every-
one,peel the potatoes!

allié   ally

Allons!   Come on!

Al-lons,mes amis! Chan-tons 'Quackquackquack.'   Come
on,my friends! Let's sing 'Quackquackquack.'

alors   well; well then

Alors! C'est as-sez.   Well! that's enough.

Alors. Qu'est-ce que c'est,mon ami?   Well then. What is it,my
friend?

Alors,qui m'appelle? Qu'est-ce qu'on fout ici.   Well,who's
calling me? What the hell's going on here.

Alors,venez avec moi KEW-MANGZ.   Well,come with me
KEW-MANGZ.

Alors,vous allez sortir.   Well then,you're getting out.

Also sprach   Thus spoke

américain   American

ami   friend

anglais   English; Englishman

apache   hoodlum

après la guerre finit   after the war is over

après la guerre finit,/soldat anglais parti,/mademoiselle que

je laissais en France/avec des pickaninee   after the war is over,/English soldier gone,/mademoiselle that I left in France/with pickaninnies.

après la soupe   after soup; after the meal

Assez!   Enough!

Asseyez-vous là,tête de cochon.   Sit there,stubborn fool.

Assieds là   Sit there

Attends,Nom de Dieu.   For God's sake,wait.

Attends,un petit moment.   Wait a moment.

Attention!   Look out!

attrapait vingt-huit jours de cabinot   got 28 days in solitary

au contraire   on the contrary

Au contraire,je veux bien.   On the contrary,I would like some.

automne   autumn

Aux armes!   To arms!

avocat   attorney; solicitor

B

bahsht! (possibly "basta!")   nothing doing!

baigné   bathed

baigneur   bath attendant

baigneur de femmes moi   me women's bath attendant

bain   bath

Balai? Vous. Tout le monde. Propre. Surveillant dit. Pas moi,n'est-ce pas?   Sweep? You. Everyone. Clean. Superintendent says so. Not me,right?

balayeur   sweeper

banque   card game similar to baccarat

Barbu   bearded one (*used as a nickname*)

Barbu! j'vais couper ta barbe,barbu!   Barbu! I am going to cut your beard,bearded one!

beau temps   good weather

belge   Belgian

Belgique   Belgium

B'en sûr.   Certainly.

bidon   tin can, drum, water-bottle, canteen

bien entendu   of course

Bis!—Bien joué!—Allez!—Vas-y!   Encore!—Well played!—Go
   on!—Go to it!

blague   practical joke, trick, hoax; blunder; nonsense

blanchisseuse   laundress

boche   German, Jerry, Kraut

Bo'jour,tou'l'monde   Good morning,everyone

bon   good

Bon. Alors,vous vous ap-pel-lez KEW-MANGZ,
   n'est-ce-pas?   Good. Well then,your name is KEW-
   MANGZ,isn't it?

Bon. Bon. Pas moi. Surveillant. Harree faire pour tout le
   monde.   Good. Good. Not me. Superintendent. Harree
   clean for everybody.

Bon,eh? Bien fait,eh?   Good,eh? Well done,eh?

bon mot   clever remark

Bon soir,Madame la Lune   Good evening,Madam Moon

Bon. Très bon. Très bien fait   Good. Very good. Very well
   done

bonhomme (bonshommes)   good-natured man (men), little
   man (men)

Bonne-nuit   Good night

bonne pour coucher avec   good to go to bed with

bons trucs   good dodges

boucherie   butcher's shop

boue   mud

bougie   candle

Boxe? Vous! Want to box? You!

brachwurst i.e. bratwurst, a mild German sausage

bureau office

C

**Ça m'est égal, parce qu'il n'y a plus d'heures—le gouverne-
ment français les defend.** It's all the same to me, because
there is no more time—the French government has forbid-
den it.

ça ne vaut rien du tout—il faut de la viande, tous les jours it's
worth nothing at all—one needs meat, every day

Ça Pue It Stinks

Ça se peut. That may be so.

Ça va mieux. That's better.

cabinet lavatory, toilet

cabinet d'aisance bathroom, comfort station

cabinot punishment cell; solitary confinement

cabinot de suite solitary at once

cachot dungeon

café coffee

café sucré sweetened coffee

Camp de Triage de La Ferté-Macé Detention Camp of La
Ferté-Macé

caoutchouc rubber

captaine de gendarmerie captain of gendarmes

carte postale postcard

casque helmet

cauchemar nightmare

ce monsieur là that gentleman there

Ce n'est pas difficile à peindre, un coucher du soleil It's not
difficult to paint, a sunset

Ce n'est pas une existence This is no sort of life

cellule   cell

Ces cigarettes ne fument pas!   These cigarettes don't burn!

Ces grands messieurs qui ne se foutent pas mal si l'on CREVE de faim, savez-vous ils croient chacun qu'il est Le Bon Dieu LUI-Même. Et M'sieu'Jean, savez-vous, ils sont tous— ***—Ils. Sont. Des. CRAPULES!   These grand gentlemen who couldn't care less if people DIE of hunger, you know each one believes he's The Good Lord HIM-Self. And Mr. John, you know, they are all—***—They. Are. Just. SCUM!

ces messieurs   these gentlemen

c'est de l'eau, monsieur?   it's water, sir?

C'est défendu.   That's forbidden.

C'est d'la blague. Sais-tu, il n'y a plus de trains?—Le conducteur est mort, j'connais sa sœur.—J'suis foutu mon vieux.—Nous sommes tous perdus, dis-donc.—Quelle heure?—Mon cher, il n'y a plus d'heures, le gouvernement français les defend.   That's clap-trap. Do you know, there are no more trains?—The conductor is dead, I know his sister.—I've had it, old friend.—We're all lost, you know.—What's the time?—My friend, there's no more time, the French government has forbidden it.

c'est d'la blague, tu sais? Moi, je connais le sœur du conducteur   that's bunk, you know? I, I know the conductor's sister

C'est dommage   It's a pity

C'est emmerdant.   It's a pain in the arse (*slang*).

C'est fini.   It's finished.

C'est joli!   It's pretty!

C'est la femme allemande qui s'appelle Lily   It's the German woman called Lily

c'est la guerre   that's war

C'est la guerre / faut pas t'en faire   That's war / don't worry

c'est la misère   this is hell on earth

C'est l'américain. It's the American.

C'est malheureux That's unfortunate

C'est moi,plan-ton! It's me,guard!

C'est pas ma faute,monsieur le surveillant! Ils m'attaquaient! J'ai rien fait! Ils voulaient me tuer! Demandez à lui It's not my fault,Superintendent! They jumped on me! I did nothing! They wanted to kill me. Ask him

C'est un bon-homme,le pauvre,il ne faut pas l'em-merd-er. He's a nice little guy,the poor fellow,you shouldn't pester him.

C'est un mauvais pays. Sale temps. It's a bad country. Nasty weather.

C'est par là? It's that way?

C'est rigolo That's funny

C'est tout. That's all

C'est un américain This is an American

c'est un menteur! he's a liar!

cette crapule that scum

chambre room

chapeau hat

Chaude Pisse gonorrhea, clap (*slang*)

chef leader, head; chef (cook)

chef de chambre room leader

chef de section section head

chez le directeur in the director's office

chez nous at our place

CHIEZ,SI VOUS VOULEZ,CHIEZ SHIT,IF YOU WANT,SHIT (*slang*)

chocolat chocolate

choux cabbages

cinque five

civil(e) civilian male (female)

cocher cabman

cochon dirty pig, swine

coif traditional headdress

coiffeur male hairdresser, barber

colique stomachache

Comme vous êtes beau How handsome you are

Comment? What?

Comment ça se pronounce en anglais? How is that pronounced in English?

Comment vous appelez-vous? What's your name?

com-pag-nie company

Comprends pas Don't understand

Comprenez vous fran-çais? Do you understand French?

Comprenez-vous: votre ami est UN SALAUD! Do you understand: your friend is A ROTTER!

con silly bastard (*slang*)

conducteur conductor

conducteur volontaire volunteer conductor

Conducteurs Volontaires, Section Sanitaire Vingt-et-Un, Norton-Harjes, Croix-Rouge Américaine Volunteer Drivers, Medical Section XXI, Norton-Harjes Ambulance, American Red Cross

confiture jam, preserves

cordonnier shoemaker, cobbler

corvée fatigue duty

corvée d'eau water duty

coup drink, swallow

couper les cheveux de suite et la barbe aussi; après il va au bain, le vieux cut his hair at once and his beard too; then he takes a bath, the old man

cour yard

cour des femmes women's yard

cour des hommes men's yard

Courage,mon ami,votre camarade n'est pas mort;vous le verrez plus tard Courage,my friend,your buddy is not dead;you will see him later

couteau knife

couverture cover, blanket

croix cross

croix de guerre war cross (military decoration)

Croix-Rouge Red Cross

cuisine kitchen

cuisinier cook

curé priest

D

de of,from

De l'eau,planton;de l'eau,s'il vous plaît Water,guard;water, please

de mes couilles by my balls (*slang*)

De quel endroit que vooz êtes? Where are you from?

de suite at once

dedans in it

défaitiste defeatist

défendus forbidden

déjeuner lunch

Demain,c'est Dimanche alors Tomorrow,it's Sunday then

demain partir de bonne heure tomorrow leaving early

démarche gait

Dépêches-toi,voici le planton Hurry up,here comes the guard

Dépêchez-vous. Savez-vous,vous allez partir de suite. Cet après-midi. Pour Paris. Hurry up. You know,you're going to leave at once. This afternoon. For Paris.

Dépêchez-vous,ceux qui vont partir. Hurry up,those who are leaving.

dépense pour   spend for

deus ex machine   a god from the machine (phrase describing the sudden appearance, in Greek and Roman drama, of a god who decides the final outcome of the plot)

Deutsche Küchen   German Kitchen

Deutsche Verein   German Association

Deux hommes pour aller chercher l'eau.   Two men to go for water.

deux sous   two sous (ten centimes)

deuxième classe   second class

Dimanche   Sunday

Directeur   Director

Dis à l'américain que je veux parler avec lui—Me voici   Tell the American that I want to speak to him—Here I am

dis donc bidon n'est-ce pas. Faut pas t'en faire   what do you know canteen. Don't let it get you down

donc   *see* Excuses donc

Dormez-bien   Sleep well

douche   shower

douille   shell case

Du pain;prenez,mes amis   Bread;take some,friends

du tabac   tobacco

durée   duration

E

Eh-bi-en   Well

embusqué   shirker (of active service)

En Amérique on ne fait pas comme ça.   In America we don't behave like that.

En avant.   Forward.

en haut   upstairs

en masse   all together

en queue   in line

en route   on or along the way

en temps de guerre   in wartime

en ville   into town

en voulez-vous?   do you want some?

enfin   at last

Enfin, nous voilà.   Here we are, at last.

ennui   weariness, boredom

ensemble   together

entre nous   between ourselves

Entrez   Come in

épaté   amazed

éplucher les pommes   to peel potatoes

espion   spy

espionnage   espionage

Est-ce que vous détestez les boches?   Do you hate the Krauts?

Est-ce que vous êtes tous ici?   Are you all here?

**Est-ce vrai! V'là, le roi d'Angleterre est malade. Quelque
chose!—Comment? La reine aussi? Bon Dieu! Qu'est-ce
que c'est?—Mon père est mort! Merde!—Eh, b'en! La
guerre est finie. Bon.**   Is it true! There you are, the King of
England is sick. Something!—What? The Queen too? Good
God! What is it?—My father is dead! Shit!—Oh, well! The war
is over. Good.

**et ma femme est très gen-tille, elle est fran-çaise et très
belle, très, très belle, vrai-ment; elle n'est pas comme
moi, un pet-it homme laid, ma femme est grande et
belle, elle sait bien lire, et é-crire, vrai-ment; et notre
fils...vous dev-ez voir notre pet-it fils...**   and my wife is
very sweet, she is French and very beautiful, very, very beauti-
ful, indeed; she is not like me, a small homely man, my wife is
tall and beautiful, she can read well, and write, really; and our
son...you ought to see our little son...

Et mes outils   And my tools

Et puis***je suis réformé....   And then***I've been invalided
   out....

Et qu'il fait beau,là-bas!   And it's so beautiful,there!

et tout   and all

**ET VOUS—PRENEZ GARDE—SI JE VOUS ATTRAPE
   AVEC LES FEMMES UNE AUTRE FOIS JE VOUS
   FOUS AU CABINOT POUR QUINZE JOURS,TOUS—
   TOUS—**   AND YOU—TAKE CARE—IF I CATCH YOU
   WITH THE WOMEN ONE MORE TIME I'LL THROW
   YOU IN SOLITARY FOR TWO WEEKS,ALL OF YOU—
   ALL OF YOU—

Excuses done   Take that back

F

fainéant   laggard

faire   to make

faire la photographie   to take a photograph

fait la putain   acting the whore

fecit   he made (it)

femme   woman, wife

femme honnête   respectable woman

fenêtre   window

fiacre   horse drawn cab

fil de fer barbelé   barbed-wire

fils de chienne   son of a bitch

Fini!   Finished!

forgeron   blacksmith

fortunati   lucky ones

fou   madman

foule   gang

foutue   lousy, rotten

français   French, Frenchman
française   Frenchwoman
fromage   cheese

G

gagnait cinq cent francs par jour   earned 500 francs a day
Garde Champêtre   rural policeman
garçon   boy
Gare   (railway) station
géant   giant
gendarme   gendarme
gendarmerie   police station
Gestionnaire   Administrator
gloire   glory, fame, pride
gonzesse   broad, chick (*slang*)
gosse   child, kid
Gottverdummer!   Goddamn!
gouvernement français   French government
gratte-ciel (les)   the skyscrapers
grève (made la)   went on strike
guéri   cured
guerre   war

H

habitué   frequenter
histoires d'amour   love stories
homme   man
hôpital   hospital

I

Ici—Mais non, ici—Mettez le ici—   Here—No, here—Put it here—

Il a écrit,votre ami,des bê-tises,n'est-ce-pas? He wrote,your friend,some foolish things,didn't he?

Il aime trop son camarade,c'est tout. He is too fond of his buddy,that's all.

il avait l'air pesant,Cézanne he had a solid appearance,Cézanne

Il est fou,le noir. He's mad,the black man.

Il est gentil,votre ami He's nice,your friend

il est tombé un dimanche—ma femme est en nourrice,elle donne la petite à téter it happened on a Sunday—my wife is nursing,she's breast-feeding the baby girl

Il fait chaud It's hot

il faut frotter bien! you must rub hard!

Il ne comprend pas français He doesn't understand French

Il ne faut pas cracher par terre You must not spit on the ground

Il ne faut pas dire ça. You mustn't say that.

Il ne faut pas rigoler de ça. Savez-vous? C'est une maladie,ça One mustn't joke about that. Do you know? It's a sickness,that is

Il n'est pas méchant. C'est un bonhomme. C'est mon ami. Il veut dire que c'est à lui,la caisse. Il parle pas français. He's not a bad sort. He's a regular guy. He's my friend. He wants to say that it's his,the box. He doesn't speak French.

Il tombe de la neige—Noël! Snow is falling—Noel!

Il vous faut prendre des douches You must take a shower

Il y a un noir! There's a black man!

Ils sont des cochons,les français They're swine,the French

Imbécile et inchrétien! Idiot and un-christian!

imperméable raincoat

J

Jamais soldat, moi. Connais toute l'armée française. Me
never soldier. Know the whole French army.

Jamais travaille, moi Me never work

jardin garden

J'avais de la chance. I was lucky

Je comprends, je comprends, c'est malheureux. I under-
stand, I understand, it's unfortunate.

**Je l'ai acheté pour six cent francs et je l'ai vendu pour qua-
tre cent cinquante***j'ai pleuré un quart d'heure comme
si j'avais un gosse morte***je dis : Bijou, quittes, au r'oir
et bon jour** I bought it for 600 francs and sold it for
450***I wept a quarter of an hour as if I'd lost a child***I
said : Bijou, go, goodbye and good luck

j'm'appelle Jean, moi me, my name is Jean

Je m'ap-pelle Monsieur Au-guste, à votre ser-vice My name
is M. Auguste, at your service

Je m'en fous de ta canne To hell with your cane

Je m'en fous pas mal I don't give a damn

Je m'ennuie pour les neiges de la Russie. I long for the snows
of Russia.

Je ne comprends pas bien I don't understand very well

Je ne comprends pas français. I don't understand French.

Je ne le crois pas, Monsieur. I do not believe that, sir.

Je suis américain. I'm American.

**Je suis content / pour mettre dedans / suis pas pressé / pour
tirer / ah-la-la-la . . .** I am happy / to put it in / am not in a
hurry / to pull it out / ah-la-la-la...

Je suis le balayeur, savez-vous? I'm the sweeper, you know?

Je vais vous voir tout à l'heure, mes amis I'll see you soon, my
friends

jet d'eau   fountain

jeune gonzesse   young broad

Jin-dobri,nima-Zatz,zampni-pisk***shimay pisk   Good day,it's nothing,shut your trap***hold your tongue

Jin-dobri,pan   Good day,sir

J'ne veux,moi.   Me don't want.

jour   day

J'suis anglais,moi. Parlez anglais. Comprends pas français,moi.   Me English. Speak English. Me not understand French.

journal (journaux)   newspaper(s)

K

képi   military cap with a round flat top and a visor

L

La Boue Héroïque   The Heroic Mud

La femme qui fume n'est pas une femme.   The woman who smokes isn't a woman.

la guerre est finie   the war is over

la justice française***la justice hollandaise   French justice***Dutch justice

La Soupe Extraordinaire   The Extraordinary Meal

la ville de La Ferté-Macé   the town of La Ferté-Macé

Là-bas!   Over there!

l'air pesant   a solid appearance

Laissez-moi tranquille!   Leave me alone!

Laissez-moi tranquille. Ils voulaient me tuer.   leave me alone. They wanted to kill me.

l'âme sensible   the sensitive soul

L'américain. Allez chez le Directeur. De suite.   The American. Go to the Director. At once.

l'américain en bas! the American downstairs!

Laquelle? Which one?

l'armée française the French army

L'automne humide et monotone The damp and monotonous autumn (a misquotation from Verlaine)

Le Bon Dieu The Good Lord, Good God

Le Bon Dieu, soûl comme un cochon... Good God, drunk as a pig...

le bras cassé the broken arm

Le bureau de Monsieur le Ministre The Minister's office

Le Directeur va vous appeler tout de suite! The Director is going to call you right away!

Le noir avait raison. The black man was right.

le noir qui comprend pas français the black man who doesn't understand French

le paradis est une maison... paradise is a house...

Le Petit Belge The Little Belgian

Le petit belge avec le bras cassé est là-bas, à la porte, il veut parler... The little Belgian with the broken arm is over there, at the door, he wants to speak...

le petit belge avec le bras cassé, le petit balayeur the little Belgian with the broken arm, the little sweeper

le petit bonhomme avec le bras cassé the little man with the broken arm

les deux américains the two Americans

les deux balayeurs the two sweepers

les deux citoyens the two citizens

les deux mangeurs de blanc the two pimps (*slang*)

les femmes descendaient***corvée d'eau, vous savez. the women came downstairs***water duty, you know.

les femmes se promènent the women are taking the air

Les français sont des cochons The French are swine

les grands boulevards the main thoroughfares

Les hommes à la promenade Men, exercise time

les hommes mariés the married men

Les landes***je les connais commes ma poche—Bordeaux? Je sais où que c'est. Madrid? Je sais où que c'est Tolède? Séville? Naples? Je sais où que c'est. Je les connais comme ma poche. The marshlands [in SW France]***I know them like the back of my hand—Bordeaux? I know where it is. Madrid? I know where that is. Toledo? Seville? Naples? I know where they are. I know them like the back of my hand.

les maladies vénériennes venereal diseases

les obus allemands, en arrière les mitrailleuses françaises, toujours les mitrailleuses françaises, mon vieux. the German shells, behind the French machine-guns, always the French machine-guns, old man.

Les pommiers sont pleins de pommes;/ Allons au verger, Simone.... The apple trees are full of apples;/ Let us go to the orchard, Simone....

les rues de Paris the streets of Paris

les rues sont tristes the streets are sad

Les Voies Urinaires The Urinary Ducts (a reference to the advertisements for medicinal cures printed in the newspaper)

Liberté. Egalité. Fraternité. Freedom. Equality. Brotherhood.

liberté, monsieur? Liberté? Freedom, sir? Freedom?

libres fiacres empty cabs

lits tous les jours (Me feeks) Me fix beds every day

lui-même himself

Lumières éteintes. Lights out.

lune moon

M

machin, là-bas contraption, there

Madame la vendeuse de café The lady coffee seller

Maintenant...c'est fini...Et tout de suite***la tête.   Now...it's
over...And right away***the head.

**Main-te-nant que la Chambre est tout propre,al-lons
faire une petite pro-me-nade,tous les trois.**   Now that
the Room is all clean,let's take a little stroll,the three
of us.

Maintenant,vous pouvez tous monter à la chambre   Now,you
can all go up to the room

Mais c'est pas là   But it's not there

Mais—mais—***—mais—vous avez de la chance!   But—but—
***—but—you're lucky!

**Mais—mais parfaitement—vous avez de la chance—uh-ah—
uh-ah—parce que—comprenez-vous—votre camarade—
uh-ah—a attrapé prison!**   But—but certainly—you're
lucky—uh-ah—uh-ah—because—you understand—your
buddy—uh-ah—got prison!

Mais,M'sieu'Jean***Vous savez elle est forte.   But,Mr.
John***You know she's strong.

Mais non!   Oh no!

Mais,on est bien ici.   It's comfortable here.

**Mais oui,ils ont cherché de l'eau et puis je leur donne du
café**   Well,they have caught water and then I give them
coffee

Mais qu'est-ce que vous avez   But what is the matter with you

Maître de Chambre   Room Leader

malheureux   unfortunate

mangeur   eater

mangeur de blanc   pimp (*slang*)

Mangez comme vous voulez   Eat as much as you want

marraine   godmother

May-errr-de,MAY-RRR-DE   *see* Merde

me promener sans   to go for a walk without

Me voici. Here I am.

mécanicien mechanic

méchant vicious

médecin major staff doctor

même even

Même le Balayeur Even the Sweeper

Même le balayeur a tiré un coup! Even the sweeper had a go!

ménage household

menteur liar

menuisier carpenter

merci thank you; thanks

Merci bien,mon ami Many thanks,friend

merci,gracias thank you,thank you

Merde Shit (*slang*)

MERDE à la France SHIT on France

Merde. Ça marche pas—***—hello Barbu. Este-ce que tu es là? Oui? Bon!—***—Barbu? Est-ce que tu m'écoutes? Oui? Qu'est-ce que c'est Barbu? Comment? Moi? qui,MOI? JEAN? jaMAIS! jamais,jaMAIS,Barbu. J'ai jamais dit que vous avez des puces. C'était pas moi,tu sais. JaMAIS,c'était un autre. Peut-être c'était Mexique—***—Hello,HEH-LOH. Barbu? Tu sais,Barbu,j'ai jamais dit ça. Au contraire,Barbu. J'ai dit que vous avez des totos—***— Comment? C'est pas vrai? Bon. Alors. Qu'est-ce que vous avez,Barbu? Des poux—OHHHHHHHHH. Je comprends. C'est mieux—***—C'est une mauvaise machin,ça—***— HEL-L-LOH. Barbu? Liberté,Barbu. Oui. Comment? C'est ça. Liberté pour tou'l'monde. Quand? Après la soupe. Oui. Liberté pour tou'l'monde après la soupe! Shit. It doesn't work—***—hello Barbu. Are you there? Yes? Good!—***— Barbu? Are you listening to me? Yes? What is it Barbu? What? Me? who,ME? JEAN? nevER! never,nevER,Barbu. I

never said you had fleas. It wasn't me,you know. NevER,it
was someone else. Perhaps it was Mexique—***—
Hello,HEH-LOH. Barbu? You know,Barbu,I never said that.
On the contrary,Barbu. I said you had crabs—***—What?
It is not true? Good. Well then. What have you got,Barbu?
Lice—OHHHHHHHHH. I undertand. That's better—***—
That's a bad thing,that—***—HEL-L-LOH. Barbu? Free-
dom,Barbu. Yes. What? That's it. Freedom for everyone.
When? After soup. Yes. Freedom for everyone after soup!

mes affaires   my belongings

mes amis,et bonne chance!   my friends,and good luck!

Mes derniers adieux à ma femme aimée,Gaby.   My last fare-
well to my beloved wife,Gaby.

messe   mass

métro   subway, underground

**Met-tez la pail-lasse ici! Qu'est-ce que vous al-lez faire? C'est
pas la peine de dé-chi-rer une pail-lasse!**   Put the mattress
here! What are you going to do? It's not necessary to tear a
mattress!

**Mettez plus que ça—C'est pas juste,alors—Donnez-moi
encore des pommes—Nom de Dieu,il n'y a pas assez—
Cochon,qu'est-ce qu'il veut?—***—Gottverdummer—**
Put more than that—It's not fair,then—Give me more
potatoes—For God's sake,there's not enough—Pig,what
does he want?—***—Goddamn—

Midi   South; Southern

midinette   young working girl

militaire   military

Mirabile dictu   Wonderful to relate

misérable   miserable, wretched; destitute

misère   misery, despair; hell on earth

mitrailleuse   machine-gun

Moi anglais*Mon père capitaine de gendarmerie,Londres. Comprends pas français,moi.** Me English***My father police captain,London. Me don't understand French.

Moi,j'suis professeur de danse. Me,I'm a dancing teacher.

mon ami my friend

mon ami et moi my friend and I

mon couteau! my knife!

Mon Dieu. Main-te-nant,c'est mieux. Il ne faut pas faire les choses comme ça. My God. Now,that's better. You mustn't do things like that.

Mon frère,me dit le coiffeur,m'a raconté une belle histoire il y a quelques jours. Il volait au-dessus des lignes,et s'étonnait,un jour,de remarquer que les canons français ne tiraient pas sur les boches mais sur les français eux-mêmes. Precipitamment il atterissait,sautait de l'appareil,allait de suite au bureau du général. Il donnait le salut,et criait,bein excité:Mon général,vous tirez sur les français! Le général le regardait sans intérêt,sans bouger,puis il disait tout simplement:On a commencé,il faut finir. My brother,said the barber,told me a fine story a few days ago. He was flying over the lines,and was surprised,one day,to observe that the French guns were not shooting towards the Jerries but at the French themselves. He hurriedly landed,jumped out of the plane,went at once to the general's office. He saluted,and cried out,very excited:My general,you are shooting at the French! The general looked at him without concern,without moving,then he said quite simply:We've begun,we must finish.

mon pauvre my poor fellow

mon père my father

mon petit jardin my little garden

mon vieux old man

Mon vieux, c'est tout-à-fait simple. Je m'en vais en permission. Je demande à aller à Paris, parce qu'il y a des gonzesses là-bas qui sont toutes malades! J'attrape le syphilis, et, quand il est possible, la gonnorrhée aussi. Je reviens. Je pars pour la première ligne. Je suis malade. L'hôpital. Le médecin me dit : il ne faut pas fumer ni boire, comme ça vous serez bientôt guéri. 'Merci, monsieur le médecin!' Je fume toujours et je bois toujours et je ne suis pas guéri. Je reste cinq, six, sept semaines. Peut-être des mois. Enfin, je suis guéri. Je rejoins mon régiment. Et maintenant, c'est mon tour d'aller en permission. Je m'en vais. Encore la même chose. C'est joli ça, tu sais.   Old man, it's quite simple. I'm going on leave. I ask to go to Paris, because there are broads there who have every disease! I catch syphilis, and, when I can, gonorrhea too. I come back. I go to the front line. I am sick. Hospital. The doctor tells me : no smoking or drinking, that way you will soon be well. "Thank you, doctor!" I go on smoking and I go on drinking and I don't get well. I stay five, six, seven weeks. Perhaps months. Finally, I am well. I rejoin my regiment. And now, it's my turn to go on leave. I go. The same again. That's fine, you know.

monsieur, c'est bon, monsieur?   sir, it's good, sir?

monsieur, combien ça coûte, monsieur?   sir, how much that cost, sir?

Monsieur le médecin, le nouveau.   Doctor, the new arrival.

Monsieur le Ministre   Minister

Monsieur le Ministre de Sûreté de Noyon   The Security Minister of Noyon

monsieur, liberté?   sir, freedom?

monsieur—monsieur—c'est cher le fromage?   sir—sir—it's expensive cheese?

monsieur, monsieur, permettez?   sir, sir, may I?

**monsieur,réformé moi—oui monsieur—réformé—
travaille,beaucoup de monde,maison,très haute,
troisième étage,tout le monde,planches,en haut—
planches pas bonnes—chancelle,tout—***—commence
à tomber,tombe,tout,tous,vingt-sept hommes-briques-
planches-brouettes-tous—dix mètres—zuhzuhzuhzuh-
zuhPOOM!—tout le monde blessé,tout le monde
tué,pas moi,réformé—oui monsieur**   sir,me invalided
out—yes sir—invalided—work,lots of people,house,very
high,third floor,everyone,planks,above—planks not
good—unsteady,all—***begin to fall,all,all,twenty-seven
men-bricks-planks-wheelbarrow-all—ten meters—zuhzuh-
zuhzuhzuhPOOM!—everyone hurt,everyone killed,not me,
invalided—yes sir

monsieur,voulez pas?   sir,don't you want?

Montez les hommes!   Upstairs,men!

morceau   piece

morceau de chocolat   piece of chocolate

morceau de pain   piece of bread

moshki,moski   yid, kike (*slang*)

moue   pout

**M'sieu'Jean,ils sont tous—les plantons et le Directeur Lui-
Même et le Surveillant et le Gestionnaire et tous—ils sont
des**   Mr. John,they are all—the guards and the Director
Him-Self and the Superintendent and the Administrator and
all—they are

M'sieu'Jean*j'ai vu QUELQUE CHOSE! Le nègre,vous
savez?—il est FORT! M'sieu'Jean,c'est un GEANT,croyez
moi! C'est pas un homme,tu sais? Je l'ai vu,moi**   Mr.
John***I saw SOMETHING! the negro,you know?—he is
STRONG! Mr. John,he's a GIANT,believe me! He's not a
man,you know? Me,I saw him.

M'sieu'Jean—quelque chose   Mr. John—something

M'sieu'Jean—un géant!   Mr. John—a giant!
Mynheer le Chef   Mister Chef
mystère   mystery

N

Naturellement je connais,pourquoi pas?   Naturally I
   know,why not?
nègre   negro
neige   snow
N'en sais rien.   Don't know anything about it.
nettoyage   cleaning
Nettoyage de Chambre   Cleaning the Room
nettoyer   to clean
n'importe   never mind
N'importe. Allez avec moi   Never mind. Come with me
n'importe quoi   anything at all
No,no,Monsieur,s'il vous plaît,pas ma barbe,mon-
   sieur   No,no,sir,please,not my beard,sir
no travaille,ja-MAIS. Les femmes travaillent   no work,ev-ER.
   The women work
No travailler moi. Femme travaille,fait les noces,tout le
   temps. Toujours avec officiers anglais. Gagne beaucoup,
   cent francs,deux cent francs,trois cent francs,toutes les
   nuits. Anglais riches. Femme me donne tout. Moi no
   travailler. Bon,eh?   No work,me. Girl works,makes
   a night of it,all the time. Always with English officers.
   Earns a lot,100 francs,200 francs,300 francs,every night.
   English rich. Girl gives me everything. Me no work.
   Good,eh?
Nom de Dieu!   God's name! For God's sake!
Nom de Dieu tirez!   For God's sake,shoot!
non   no

Non. J'aime beaucoup les français. No. I like the French very much.

Non,non. Plus tard,peut-être. Pas maintenant. No,no. Later,perhaps. Not now.

noir black man

noir qui était plus fort que six français black man who was stronger than six Frenchmen

N'oubliez pas,M'sieu'Jean! Et dépêchez-vous! Don't forget,Mr. John! And hurry up!

nous allons voir we will see

nous étions toujours ensemble,mon ami et moi we were always together,my friend and I

nouveau(x) new arrival(s), new one(s)

O

officer anglais English officer

Oh peut-être un jour,deux jours,je ne sais pas. Oh perhaps a day,two days,I don't know.

où—où? Kis! (possibly "Kiste!") where—where? Chest!

oui yes

Oui,c'est du fromage. Yes,it's cheese.

Oui,c'est le nouveau. Yes,it's the new one.

Oui? Je ne le savais pas. Yes? I didn't know it.

OUI! JE VIENS! YES! I'M COMING!

Oui,j'suis américain,Monsieur. Yes,I am American,Sir.

Oui,Monsieur Yes,Sir

Oui,Monsieur le Surveillant. Yes,Superintendent.

ouvrier workman

P

paillasse mattress stuffed with straw

pain sec dry bread

pantalon trousers

papierosa cigarette (Russian)

paquebot liner, steam ship

paquet bleu blue pack (cigarettes)

paquet jaune yellow pack (cigarettes)

par année a year, yearly

Par ici! This way!

Par-ce-que je n'en a-vais pas le moy-ens. Je ne suis pas un mil-lionnaire,mes-sieurs. Because I didn't have the means. I am not a millionaire,gentlemen.

Parfaitement Certainly

Parisienne Parisian woman

parle pas français,moi me don't speak French

parti departed; one who has left

pas not

Pas bon. Not good.

Pas de quart,vous? Have you no cup?

pas difficile not difficult

pas méchant not vicious

patrie native land

patronne proprietress

pauvre poor

pelisse long coat made of or trimmed with fur

per diem daily

permission leave

permission de sept jours seven days' leave

permissionnaire soldier on leave

petit balayeur little sweeper

petit belge little Belgian

petit femmes sweethearts; prostitutes

peuplier poplar (tree)

peut-être perhaps

photographie photography

pièce de résistance main feature

pinard strong, cheap, ordinary wine

planton guard; soldier assigned to non-combat duty

Plan-ton! C'est im-possible de dor-mir! Guard! It's impossible to sleep!

planton voleur thieving guard

poêle stove

poilu ordinary French soldier

poilus divins divine soldiers

Poilus en permission soldiers on leave

pommier apple tree

Porte de Triage Detention Center

pour la durée de la guerre for the duration of the war

pour la durée de la guerre: le gouvernement français a bein fait! for the duration of the war: the French government did well!

pour moi, monsieur? for me, sir?

pour voir les femmes to see the women

POURQUOI? WHY?

Pour-quoi êtes-vous ici, KEW-MANGZ? Why are you here, KEW-MANGZ?

Pourquoi qu'il est ici? Why is he here?

Pourquoi vous êtes ici? Why you are here?

premier first

première classe first class

Prenez, ell dit, vous êtes fatigué.—Madame, répondit le soldat allemande en français, je vous remercie—et il cherchait dans la poche et trouvait dix sous. Non, non, dit la jeune fille, je ne veux pas d'argent; je vous donne de bonne volonté—Pardon, madame, dit le soldat, il vous faut savoir qu'il est défendu pour un soldat allemand de prendre

quelque chose sans prayer.   Take it,she said,you are tired.—Madam,replied the German soldier in French,I thank you—and he searched his pocket and found ten sous. No,no,said the young girl,I don't want any money;I give it willingly—Excuse me,Madam,said the soldier,you must know that it is forbidden for a German soldier to take something without paying.

Prenez,monsieur   Take it,sir

Prenez votre paillasse.   Take your mattress.

prisonnier   male prisoner

prisonnière   female prisoner

promenade   walk, stroll, exercise

promenade de hommes et des femmes   men's and women's exercise

peu   little

punition   punishment

putain   whore

Q

Quand meme   Nevertheless

Quand vous arrachez ma barbe,il faut couper ma tête   When you tear out my beard,you must cut off my head

Quatre heures.   Four o'clock

quel idiot   what an idiot

quelle heure qu'il est?   what time is it?

Quelque chose à boire,s'il vous plaît.   Something to drink,please.

quelques sous   a little money

Qu'est-ce que ça veut dire?* * *m'en vais à Calais,moi,travailler à Calais,très bon!   What does that mean?* * * me going to Calais,to work in Calais,very good!

Qu'est-ce que c'est!   What is it!

Qu'est-ce que vous avez foutu avec cette machin-là? What the hell are you doing with that contraption?

Qu'est-ce que vous faites là? Nom de Dieu!—Pardon. Les douches What are you doing there? God's name!—Excuse me. The showers

Qu'est-ce que vous foutez What are you doing

Qui dit ça? Moi? Jean? Jamais,ja-MAIS. MERDE à la France! Who said that? Me? Jean? Never,nevER. SHIT on France!

Qui m'appelle? Mexique? Est-ce que tu m'appelles,Mexique * * * —Est-ce tu m'appelles,toi? Who's calling me? Mexique? Are you calling me,Mexique? * * *—Are you calling me,you?

qui n'aime que son mari,qui n'attend que son mari who loves only her husband,who's only waiting for her husband

qui se trouvaient dans la zone des armées that are found in the battle zone

qui vaut trois fois that is worth three times

quinze jours fortnight, two weeks

R

réformé invalid; invalided, war wounded, disabled
rien à faire nothing to do
rixe fight
rue street

S

sabot wooden shoe
sac bag
Sais pas. Don't know.
salle à manger dining room, dining hall
sans without

sans blague   no crap (*slang*)

Sar va, Sar marche, Deet donk moan vieux   O.K., It's all right, I say, old friend (phonetic spelling of A.'s badly spoken French)

saucisse, fromage, pain, chocolate, pinard rouge   sausage, cheese, bread, chocolate, red wine

savez-vous   do you know

se promener   to go for a walk, to take the air

se trouvait   was to be found

seau   pail

secrétaire   secretary

section sanitaire   medical section

see-cent francs   600 francs

seidel   large beer mug with hinged lid

sensibilité   sensitivity

sergent de gendarmerie   sergeant of gendarmes

sergent de plantons   sergeant of guards

sergent de plantons lui-même   sergeant of guards himself

serviette   towel

si   if

Si tout-le-monde marche dou-ce-ment nous al-lons ar-ri-ver plus tôt! Il faut pas faire comme ça!   If everyone walks slowly we'll get there sooner! You mustn't act like that!

Si vous avez une lettre, sais-tu, il faut dire.   If you have a letter, you know, you must say so.

Si vous met-tez vos chaus-sures au de-sous de la pail-lasse*vouz al-lez bien dor-mir.**   If you put your shoes under the mattress***you'll sleep well.

Si vous passez par ma vil-le/n'oubliez pas ma maison:/on y mang-e de bonne sou-pe Ton Ton Tay-ne;/faite de merde et les onions, Ton Ton Tayne Ton Ton Ton   if you pass by my town/don't forget my house:/there's good soup to eat Ton

Ton Tay-ne;/made of shit and onions, Ton Ton Tayne Ton
Ton Ton

S'il vous plaît   please

SIX CENT SIX   606 (Salvarsan or arsphenamine), specific
remedy for syphilis discovered by Dr. Paul Ehrlich in 1909

soi-même   oneself

soirée   evening party

soldat   soldier

sont fait de la poussière du tabac   are made of tobacco dust

soupe   soup, meal

sou   five centimes

sous-lieutenant   second-lieutenant

Soyez prêts partir demain matin de bonne heure   Be ready to
leave tomorrow morning early

Surveillant   Superintendent

suspecte   suspect

T

Ta gueule   Shut up

Ta môme.   Your gal.

tête de cochon   pig head

têtes d'obus   shell heads

Tiens. Prends ça. Vite.   Look here. Take this. Quick.

**Tombé pour désert. Six ans de prison—dégradation mili-
taire.**   Condemned for desertion. Six years prison—military
degradation.

toujours l'enfer   always hell

tous   all of them

tous les généraux, tous   all the generals, all of them

tous les matins   every morning

tous les trois mois   every three months

tout-à-coup   suddenly

tout de suite   immediately, right away

tout le monde   everyone

Tout le monde en bas   Everyone downstairs

Tout le monde en haut   Everyone upstairs

**Tout le monde me fout au cabinot parce que je suis
    noir.**   Everyone throws me in solitary because I'm black.

travaux forces à perpetuité—verbum sapientibus   hard
    labour for life—a word to the wise

très ennuyé   very annoyed

très fâché   very angry

très gentil   very nice

troisième classe   third class

troisième étage   third floor

Trop tard pour la soupe!   Too late for soup!

tu comprends,le matin il ne fait pas chaud   you under-
    stand,in the morning it's not warm

tu sais   you know

**Tu vas au cabinot,mais tu vas revenir tout de suite. Je sais
    bien que tu as parfaitement raison. Mets cela—***Voici
    mes cigarettes,Jean;tu peux fumer comme tu veux**
    You're going to solitary,but you're coming back right away.
    I know very well that you are perfectly right. Put that
    on—***Here are my cigarettes,Jean;you can smoke as
    much as you want

tuyau   pipe, tube

U

Übermensch   superman

Un ami de son père,un anglais,bon!   A friend of his father,an
    Englishman,good!

**Un canard,déployant ses ailes/Il disait à sa cane fidèle/
    Il chantait/Il faisait/Quand/finiront nos desseins**   A

drake,unfolding his wings/He said to his faithful duck/He
sang/He made a noise/When/our plans are completed

Un Mangeur de Blanc   A Pimp (*slang*)

Un peu,Monsieur   A little,Sir

un section pour les femmes   a section for the women

Une cuiller,s'il vous plaît.   A spoon,please.

**Une femme entre. Elle se lève les jupes jusqu'au menton
et se met sur le banc. Le médecin major la regarde. Il
dit de suite 'Bon. C'est tout.' Elle sort. Une autre entre.
Le même chose. 'Bon. C'est fini'…M'sieu'Jean:prenez
garde!**   A woman comes in. She raises her skirts up to her
chin and gets onto the bench. The staff doctor eyes her.
He says at once 'Good. That's all.' She leaves. Another
comes in. The same thing. 'Good. That's all'…Mr.
John:take care!

**Une section mesdames! A la gare! Aux armes tout le
monde!**   A ladies' section! To the station! Everyone to arms!

V

va attraper quinze jours de cabinot   going to get two weeks of
solitary

verger   orchard

vespasienne   street urinal, pissoir

veuve   widow

viande   meat

vieux   old man

ville   town

vin rouge   red wine

vingt   twenty

vingt diplômes   twenty diplomas

Vingt-et-Un   twenty-one, XXI

vis-à-vis   person opposite, partner

Vive Jean   Long live Jean

Vive la bourgeoisie   Hurrah for the middle class

Vive la liberté   Hurrah for freedom

Vive le patriotisme   Hurrah for patriotism

Vive les plantons   Long live the guards

Vive la Pologne   Long live Poland

voiture   vehicle, cart

voleur   thief

Voo parlez bien   You speak well

Voo parlez français.   You speak French.

Voo poovez aller. Je vooz appelerai.   You can go. I'll call you.

Votre ami est mauvais, très mauvais, SAVEZ-VOUS?   Your
   friend is bad, very bad, YOU KNOW THAT?

votre camarade   your buddy

**Voulez-vous me prêter dix sous? Je vais acheter du tabac à
   la cantine.**   Will you lend me ten sous? I am going to buy
   some tobacco at the canteen.

Vous allez partir?   You're going to leave?

Vous avez faim?   Are you hungry?

Vous en aurez besoin, croyez-moi.   You will need it, believe me.

Vous êtes chef de chambre   You are room leader

Vous êtes KEW-MANGZ?   You are KEW-MANGZ?

Vous êtes le nouveau?   You're the new arrival?

**Vous êtes libres, mes enfants, de faire l'immortalité—
   Songez, songez donc—L'Eternité est une existence sans
   durée—Toujours le Paradis, toujours l'Enfer***Le ciel
   est fait pour vous**   You are free, my children, to become
   immortal—Think, think now—Eternity is an existence with-
   out duration—Always Paradise, always Hell***Heaven is
   made for you

Vous êtes uh-ah l'am-é-ri-cain?   You are, uh-ah, the
   American?

Vous êtes un nouveau?   You are a new one?

Vous n'avez pas de tasse?—Non   Do you have a cup?—No

Vous ne voulez pas de café?   You don't want any coffee?

Vous parlez anglais? Moi parlez anglais.   You speak English?
Me speak English.

vous savez   you know

vraiment   really

W

Wie geht's   How are you

Wilhelm,Ober,Olles   Wilhelm,Above,All (play on the name
of the German Kaiser and the national anthem,"Deutsch-
land über alles" as well as "double O"—"OO"—German
symbol for a public toilet)

Z

zone des armées   battle zone

Afterword

RICHARD S. KENNEDY

The Enormous Room, along with John Dos Passos' *Three Sol-diers* and Hemingway's *A Farewell to Arms,* is one of the clas-sic American literary works which emerged from World War I. It has been in print continuously since 1922 when it first appeared in an edition which, by omission and alteration, did not follow the author's manuscript. When E. E. Cummings saw his first copy, he was outraged and demanded that the book either have the origi-nal text restored or that it be "immediately suppressed,thrown in a shittoir." His angry message, sent from Paris, never reached his American publisher, and it was not until 1928, when Cummings prepared a completely new typescript for an English edition, that the corrections were made, including the restoration of some of the original French phrases. Over the years both of these versions in varying editions have been on sale in American bookstores, but no publisher ever agreed to include any of the sketches which Cummings offered to supply for the book. It is, therefore, a great pleasure to have the book available now in the form the author intended, including a generous sampling of the drawings from his sketchbooks and featuring a definitive text prepared by George

Firmage, Cummings' official bibliographer. This new edition also retains the Introduction to the first edition by Edward Cummings, who describes, largely by means of letters, the bureaucratic drama that was enacted before he could get his son released from the French *Depôt de Triage* where he had been imprisoned.

Besides having the new text and the drawings to enhance our reading of *The Enormous Room*, we can respond more fully today to the experiences Cummings describes in his book because we know a great deal more about the author now. It is possible to recreate the E. E. Cummings of 1917 so that the reader can be aware of the attitudes he held and can better understand what he has to tell us and why he tells his story in the unusual way that he does. He had been living happily in New York, seriously at work as a cubist painter. He had just completed five years at Harvard (B. A. 1915; M. A. 1916), where Greek and English literature had been his specialties. He had recently been experimenting with poetry and developing new styles of expression. Some were colloquial, even slangy; others adopted a syntactically radical method of literary cubism which wrenched words into new meanings and created startling juxtapositions of phrasing. He was not interested in politics or international affairs. Nevertheless, the controversies about neutrality, sympathy for the Allied cause, "preparedness," and atrocities in Belgium which were then raging did make their impact upon him.

During most of his youth, he had breathed a heavy atmosphere of pacifism. His father, a Unitarian minister in Boston, was the Executive Secretary of the World Peace Foundation. His friends at Harvard were mostly pacifists. But when President Wilson's war message to Congress called for the United States entry into the European war, declaiming "that the world must be made safe for democracy," and when war was declared on April 6, this atmosphere changed. His father strongly supported Wilson, and his friends very soon began to don one sort of uniform or another.

On April 7, Cummings himself volunteered for duty with the Norton-Harjes Ambulance Service, a Red Cross unit serving the French army. He took the step for a complex of reasons. In the first place, conscription threatened to take single and unemployed men of his age into the army. But the prospect of adventure was a strong attraction, too, for Norton-Harjes sent its groups to France as soon as they were formed. As Cummings wrote to his father: "I'm glad to be out of here by the 1st of May, when everybody is to be tabulated on pink, violet, yellow, (and I dare say orange) cards, for the benefit of conscription. It will mean everything to me as an experience to do something I want to, in a wholly new environment, versus being forced to do something I don't want to & unchanging scene. I only hope I shall see some real service at the front."[1]

The choice of the ambulance service by young intellectuals and especially by young literary men is quite understandable. They usually were pacifist by inclination and this was noncombatant duty. They were classed as officers, yet did not have to bear the burdens of command or the responsibilities of giving orders to others. The ambulance service carried all the prestige of dangerous military duty with a minimum of risk. It required no long, dull training period; anyone could drive a car. They signed on for only six months, and if they did not like it, they could get out, rather than having to endure two to six years of service. Most important, they would share in the experience of their time, yet do so on their own terms with the least amount of regimentation and the maximum amount of freedom.

Soon after Cummings sailed for France, he struck up a friendship with William Slater Brown, a college student from the Columbia School of Journalism, who had just returned from

1. Unpublished letter, 18 April 1917, in the Cummings collection of the Harvard Library.

a pacifist demonstration in Washington and had joined the
ambulance unit with a mixture of impulses similar to those that
Cummings followed. They both shared many interests in liter-
ature and the arts, and as lively, witty companions they made a
good team.

Through a mishap on their arrival in Paris, they were sepa-
rated from their unit and, as a result, spent five glorious weeks
on an impromptu holiday while waiting to be assigned to duty.
Their pleasures ranged widely, from attendance at the Ballet
Russe (where they saw Stravinsky's *Pétrouchka* twice) to the
Folies Bergères and the Olympia Music Hall. In their favorite
restaurants and in the company of beautiful French girls, "the
finest girls god ever allowed to pasture in the air of this fresh
earth," they became fluent in the French language. In time, they
became the daily companions of two handsome streetwalkers
who patrolled the *Boulevard des Italiens,* and from them learned
the argot of the streets.

When they were finally sent to the Front, to *Section Sanitaire*
XXI at Germaine, a small village between St. Quentin and Ham
from which the Germans had withdrawn in the spring, they
found the life of an ambulance driver was not as exciting as they
expected. The sector was very quiet during the three months that
Cummings and Brown stayed there, and the ambulance group
and its twenty vehicles spent most of the time merely standing by
in one muddy French village or another. Duty assignments came
seldom, much of the time was occupied in cleaning mud from the
vehicles, the food was poor.

But the real problem was their fellow Americans. Cummings
and Brown loathed the men in their outfit—Midwesterners who
were not college graduates, whom they regarded as provincial
and uncouth—and they hated their *chef de section,* a Mr. Ander-
son, whom they found stupid and overbearing. As a conse-
quence, they spent a great deal of time with the eight Frenchmen

who were assigned to their unit as cooks, auto mechanics, and menials. Unlike their compatriots, they now spoke French with colloquial ease and they used their ability well. From the French soldiers of the nearby units, they heard, over bottles of wine, all the gossip of the French Army. They heard all the bitterness that boiled up in the ranks, and in particular they learned the details about the best-kept secret on the Western Front, the mutiny in the French Army after General Nivelle's disastrous campaign on the Aisne. Their talk about what they heard and their pacifist views in general did not go down well with the Americans in *Section Sanitaire* XXI.

Also, this fraternization with the French was a violation of the wishes of the *chef de section*, who wanted "to show those bastards how they do things in America" by keeping spic and span and pretending superiority. Cummings and Brown preferred relaxation and mud-stained, grease-marked uniforms—and wine when they could get it. They were welcomed and questioned by the French, especially as they displayed a friendliness that had not usually been found among the English in that Sector. One time in Chevincourt, they had a hilarious drinking session with the neighboring French soldiers, who wanted to learn songs in English. Brown and Cummings did not know the words to most of those which were requested, but Cummings improvised anyway. Brown remembers himself and Cummings standing on a table, with Cummings leading the singing:

And to her maidenhead
He very softly said:
It's a long way to Tipperary
It's a long way to go.[2]

2. I am grateful to William Slater Brown for his reminiscences of the months that he spent in France with Cummings.

Their dislike of the group they served with, plus problems with the censorship of outgoing mail, combined to cause real trouble for them as time went by. Brown and Cummings, having heard of the Lafayette *Escadrille*, had hoped perhaps to get out of their ambulance unit by joining the French army as aviators. On the advice of a friendly French lieutenant, they naively wrote a joint letter to the under-secretary of French aviation volunteering their services but expressing their reluctance to kill Germans. This strange proposal alerted the censors, who then watched their mail carefully. Brown was writing to friends in the United States and, in a manner that looks like a deliberate teasing of the censors, he reported a good deal of the gossip of the French troops. He reported that "the French soldiers are all despondent and none of them believe that Germany will ever be defeated."[3] This and other opinions about the spirit of the troops and the progress of the war made him appear dangerous to the jumpy French intelligence authorities. They ordered the arrest of Brown and his accomplice. The oddity of Cummings' arrest merely because he was Brown's friend made Cummings realize that Anderson, too, played some part in the decision. Thus began the series of events that form Cummings' autobiographical narrative *The Enormous Room*.

II

Cummings' whole career is marked by creative surprise and his first book is no exception: he produced a unique work. Here was a story of oppression, injustice, and imprisonment presented in a high-spirited manner as if it were a lark. Nothing in the

---

3. Charles Norman, *E. E. Cummings the Magic Maker* (New York: Bobbs-Merrill, 1972), pp. 83–88, prints in full the three letters Brown wrote which troubled the censors.

book is handled in any way that could be expected—the experience is peculiar, the linguistic style is experimental, the mixing of French words and sentences in with the English is a practice that no modern literary work had attempted, the characters are a crew of incredible grotesques, and, finally, Cummings even forbids the reader from interpreting his release and return home as a "happy ending."

All this is most appropriate for a work whose central theme is romantic individualism. Earlier, Cummings had tried, not quite successfully, to set forth his outlook on life when he wrote an appraisal of the sculptor Gaston Lachaise in *The Dial* magazine. It can perhaps be called "a child's vision of the world," for it proclaims the virtues of the untutored mind responding to phenomena and not reasoning about them. In dealing with life, the natural intelligence, he says, functions "at intuitional velocity." It expresses itself like "the child who has not yet inherited the centuries" and like "the savage whose identity with his environment has not yet become prey to civilization."

In *The Enormous Room* Cummings works this primitivistic view of life into his autobiographical narrative very skillfully. He not only upholds the child's vision of the world when he considers human behavior but he even carries it to the heights of political anarchism, seeming to echo Thoreau's basic position, "That government is best which governs not at all." In the book, Cummings mounts a symbolic attack upon all governmental structures whatsoever; indeed, he offers the proposition that authority of any kind stifles the development and the expression of individual being.

In *The Enormous Room*, Cummings is quite explicit about what that essential being of each person is. Different words have been used for centuries to describe an essential self—Socrates called it a daimon, Plato called it a psyche, Duns Scotus called it thisness, Shelley called it genius, Bernard Shaw called it life force, Freud called it Id. Cummings called it an "IS." One can best understand what he means by looking at a series of notes that he jotted down sometime in 1921:

IS=the cold 3rd singular of the intense live verb,to feel.
Not to completely feel=thinking,the warm principle.
incomplete thinking=Belief,the box in which god and all other nouns are kept.[4]

Once we recognize the pejorative coloration that he throws over the word "belief," we can understand more clearly his description of the IS as he applies it to the character named Zulu, who exhibits "an effortless spontaneity":

There are certain things in which one is unable to believe for the simple reason that he never ceases to feel them. Things of this sort—things which are always inside of us and in fact are us and which consequently will not be pushed off or away where we can begin thinking about them—are no longer things;they,and the us which they are,equals A Verb; an IS.

The book, without ever saying so, presents the narrator as an IS in action. In discussing the book I am going to refer to the narrator as C. in order to distinguish my comments about him as a character from those about Cummings as the creator of this work.

The structure of *The Enormous Room* is fairly simple, dividing into three main parts. Part I covers the arrest of C. and his journey to the detention center at La Ferté-Macé. It jumps right into

---

4. Unpublished notes in the Cummings collection, Harvard Library.

the incident of the arrest without any preliminaries and later we gradually learn the details of the problem. The bouncing jollity of Cummings' language scarcely hints of his predicament as he is driven off to Noyon by car, escorted by a helmeted soldier. But when the driver's hat blows off and C. helpfully starts to get out to retrieve it, he is in for a sudden shock. The soldier draws his pistol to stop him. The narration continues to be ebullient, however, through the next episodes: his eating *déjeuner* under detention, his being scarched, and his interrogation at a security hearing in the *Gendarmerie*. During the questioning he passes his first test: he refuses to be in any way deferential toward his examiners, and when he is asked the crucial question that will determine his case, "Do you hate the Germans?" his own Socratic daimon rises up and forbids him to say yes.

When the door of his jail cell in Noyon slams upon him, he has no misgivings. "I put the bed-roll down. I stood up. I was myself." The whole sequence of this first day in jail reverberates with joy, although the grimmest details are available for an indulgence in self-pity. When he inspects a toilet can in the corner of the cell, he is filled with a sense of human companionship upon finding a recently deposited turd. It reminds him of Robinson Crusoe's discovery of a footprint in the sand. Such is the emphasis on life in this book that an animism frequently transposes things into beings: the toilet can gets a name, *Ça Pue* (It Stinks), and becomes an animate presence in the cell. A surge of pleasure at reunion with his friend B. comes over him when he hears someone in another cell whistling a melody from *Pétrouchka*. He answers the whistle and they communicate musically as he remembers the satisfactions of Paris and of friendship. He soon has the pleasure of more company, "a little silhouette" who comes along the windowsill and nibbles at a piece of his chocolate. "He then looked at me, I then smiled at him, and we parted, each happier than before." Night falls; a sliver of a moon appears—another animation, feminine this time, not *Madame la Lune,* as in the song, but Mademoiselle. He is happy. Imagination provides him company, "My friends:the silhouette and la lune, not counting Ça Pue, whom I regarded almost as a part of me."

As the series of ordeals continues, a literary development takes place which adds extra dimension to the work. Cummings begins a series of allusions to Bunyan's *Pilgrim's Progress,* the best-known allegory in English literature, and this continues throughout the book. Bunyan's story of Christian, who leaves home, wife, and children, setting out on a journey to the Celestial City, is filled with allegorical episodes. Christian falls in the Slough of Despond, he is imprisoned in the castle of the Giant Despair, he has to do battle with the monster Apollyon in the Valley of Humiliation, but at length he reaches the Delectable Mountains and attains the Celestial City.

But Cummings does not use Bunyan's work as a structural device the way Joyce did with the *Odyssey.* He does not duplicate all the episodes and significances of *Pilgrim's Progress.* Rather he merely employs an accumulation of allusions in order to elevate and intensify the misadventures that befall the narrator. Because of the reference to *Pilgrim's Progress,* the heavy load of gear which C. has to carry on his three-day journey to La Ferté-Macé is seen to be like the burden that Christian must carry and thus becomes heavier and mythically more credible (150 pounds is the weight given) as C. staggers with it from station to station. The muddy area of the ambulance unit in which he and B. are stuck without getting any *permission* (leave) is made muddier and more dispiriting by the allusion to the Slough of Despond. The cruel *Directeur* at La Ferté-Macé seems the more threatening because he is referred to as Apollyon. And so on. But these are selective allusions and we would do wrong to see the whole narrative in terms

of Christian's journey or to look among the characters for repre-
sentations of Mr. Worldly Wiseman, Mr. Facing-Both-Ways, and
all the rest of Bunyan's personifications.

This raising of the narrative above the level of realism has
made possible other variations in the fictional mode. As C.
makes his way to La Ferté-Macé in the custody of the two stupid,
prodding gendarmes, he is given help and comfort by a series of
strangers, and Cummings lets the characters take on a mythic
nimbus by using the language of religious supernaturalism. On
the train another prisoner, a "divine man," humble in speech and
demeanor, helps him with his burden and shares with him his
wine and sausage. A kindly woman in Noyon who serves him
food and offers comforting words is revealed to be the *marraine*
(godmother) of all the prisoners: "I love them and look after them.
Well, listen:I will be your marraine too." When the train reaches
Paris, it is a holy place: The people on the streets are "divine,"
a motherly woman sells C. coffee, a "sacredly delicious" brew.
All these figures draw strength from association with Christian
folklore, which is full of tales of sudden appearances of saintly
helpers or even of Jesus himself. In a scene no doubt inspired by
the episode in which Christian is relieved of his burdens when
he stands before a cross, Cummings arranges a final beatification
for the narrator himself, carrying the religious identification a
good deal farther now than he has with the minor characters. In
a passage full of cubistic obliquities, he identifies the suffering
C. with the Christ figure and the two gendarmes with the two
thieves who were crucified on either side of Him. The scene takes
place at night near the end of the journey to La Ferté-Macé when
the prisoner and his guards come upon a large roadside shrine:

I banged forward with bigger and bigger feet....Uphill now. Every
muscle thoroughly aching, head spinning,I half-straightened my

no longer obedient body;and jumped:face to face with a little wooden man hanging all by itself in a grove of low trees.

—The wooden body clumsy with pain burst into fragile legs with absurdly large feet and funny writhing toes;its little stiff arms made abrupt cruel equal angles with the road. About its stunted loins clung a ponderous and jocular fragment of drapery. On one terribly brittle shoulder the droll lump of its neckless head ridiculously lived. There was in this complete silent doll a gruesome truth of instinct,a success of uncanny poignancy, an unearthly ferocity of rectangular emotion....

Who was this wooden man?...I had seen him before in the dream of some mediaeval saint,with a thief sagging at either side,surrounded with crisp angels. Tonight he was alone;save for myself,and the moon's minute flower pushing between slabs of fractured cloud.

I was wrong, the moon and I and he were not alone....A glance up the road gave me two silhouettes at pause. The gendarmes were waiting.

Part II of the book begins in the *Depôt de Triage* when C. wakes to find himself in the new world of *The Enormous Room* and is reunited with B. We are taken through his bewildered introduction to this world, its laws and punishments, its meager recreations, and its remarkable inhabitants, Harree, Pom-Pom, Bathhouse John, the Schoolmaster, Garibaldi, the Machine-Fixer, and all the rest who bear the colorful labels by which B. and C. identify them. It is in Part II that we get the most explicit presentation of the world-view of the book.

It is a world in which everything is upside down. Although they are imprisoned, it is "the finest place on earth." It is a fine place for B. and C. because they have escaped from the oppressive ambulance unit, but it is a fine place for the group as a whole because they are in a limbo away from the world at war. In the world outside, it is suggested, the Schoolmaster was perhaps considered a corrupter of youth for telling "the children that there are such monstrous things as peace and goodwill." Civilization is seen as a bad kind of development for nations, compared to a place like Algeria, "uncivilized, ignorant, unwarlike." The harsh rule of the *Depôt de Triage* and the oppression and injustice that it perpetrates are very gradually seen as symbolic of all governmental structures. Although it is identified with and apostrophized as the French government, it stands for civilized governments all over the globe. When Bill the Hollander is returned to the Netherlands to be jailed as a deserter, the narrator remarks, "Much as le gouvernement français would like to have punished Bill on its own account and for its own enjoyment,it gave him up—with a Christian smile—to the punishing clutches of a sister or brother government."

In spite of the earnest social criticism, the thematic emphasis in *The Enormous Room* is rather upon affirmation and particularly upon the values of individualism and the virtues of primitivism. The characters who become friends of B. and C. are simple, gentle, harmless people—even Christlike. They are especially pathetic because of their vulnerability—they are weak, or small, or crippled, or illiterate, or mentally deficient—and they are in one respect or another childlike.

This is especially true of those venerated companions whom C. has designated the Delectable Mountains. For example, the little man named Surplice is, B. and C. think, Polish, but "nebbish" is a word more applicable. He is the one who is always ignored, forgotten, silent in the background—except when selected for group derision and teasing, when he becomes wide-eyed with bewildered wonder that anyone would notice him. He has an intuitive talent for music, and a childish toy, the harmonica, is his special instrument. As the characterization develops he becomes an archetype of the Holy Fool. He is "intensely religious" and so oblivious to the things of this world that he does not know there is a war going on. What Cummings emphasizes is his ignorance of the terrible things that civilization has developed—like submarines. He is not only childlike in his naiveté, but also oblivious to dirt, as if he were a three-year-old still picking up anything he finds on the floor or still fascinated with paddling in feces. Surplice sweeps up the spilled sand from the spitting box; he salvages the saliva-soaked cigarette butts for his pipe; each day he voluntarily carries down to the sewer the pails of solid excrement.

If the holy child Surplice is pathetic, Jean Le Nègre is the comic child, full of natural high spirits. He likes to pretend—he tells outrageous stories of his life and exploits. In his play he invents games in which he can play a role. He reads aloud nonexistent news out of a newspaper. He carries on a hilarious conversation with a friend through the imaginary telephone of a stove pipe. But he can also throw tantrums or have periods of the sulks.

In developing the character, Cummings intensifies the feeling about Jean by beginning with high-jinks and then dropping down to the troubles that beset him. The sequence is brought to its crisis in the account of an unjust punishment of solitary confinement. It is here that Cummings brings in poignantly the basis of the child's emotional disequilibrium. He wails, "Everybody puts me in the cabinot because I am black" and smashes his head against a pillar. C. cements his friendship with Jean by defending him against the punishment and, when he is powerless to prevent it, by personal gifts including the coat off his back. It is one of those moments, frequent in American literature, of interracial masculine bonding.

Part II is a relatively static section of the book. In prison, time stands still. Every day is like the next. The only things worth considering are the people who inhabit the prison and the variations from the prison routine. Thus this middle section of the book is filled with portraits and anecdotes. Part III picks up the narrative again and moves the story to its conclusion. Change comes with the verdicts of the examining commission. B. is sent to a permanent prison and C. is to be freed but placed under surveillance in a French town. With this turn of events, C.'s mental attitude changes too. With the departure of B., the *Depôt* is no longer "the finest place on earth." C. goes about in a numbed state, captured, we might say, by the Giant Despair. From those clutches he is rescued by a *deus ex telegramma*: he is ordered released to the American embassy and sent on his journey home. The final allusive detail comes when the return by ship to New York is described as if it were a cubist view of the spires of the Celestial City: "The tall,impossibly tall,incomparably tall,city shouldering upward into the hard sunlight leaned a little through the octaves of its parallel edges...."

III

A narrative of the sort we have just examined would have had its vogue in the 1920s and then faded into the obscurity of a wartime document were it not for the fact that it was written by an artist who had plunged himself fully into the modern movement as an experimental poet and a cubist painter. By 1920, when *The Enormous Room* was written, Cummings had already completed the first volume of poems, *Tulips & Chimneys* (see the complete version published by Liveright in 1976), and some of his radically arranged and unusually punctuated poems had begun to appear in *The Dial*. He was spending most of his time painting and had exhibited for the first time in the Society of Independent Artists Show of 1919 with two controversial cubist canvases, "Noise" and

"Sound." The spirit of twentieth-century poetry and art, then, invigorates *The Enormous Room*.

Cummings brings the narrative alive by recording sensations whenever he can. He makes us see and smell and sometimes hear, taste, and touch. We experience vividly the daily life in the *Dépôt de Triage*—its oozing walls, its overflowing pails of urine, its encrusted dirt, its greasy soup, the piercing cold, the noise and confusion. To give a sense of what it was like to be surrounded by sounds of a foreign language, Cummings judiciously laces his text with simple French words and phrases, most of which are understandable from the context. Even the punctuation and other features of the styling for print are adapted to the narrative: no spaces occur after the commas, a practice which creates a faster flow of the words; when dashes separate dialogue within a paragraph, the give-and-take becomes more dramatic; abbreviation or unusual capitalization conveys special meaning or emphasis.

The linguistic exuberance of the style is in harmony too with the philosophy of individualism and it immediately comes into conflict with the prevailing wartime rhetoric. On the very first page, Woodrow Wilson's "characteristic cadence" is made fun of in the summary of the trouble with Mr. A. As the narration goes on, the slanginess gives vigor, and the occasional lift into formal circumlocution provides irony. More than this, lively and unusual figures of speech give ready bounce to passages over and over again: C. waits in a moment of excitement: "my blood stood on tiptoe"; a gendarme gets ready for duty: he "buckled on his personality." Surplice speaks with a "shrugging voice"; an ineffective and isolated prison guard stands "like a tragic last piece of uneaten candy in his box at the end of the cour"; the gypsy's little son has "lolling buttons of eyes sewn on gold flesh."

There is no standard narrative style. Cummings tries out

everything. We have, for instance, impressionism, a style invented by Stephen Crane and developed by Joseph Conrad, in which the impressions are recorded as falling on the consciousness of the narrator. This is a view of the jail at Creil:

A wall with many bars fixed across one minute opening. At the opening a dozen,fifteen,grins. Upon the bars hands,scraggy and bluishly white. Through the bars stretchings of lean arms,incessant stretchings. The grins leap at the window,hands belonging to them catch hold,arms belonging to them stretch in my direction...an instant;then new grins leap from behind and knock off the first grins which go down with a fragile crashing like glass smashed:hands wither and break,arms streak out of sight,sucked inward.

That style carried further can become interior monologue, a very good means for conveying unusual states of mind. Here is the narrator, dazed by his sudden release, leaving La Ferté-Macé by train:

A wee tiny absurd whistle coming from nowhere,from outside of me. Two men opposite. Jolt. A few houses a fence a wall a bit of neige float foolishly by and through a window. These gentlemen in my compartment do not seem to know that La Misère exists. They are talking politics. Thinking that I don't understand. By Jesus,that's a good one. "Pardon me,gentlemen,but does one change at the next station for Paris?" Surprised. I thought so.

He tries out his synaesthetic style, in which he merges, linguistically, the words which apply to one of the senses with those which apply to another (the sort of writing better known in some of his poems, such as "i was sitting in mcsorley's"). For example, the description of C.'s first observation of the prison chapel when the *Surveillant* leads him through it in the darkness.

The shrinking light which my guide held had become suddenly minute;it was beating,senseless and futile,with shrill fists upon a thick enormous moisture of gloom. To the left and right through lean oblongs of stained glass burst dirty burglars of moonlight. The clammy stupid distance uttered dimly an uncanny conflict—the mutterless tumbling of brutish shadows. A crowding ooze battled with my lungs. My nostrils fought against the monstrous atmospheric slime which hugged a sweet unpleasant odour. Staring ahead,I gradually disinterred the pale carrion of the darkness—an altar....

There are passages, too, as we have seen, that are somewhat like set pieces, done in variations of his cubist style—the description of the roadside crucifix and the culminating portions of each of his views of a Delectable Mountain.

It is this linguistic display, along with the allusions to *Pilgrim's Progress* and the hints of a mythic dimension, that takes *The Enormous Room* out of the humble category of the war memoir and that keeps it out of the workaday category of the realistic novel. It is then merely a prose work of literary art. There had never been anything quite like it before and there has never been anything like it since.

Temple University
September 1976

A Note on *The Enormous Room*

GEORGE JAMES FIRMAGE

Partial drafts of seven chapters, three complete fair copies, and two carbon copies of *The Enormous Room* manuscript have survived the half century since the book's publication. A detailed examination of these drafts and copies and the family correspondence in The Houghton Library, Harvard University, and the Clifton Waller Barrett Library, University of Virginia, reveal that the earliest of the drafts—a nine-page version of Chapter One typed on the family typewriter and heavily corrected in the author's hand[1]—was probably written in Cambridge, Massachusetts, sometime after Cummings' return to the United States from La Ferté-Macé on New Year's Day 1918 and before his departure two months later for New York City to find living quarters of his own. At least one thing is certain: on March 5, 1918, Cummings reported from New York to his father in Cambridge "that [the manuscript] progresses gradually,tho'possibly not at the 20th C[entury] L[i]m[i]t[e]d speed which you dictaphone my so-called conscience." In his reply of the nineteenth, the author's father

1. Clifton Waller Barrett Library, University of Virginia, Deposit 6246-a.

reminded his son of "the manuscript you contracted to produce as rapidly as circumstances would permit. . . . But I daresay your silence covers a multitude of type-written pages. With which oracular utterance, I leave you to your conscience. . . ."[2]

While little progress was made on the manuscript itself during the months that followed, William Slater Brown's return to the United States on March 12, 1918 and his reunion with Cummings early in May did give the fellow-prisoners an opportunity to talk at length about their experience in La Ferté-Macé. "W," Cummings wrote to his father on May 8, "is very amusing noting down the thousand et one incidents of ex-convictdom in the course of let us say a two hour conversation....Soon I shall have a pretty fair skeleton on which to erect as I see fit." But any plans he may have had to continue his work had to be abandoned when he was drafted and, on July 26, left for Camp Devens, Massachusetts. Cummings was stationed at Camp Devens until his discharge on January 18 the following year.

There does not appear to be any further mention of the manuscript in the family correspondence until November 3, 1919 when, in a letter to his mother, Cummings reports that "The 'French Notes' are by no means in their final shape,but should near it presently." This statement apparently raised hopes in Cambridge for the book's early completion, so much so that on the twenty-fifth of the month, the author was obliged to explain:

As for the Story Of The Great War Seen From The Windows Of Nowhere,please don't expect a speedy conclusion or rather

---

2. All quotations from the letters of E. E. Cummings and Edward Cummings are taken from the copies in The Houghton Library, Harvard University. Edward Cummings' letters are cataloged under bMS Am 1823 (296), 1823.10 (12), and 1892 (193). E. E. Cummings' letters are cataloged under bMS Am 1823.1 (152) and 1892.1 (32).

completion of this narrative;for this reason:that in consent-
ing(it almost amounted to that)to "do the thing up" I did not
forego my prerogative as artist,to wit—the making of every para-
graph a thing which seemed good to me,in the same way that a
"crazy-quilt" is made so that every inch of it seems good to me.
And so that if you put your hand over one inch,the other inches
lose in force. And so that in every inch there is a binding rhythm
which integrates the whole thing and makes it a single moving
ThingInItself.—Not that I am held up in my story,but simply that
progress is slow. I am sure the result will say(eventually that is)
that no other method was possible or to be considered. It is not
a question of cold facts per se. That is merely a fabric:to put this
fabric at the mercy of An Everlasting Rhythm is somethingelse.

Cummings' other interests, particularly an opportunity to
enter a painting in the Spring 1920 exhibition of the Society of
Independent Artists, further delayed his work on the manuscript.
"Until I get ready for the Independent," he wrote his mother on
January 29, "the French notes will remain(as all else)in the back-
ground." And there the manuscript remained until June 26 when
his father wrote to report the safe return of Cummings' mother
from a visit to New York and to confirm an offer to finance a trip
to South America for his son and Slater Brown. "I have not had
time," Dr. Cummings noted, "to look at the French notes which
your mother brought back. If you will only put those in shape for
publication, I will show you how the record of one voyage can be
made to pay the cost of another."

By the middle of July 1920 the author was back with his family
in Cambridge and, by August 1, in Silver Lake with Brown work-
ing on the "French notes." It seems likely that a complete rough
draft of the book was ready sometime in September; for when
Cummings' father and mother went back to Cambridge at the

end of that month, they took with them the final draft of the first four chapters.[3]

On October 4, Dr. Cummings wrote:

I am sending you 21 pages of your own manuscript and the 33 pages of fair copy. We will try to ship you some more tomorrow night. You will observe that I am retaining one of the fair copies. Miss [Mary J.] MacDonald and I hope that your rather miscropic [microscopic] interlinear notes have been interpreted with some degree of success.

The initial installment of the first "fair copy" and the corresponding pages of the final draft reached Silver Lake by October 6 when Cummings wrote to say "thanks for your kind not to say appreciative efforts!...Also the paper(which is first-rate)and the MS. I have already got some 30 more pages typewritten, which I will send you when Miss MacDonald and yourself have waded through the original as far as La Ferté-Macé Itself." Then on the eighteenth Cummings informed his father:

Last night,you will be pleased to learn,I completed the final chapter of my French notes. Not that it,as well as others,will not have to be worked over. Nor that certain insertions will not have to happen here and there.

As I expect to leave in a few days,please don't send any more copy than you have already placed on the way. The two chapters

3. Only six incomplete chapters of the author's final draft have survived: Chapter IV (7 pages), The Houghton Library, bMS Am 1892.6 (25), and the University of Virginia, Deposit 6246-a; Chapter V (2 pages), The Houghton, bMS Am 1823.4 (3); Chapter VI (6 pages), The Houghton, bMS Am 1892.6 (26); Chapter VII (8 pages), The Houghton, bMS Am 1823.4 (3) and 1892.6 (26); Chapter XII (1 page), The Houghton, bMS Am 1823.4 (3); and Chapter XIII (3 pages), The Houghton, bMS Am 1823.4 (3).

which I have done since you left with Mother a few days since make together sixteen pages. I may place another chapter after these,summing up my impressions in general—but I doubt it. In any event there is nothing more to be done till I can work over the copy as a whole in New York—I mean the entire book,or all the chapters together.

If I don't find any more MS in today's mail, no matter at all : in fact,just as well.

Three days later, on October 21, Brown and Cummings left Silver Lake for Cambridge and, after a brief visit, returned to New York where Cummings moved in with his friend and Harvard classmate John Dos Passos.

By the eighteenth of November, Dr. Cummings was able to report that he and Miss MacDonald—a typist for the World Peace Foundation of which the author's father was then General Secretary and on the back of whose discarded letterhead most of the first fair copy of the manuscript had been typed—"are getting about through with your French notes." Without the chapter entitled "Jean Le Nègre," which Cummings had taken with him to New York, "there will be about 250 pages of our fair copy." The initial typing of all but the missing chapter was finished by the end of the month; and sometime between the first and the fourteenth of December, the missing chapter itself was complete, copied and posted to the author in New York. In this first "fair copy" of the manuscript, the nineteen pages devoted to "Jean Le Nègre" are numbered "208a" to "208s."[4]

4. The 265-page original of the first "fair copy," with the author's holograph corrections and alterations and his typed additions to the text, is at The Houghton Library (bMS Am 1892.12) together with Chapters XII and XIII of the carbon copy (bMS Am 1823.4 (2)). The remaining chapters of the carbon copy are at the University of Virginia (Deposit 6246-a).

Cummings apparently read through the "fair copy" of the manuscript almost at once, correcting, amending, and altering as he went along. By the twenty-eighth of December at least some of the corrected copy must have been sent to Dr. Cummings for the latter to write that, following a visit to the Boston publishers Ginn and Company, "we have started in making two copies according to . . . specifications" they had given him.

The second "fair copy," incorporating all of the author's earlier corrections and alterations, was probably completed by February 1, 1921 when the author's father wrote to suggest that Cummings contact Will D. Howe, "formerly of Harcourt, Brace & Howe, and now of Scribner's," with whom Dr. Cummings had discussed the as yet untitled· manuscript. Whether Cummings got in touch with Howe or any other publisher is not recorded. All we know for certain is that by the end of February the author and his friend Dos Passos had made plans to go to Paris via Lisbon and Madrid; and after a brief visit to Cambridge, they sailed for Portugal on the sixteenth of March. The second "fair copy" of the manuscript, to which Cummings had added some final revisions[5] and which Brown wanted to read, was left in the latter's care with instructions to forward the corrected copy, together with "two note-books, containing drawings à propos," by registered mail to the author's father, who received them sometime after the twenty-sixth of March.

Harper's, to whom Dr. Cummings had sent a copy of the manuscript, turned it down, as had Harcourt. Then on March 21, Horace B. Liveright of Boni & Liveright wrote to inquire about

---

5. The 280-page original of the second "fair copy," with Cummings' final corrections and alterations and his father's "Introduction" to the first edition, is at The Houghton Library (bMS Am 1823.4 (1)). The University of Virginia holds the carbon copy of this manuscript (Deposit 6246-a).

the book at the suggestion of Mary Heaton Vorse, another Live-right author who had read Cummings' manuscript and enthusi-astically recommended it. "I believe," wrote the publisher, "it is an account of his experiences in a French prison. If you have not already arranged for publication of this book, I'd like very much to read it with a view of publishing it." A copy of the manuscript was sent to Boni & Liveright sometime after July 7, on which date Dr. Cummings wrote to Will Howe of Scribner's, who were considering publication themselves, to ask him to forward it on. Liveright must have read the manuscript shortly after he received it; for on the twenty-sixth of August he wrote to Cummings' mother in Silver Lake—Dr. Cummings was in Europe attending a World Peace Foundation meeting in Geneva—to inform her of his decision to publish the book. Dr. Cummings himself acknowl-edged the good news on the seventeenth of October following his return to Cambridge and, with an authorization from his son, whom he had visited in Paris, he asked Liveright to draw up the contract. The contract was signed and returned to the publisher on the fourth of November.

A letter from Liveright that accompanied the contract states that he was anxious "to set this book up as soon as possible and get all the advance publicity we can." All that remained for Dr. Cum-mings to do was to forward the drawings his son had selected to illustrate the book and a two-paragraph addition to the "Jean Le Nègre" chapter Cummings had written in Paris to Liveright, which was done on the twelfth of November, and help the pub-lisher choose a title for the book. Liveright suggested the book be called "Hospitality," a title that Dr. Cummings thought "would be attractive" but believed he could improve upon given the time. A list of twenty-six suggestions followed on the fifteenth of Novem-ber: "The Enormous Room," "Held on Suspicion," "Caught in the French Net," and "Unwilling Guest," among them. The author, however, had the final word. On the morning of November 25 a cable reached Dr. Cummings from Paris. It read: "Title of book The Enormous Room."

The Boni & Liveright edition of *The Enormous Room*, which was published on April 27, 1922, used only one drawing by the author on its dust wrapper; and the text, which omitted passages equivalent to twelve pages of the final "fair copy" of the manuscript, translated many of the French passages into English, and restored most of the punctuation that had been deliberately removed by the author, raised temperatures on both sides of the Atlantic. But in the absence of any firm evidence, it is impossible to apportion the blame for these "omissions, mistakes in punctuation, and other stupidities," as Cummings referred to them in an undated letter to his father. The changes, alterations, and deletions were probably made in the first set of galley proofs by some well-meaning copyeditor and passed on to Cummings' father, who accepted them without comment.

The Jonathan Cape edition, which was published in England in July 1928, and the "Modern Library" edition, which was based on the English text and published on January 25, 1934, are both textually complete. However, the manuscript from which the Cape edition was set—a reasonably accurate retyping of the corrected second "fair copy" of the original—shows many signs of "editorial" tampering with Cummings' punctuation and improvements, rather than corrections, of his French.[6] Neither of these later editions includes any of the author's drawings.

The present edition, it is hoped, represents *The Enormous*

---

6. The printer's copy used for the text of the first English edition is at the University of Virginia (Deposit 6246-a). It includes copies of Robert Graves' "Introduction," Edward Cummings' "Foreword" (the "Introduction" to the earlier American edition), and a set of designs for the layout of the book.

Room as its author would have wished to see it published. Typographically, it reproduces the text as Cummings himself created it in the final draft he typed for his father; i.e., without a space after medial punctuation marks and without the added emphasis of italics for the French and other languages of La Ferté-Macé. The absence of space after punctuation marks in Cummings' work has long been an accepted element of his style; however, it now appears that this "style" is equally applicable to the author's prose writings, even his type-written letters and notes. Since it is the intention of the present edition to present the text of *The Enormous Room* as Cummings wrote it, *his* "style," rather than that of his father's typist and the book's previous publishers, has been followed throughout. This is also the reason for printing the foreign terms in the text in a roman face. The copy of the manuscript upon which the text is based reveals that the use of italic for languages other than English was an editorial decision of the publishers and not the author.

Textually, this edition follows the second "fair copy" of the manuscript and incorporates all of the corrections, additions, and amendments in the author's hand. Only three kinds of changes have been made to the text: (1) Anglo-Saxon four-letter words have been printed in full, as they were in Cummings' final draft; (2) obvious misspellings of words, especially place names, have been corrected; and (3) clearly unintentional inconsistencies in spelling and capitalization have been made to conform with the manuscript's established style. Dr. Cummings' suggested change of name for the character now known as "Judas"—he was called "Jesus Christ" in the final draft—has been retained.

The illustrations by Cummings that adorn the text have been taken from the "two note-books,containing drawings à propos" referred to earlier, and thirteen other notebooks, all in The Houghton Library's collection of the "Papers of Edward Estlin

Cummings."[7] The fifteen notebooks have been identified as dating from the period of the author's stay in France in 1917 and contain hundreds of drawings in pen and pencil associated with his stop-over in Paris, his impressions of the front, and his internment in La Ferté-Macé. For the present edition, only drawings associated with matters relevant to the text have been used. The titles that appear are Cummings' own.

7. bMS Am 1823.7 (7–20) and 1892.8 (1).